CONTROLLING VENDOR TRANSACTIONS

CONTROLLING VENDOR TRANSACTIONS
A GUIDE FOR AUDITORS AND ACCOUNTANTS

**HERMAN H. HALE
ROBERT M. ATKISSON**

THE WILEY/INSTITUTE OF INTERNAL AUDITORS
PROFESSIONAL BOOK SERIES

JOHN WILEY & SONS, INC.
New York • Chichester • Brisbane • Toronto • Singapore

In recognition of the importance of preserving what has been written, it is a policy of John Wiley & Sons, Inc., to have books of enduring value published in the United States printed on acid-free paper, and we exert our best efforts to that end.

Copyright © 1992 by John Wiley & Sons, Inc.

All rights reserved. Published simultaneously in Canada.

Reproduction or translation of any part of this work beyond that permitted by Section 107 or 108 of the 1976 United States Copyright Act without the permission of the copyright owner is unlawful. Requests for permission or further information should be addressed to the Permissions Department, John Wiley & Sons, Inc.

This publication is designed to provide accurate and authoritative information in regard to the subject matter covered. It is sold with the understanding that the publisher is not engaged in rendering legal, accounting, or other professional services. If legal advice or other expert assistance is required, the services of a competent professional person should be sought.

From a Declaration of Principles jointly adopted by a Committee of the American Bar Association and a Committee of Publishers.

Library of Congress Cataloging-in-Publication Data:

Hale, Herman H.
    Controlling vendor transactions : a guide for auditors and accountants / Herman H. Hale, Robert M. Atkisson.
      p.   cm. — (The Wiley Institute of Internal Auditors professional book series)
    ISBN 0-471-82726-6
    1. Purchasing—Accounting. 2. Purchasing—Auditing.
3. Industrial procurement—Accounting. 4. Industrial procurement—Auditing. I. Atkisson, Robert M. II. Series.
    HF5681.B9H35   1992   92-8813
    657'.45—dc20   CIP

Printed in the United States of America

10 9 8 7 6 5 4 3 2 1

ABOUT THE AUTHORS

Herman Hale is founder and president of Herman Hale & Associates, Inc., a nationally known consulting firm specializing in management controls systems development. The firm has fourteen offices nationwide that conduct operational audits of client fiscal controls over their procurement functions. Among these clients are many Fortune 500 companies, public utilities, railroads, and major healthcare institutions.

Mr. Hale is a graduate of Miami University (Ohio) and holds a degree in marketing. Before starting his own business, he was a vice-president of the Harry Camp Company, a national retailer with buying offices in the New York and Chicago garment centers.

Robert M. Atkisson, a certified internal auditor, is a regional associate and member of the board of directors of Herman Hale and Associates, Inc., a firm that specializes in reviews of procurement controls for private industry and nonprofit organizations.

Mr. Atkisson has served as an adjunct faculty member for KPMG Peat Marwick's Executive Education program, leading seminars on internal auditing and auditing operations. He is the former director of education for the international headquarters of The Institute of Internal Auditors. He has extensive experience as a consultant, specializing in internal audit management and training, and has worked in internal audit management and training in both the public and private sectors.

His contributions to auditing and accounting literature include a seminar, "Establishing and Managing the Internal Audit Function," *American Institute of Certified Public Accountants*; "Review Digest for Certified Internal Auditors (Part IV)," *The Institute of Internal Auditors*; "The Case for Internal Auditing in Local Government," *The Institute*

ABOUT THE AUTHORS

of Internal Auditors; and a seminar, "Operational Auditing," *KPMG Peat Marwick*. In addition, Mr. Atkisson is managing author for the textbook *Modern Internal Auditing* (CPE Edition), by Robert M. Atkisson, Victor Z. Brink, and Herbert Witt, published by John Wiley and Sons, Inc., in 1986.

PREFACE

The primary objective of this book is to present meaningful concepts that can provide for a well-controlled procurement process. Also presented are approaches that may be gainfully used by auditors and financial managers in the evaluation of the efficiency, economy, and effectiveness of an organization's procurement controls.

To that end, this book focuses on three major areas:

- An approach to controlling vendor transactions that is economical, efficient, and free of incompatible duties
- Proper approaches to adjusting vendor accounts
- Related policies, procedures, and practices that should be used in a well-run financial division.

The coauthors are members of Herman Hale and Associates, Inc., which specializes in procurement control reviews. This firm's activities, some of which are described in this book, are an extension of concepts developed by major retailers and mass merchandisers in recent years. In their hundreds of thousands of transactions involving drop shipments to widely spread outlets, transaction controls have received a higher priority than generally found in other industries. With the recognition of the problems of controlling transactions with vendors, mass merchandisers have an established lead in developing solutions to these problems.

The authors' experiences as consultants in hundreds of organizations indicate that the large majority of managers have yet to recognize many of the problems inherent in controlling vendor transactions. And where there is an awareness, many believe that such problems are so inconsequential as not to merit greater attention from those in management. As an example, financial management

PREFACE

may be so preoccupied with the revenue side that disbursement decisions are, at best, relegated to the supervisory level or lower. Seldom can one find a controller who cannot quote the number of days in sales represented by customer accounts; however, not often is one found who understands the concept of "prox" terms and the advantage that these terms represent to cash flow and the bottom line.

This book is couched in terms of business organization, for convenience only. In truth, all organizations—business, nonprofit, and governmental—have needs in the areas of protection and control to which the concepts apply.

The controls advocated in this book are equally as effective in an automated as in a manual environment. As advances in technology bring us ever closer to a paperless sytem (the process of exchanging business transactions electronically, for example), we must be ever mindful that risks and control procedures undoubtedly will change, but control objectives should remain firm.

An Audit Guide follows each of the three sections of this book. Each guide is intended as a summary of the major audit points covered in the preceding chapters. The questions in the guides are not intended to elicit simply a positive or negative response. They are meant to spark a critical review of the individual questions raised, with the goal of bettering the operation in some manner.

The Appendix contains a set of Policies and Procedures that may assist the internal auditor or consultant in formulating various approaches to improving operations.

HERMAN H. HALE
ROBERT M. ATKISSON

Avon Park, Florida
Winter Park, Florida
March 1992

I would like to dedicate my efforts in developing and coauthoring "Controlling Vendor Transactions" to Dr. Joseph Seibert, Miami University (Oxford, Ohio), without whose knowledge of market research, this book could not have been written.

HERMAN H. HALE

CONTENTS

1	**The Concept**	**1**
	A Changing World: Controls Can Be Streamlined	3
	Transaction Controls: Improve Them—and Boost Your Bottom Line	9
	Internal Auditors: Go for the Jugular	11
	Audit Guide	29
2	**Controlling Adjustments to Vendor Accounts**	**33**
	Vendor Credit Invoices vs. Chargebacks (Debit Memos)	35
	Chargeback (Debit Memo) Procedure	41
	Tolerances	49
	Adjustments to Vendor Accounts	51
	Audit Guide	59
3	**Policies, Procedures, and Practices**	**63**
	Financial Discounting and Payment Practices	65
	Trade and Volume Discounts	75
	Freight Control Analysis	83
	Filing Systems	97
	Accounts Payable Department Analysis	101
	Audit Guide	107
Appendix		**111**
Index		**145**

CONTROLLING VENDOR TRANSACTIONS

PART I

THE CONCEPT

1

A CHANGING WORLD:
Controls Can Be Streamlined

American corporations have developed a propensity for "paper shuffling." If a simple administrative process can be made into a complex one, corporations have historically taken that direction. Under the guise of "corporate management," whole departments have been created to solve the most elementary control problems: the result is extremely top-heavy corporate structures. The costs of such structuring have become most excessive. And as these costs are necessarily passed on to the consumer, many major companies have found themselves in undesirable competitive situations.

As a result, industrial giants across America are currently in the process of effecting administrative cost reductions. The business sections of newspapers continually announce the institution of early retirement programs for white-collar personnel within the corporate staffs of familiar "blue-chip" companies. What was referred to as "downsizing" in the 1980s is appropriately called "rightsizing" in the 1990s.

The accomplishment of administrative cost reductions requires streamlining procedures by the elimination of redundant document routing among departments. To affect these reductions, without the accompanying loss of effective control, many major industries are borrowing a page from their counterparts in the retailing industry.

Years ago, an internal auditor for a major retail chain was assigned to conduct an operational audit of his company's purchasing function. As the result of great insight (or perhaps due to basic laziness on his part), the auditor bypassed the more traditional audit approaches. Instead of observing and reviewing the negotiating,

A CHANGING WORLD

vendor selection, requisitioning and order placing procedures, he went straight to the archives (the accounts payable paid invoice files). There, an evaluation was made of the results of past and current activities with his company's vendors.

In addition, the auditor used an extremely unique approach in reviewing transactions. He looked at each transaction as if *he* owned the company. And, in that light, determined whether the individual transactions made good sense. He discovered that a substantial number of the transactions and resulting vendor payments did not stand up to his type of scrutiny—despite the fact that they carried the correct control stamps and authorized signatures. In fact, so many fell short that overpayments to vendors were found that exceeded one million dollars!

How can any company's fiscal controls be that ineffective? Very easily—and this happens with surprising frequency. To understand how, we have only to look at the methods used to produce the policies and procedures manuals for controlling vendor transactions.

Sometime in its history, nearly every company has had to create "policy and procedure" directives for the various functions within the organization. This action usually resulted after an organization's president had attended a scholarly seminar held at a prestigious university, in which "policy and procedure" manuals were considered a "must."

After returning from such a seminar, the president would usually ask the firm's department heads to create appropriate policies and procedures for their individual areas of responsibility. Naturally (or so it seems), the purchasing director would most likely be assigned the task of creating directives covering the procurement cycle. And therein lies the root of the problem: *The fox was designing the locks for the henhouse.*

Interestingly, this is not an unusual scenario. Reviews of the average corporate procurement policy and procedure manuals usually disclose that any changes and additions have been initiated by the *purchasing department*—despite the fact that these manuals deal extensively with financial controls, the rightful domain of the controller.

A LESSON FROM THE RETAILING INDUSTRY

A look at the retail industry in the United States will help to illustrate the importance of proper development of corporate controls. In the early 1960s, as mass merchandisers throughout the nation expanded by opening large numbers of branches and developing central buying and warehousing operations, they were forced to simplify and strengthen control disciplines. As a consequence, retailers have moved far ahead of other industries in this regard.

To fully understand the scope of the control problems faced by even a moderate-sized retailer, consider the logistics for a typical "small shop" operation with about $100 to $300 million in sales. Such an operation would consist of

- 500 to 600 retail outlets, geographically dispersed, each representing a receiving location
- 30 to 50 merchandising buyers located in varied market centers
- A centrally located accounts payable department including 10 to 25 individuals

A sample order for one set of an item selling for $30 per dozen going to each outlet could produce

- 600 shipments to as many locations
- 600 receiving documents
- 600 invoices and payments made by an accounts payable department as far as 1000 miles away from the average outlet, and at an equal distance from those placing the order

No wonder that the retail industry has been so far ahead of most others in the development of fiscal controls and disciplines of purchase order transactions. Clearly, the sheer volume of transactions with vendors has forced the entire retail industry to join in the development of practical and efficient systems of controlling transactions with their vendors. If any retailer's controls are inadequate, the very frequency of transactions can produce tremendous cumula-

A CHANGING WORLD

tive losses even on purchases that would be considered immaterial by other industries.

We have observed that control of procurement transactions with vendors has received much more attention from top management within retailing than in other industries. No longer is the buyer "king." In the late 1940s and early 1950s, department store buyers were under contracts with salary and performance bonus arrangements. *How* they produced was not a principal concern of management. Buyers received the goods they bought, ran their own marking rooms, and issued receiving documents as a part of "prepping" invoices for payment. In this arrangement

- The accounts payable department made all payments at the direction of the buyer.
- Resulting fiscal controls were virtually nonexistent.

COMING TO TERMS

Sophisticated retailers have adopted policies and procedures that "render unto Caesar that which is Caesar's." No longer are buyers allowed sole discretion on all transaction matters—and rightly so. It is impractical to expect even the best merchandising buyer to be a financial wizard, a master of cash flow, and a traffic expert as well.

Consider a classic situation that occurred often in the "old days" (and may still occur in less sophisticated organizations). The accessory buyer goes to the market to place a special-event order for the store's anniversary sale. The payment terms standard for accessory purchases at the time are 7% 10 EOM. The purchaser is allowed to discount the payment by 7% if payment is made by the 10th of the month following the month in which the purchase was invoiced or shipped. Or, net payment is due by the 10th of the second month.

In our story, the buyer is offered the vendor's hottest selling item at a 20% special discount. After writing a substantial order, the buyer is told by the vendor's salesman that because of the special price, payment terms of Net 30 days will apply to this order. The buyer accepts the less favorable terms in order to get the price. Thus, the resulting net discount to the purchasing corporation is only 13%—not the full

COMING TO TERMS

20% plus the opportunity to also realize the 7% financial discount. Despite this, the buyer is not concerned. Cash flow and financial discount realization are not among the buyer's strong points. All that matters is that the gross margin (which is the buyer's responsibility) is going to be on target.

The solution to this problem is simple. So simple, in fact, that we find it unbelievable that it has not been applied in every industry. In the sophisticated operation, all purchases must be made *based on the vendor's most favorable financial discount, freight, and other terms* at *all* times, unless specifically negated on the body of the purchase order. Thus, if a buyer is going to make a foolish mistake, he or she must go on record to do so.

One major industrial client has gone a step further: any reductions in favorable terms accepted by the buyer must be fully justified to the financial division. The results have been excellent. This policy has so stressed the need for favorable terms that the negotiation of terms, in addition to price and delivery, has been given added emphasis by the purchasing department. This multibillion-dollar manufacturer and supplier to the automotive industry negotiated extended terms from enough suppliers to effectively add 20 days to its payment history. Using only a 10% figure as an opportunity money cost, the 20-day extension resulted in a net value to the corporation of over $4,000,000 per year in just one division.

We estimated the value of this extension of credit by applying the following series of computations:

$$10\% \text{ effective interest rate per annum}$$
$$.10/360 \text{ days per year} = .000277 \text{ per day}$$
$$20 \text{ days @ } .000277 \text{ per day} = .00554$$

An average of $800,000,000 in total payments to vendors was made through the division's accounts payable department each year.

$$.00554 \times \$800,000,000 = \$4,432,000$$

The corporation felt this to be an excellent return for having made only a simple change in policy.

A CHANGING WORLD

Another client's buyers admitted that they did not regularly discuss payment terms with their vendors, because doing so might detract from their main objective: negotiating price and delivery. These are admittedly crucial objectives, but they should not be permitted to dominate the entire procurement process.

2

TRANSACTION CONTROLS: Improve Them—And Boost Your Bottom Line

In general, business owners are not concerned with *what* causes losses in vendor transactions. Whether losses are attributable to inadequate controls or to theft or fraud, the final results are the same—*reduced profits* for the owners to share.

Losses incurred during the purchase order process are usually hidden losses. They generally stem from a "sin of omission," such as

- Failure to receive volume or trade rebates due from vendors
- Certain earned freight allowances not given on invoices
- Advertising allowances overlooked

It is no surprise that during the 1970s' furor caused by the exposures of corporate slush funds, political payoffs, kickbacks, and the laundering of monies, leading to passage of the Foreign Corrupt Practices Act, it was revealed that many such funds were created from monies flowing to and from corporate suppliers coincidental to procurements. Executives who created such funds generally refrained from manipulating accounts receivable or established cash accounts. Controls in such areas are usually too positive and stringent to allow easy manipulation. Instead, they used the procurement process, for obvious reasons.

TRANSACTION CONTROLS

For example, there was no real accountability for the sources of funds received from suppliers. Such sources included rebates, advertising allowances, freight allowances, and so on. Unless purchase orders were specifically written to provide for the recoveries of funds due the purchasing corporation from these sources, any funds so received could easily be diverted and directed to any use at the whim of those receiving them.

Surprisingly, few organizations have learned anything from the revelations of the 1970s. The average corporate controls and procedures used to discipline vendor transactions remain disjointed and largely apologetic, without any focal point of control. Audit trails range from difficult to nonexistent in many sizeable corporations.

3

INTERNAL AUDITORS:
Go for the Jugular

Too often, the internal auditor approaches an operational audit of purchasing by making evaluations concerning a number of factors, such as

- Vendor selection
- Purchasing department adherence to competitive bid requirements
- Authorizing signatures
- Adherence to established tolerances

This approach appears sophisticated, but stops short of an acceptable degree of substance. A better solution is to "go for the jugular"— the accounts payable department. If corporate policies and procedures regarding vendor payments for purchase-ordered materials provide even mildly effective controls, the paid invoice files for each vendor should contain vital information, such as copies of the individual purchase orders, complete receiving documentation, and a concise record of the individual payments relating to the purchase orders.

Once you are in the paid invoice files, *for the purposes of this specific type of review, forget the standard audit procedures.* Do not be concerned with whether individual documents carry proper authorizing signatures. If vendor compliance with established industry terms and conditions of purchase are slipshod, or if fraud is occurring, the fault usually lies with those whose signatures *are* on transaction-related documents, rather than the absence of such signatures.

The auditor should identify the type of controls being used by the corporation. This can be accomplished only by determining exactly what is happening at each step in the flow of transaction-related documents, not merely by seeing whether published procedures are being followed. During this familiarization phase, the auditor should conduct an evaluation, identifying the actual disciplines and control procedures.

To properly evaluate the effectiveness of any organization's transaction controls, the first step is to define the various types of controls in use. Until recently our firm could not find any sources properly categorizing the different types of control procedures. So we developed our own. The following are categories of control systems that we have encountered during our review of clients' transaction controls. Appropriate flow charts and definitions have also been developed to help you understand the three different categories:

- Payable by Authorization (Figure 3.1)
- Payable by Approval (Figure 3.2)
- Payable by Direct Purchase Order Control (Figure 3.3)

(See the Figure 3.4 at the end of this chapter for an explanation of the symbols used in flowcharts in this book.)

PAYABLE BY AUTHORIZATION

Under this category, upon receipt, all invoices are sent directly to those departments that originally initiated the purchases. There they are matched with the purchase orders. During this initial processing, any necessary terms disciplines (for price, freight, or payment) are established, as in the following examples:

- The invoices are actually "prepped" for payment by the user (or purchasing) department.
- The invoices and related documents are *authorized* for payment and forwarded to the accounts payable department with appropriate signatures.

PAYABLE BY APPROVAL

- The accounts payable department makes all payments in the manner and amounts directed by the authorizing department.

The theory behind this type of supposed "control" procedure is that certain purchases are so complex that only those individuals *directly* involved can properly discipline vendor compliance with the specific terms and conditions of the purchase. In actuality, it is possible to provide glossaries of the terms used in such purchases so as to define precise applications of the terms for the use of those charged with their discipline.

We have seen corporations with multibillion dollar revenues in which the purchasing departments are actually responsible for vouchering invoices for payment. The accounts payable department's functions are relegated to merely inputting these vouchers into the system for payment.

PAYABLE BY APPROVAL

The second control system category, Payable by Approval, appears sophisticated, but, in reality, it merely whitewashes the obvious control deficiencies of Payable by Authorization procedures. By specifying that all invoices received from vendors be routed directly to the accounts payable department, this method seems to provide certain fiscal checks and balances along with stronger control measures. However, the exact opposite often results, with accompanying high administrative costs. In organizations using the Payable by Approval system,

- The accounts payable department is provided with a control copy of all purchase orders as issued.
- Invoices are sent from the mailroom directly to the accounts payable department.
- Receiving documents are routed by the receiving department directly to the accounts payable department.

Under this system, accounts payable department personnel match invoices with receiving reports and control copies of purchase orders. Apparent purchase order violations are supposed to be de-

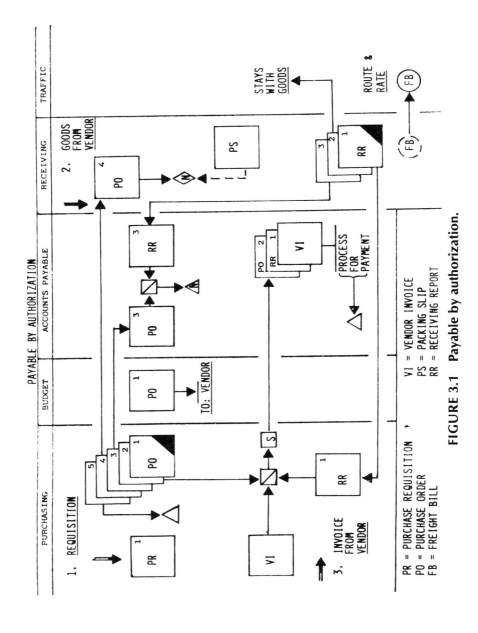

FIGURE 3.1 Payable by authorization.

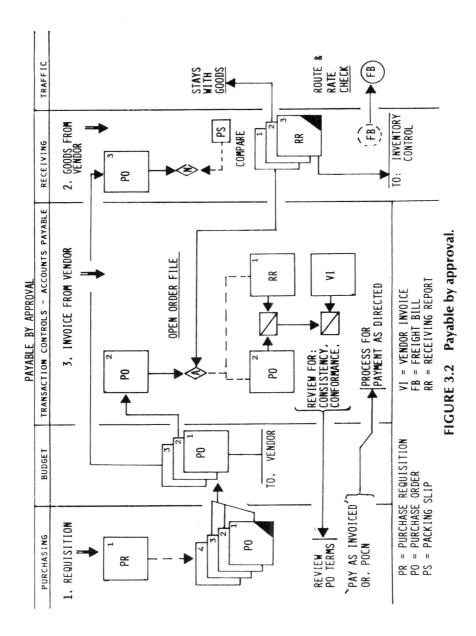

FIGURE 3.2 Payable by approval.

tected during this matching process. It is at this point that any effective fiscal control breaks down.

Invoices found to have apparent purchase order violations are sent to purchasing (or other initiating authority) for direction and *approval* before final processing for payment. Upon their return to the accounts payable department, the documents are processed for payment as directed. The end result is that nothing has really changed, as compared with the Payable by Authorization process, and accounts payable will end up making payments as directed by those responsible for the purchase.

In the Payable by Approval System, duties only *appear* to be separated. The very "approval" process reverts almost total control back across the lines established to provide the desired checks and balances. The person who initiated the purchase ends up *directing* the payment through an "approval" response to the query from the accounts payable department.

This very control procedure resulted in one client's discovering that his buyer was "on the take" when the individual was indicted by the Internal Revenue Service for failure to declare as income the kickbacks received from a major chemical supplier. In this situation, the "pay as invoiced" directions given to the accounts payable department under the approval procedure were actually approving payment for overcharges. The overcharges were ultimately funnelled back to the buyer as kickbacks.

In another company, a buyer received indirect reimbursement (in the form of an after-retirement consulting contract) from a favored vendor in return for helping to subvert his company's contract award procedures for major commodity purchases.

This company's procurement policies and procedures manual required that raw material purchase contracts exceeding $3,000,000 be executed through vendor bidding procedures reviewed by an executive committee. The favored vendor, with assistance from the buyer, made the low bid and received the desired contract—and then proceeded to invoice at a higher price. Under the purchaser's Payable by Approval control procedure, each invoice (varying from the purchase agreement) was sent to the buyer and "approved" for payment "as invoiced."

Granted, most Payable by Approval procedures manuals will place myriads of restrictions on the "approval" authority. However,

INTERNAL AUDITORS

these restrictions are often complex and, thus, are continually revised and restated. The restrictions end up as crutches, propping up a system that is itself flawed.

In addition, the system has other basic inefficiencies:

1. Excessive administrative expense can result from the requirement that both the accounts payable department and the purchasing department handle all documents with apparent violations at least *twice*.
2. Increased costs are incurred by routing documents to the approving authority and subsequently returning them to the accounts payable department.
3. There is increased potential for missing discounts because of delays in document processing resulting from excessive routing.
4. For proper evaluation, the entire transaction containing the apparent terms violation may require thorough research by the approving authority. In this case

    - The documents are more often than not received for approval out of context. In other words, invoices are received in the purchasing department in June for "approval" that relates to purchase orders placed back in May.
    - Much of the information required for an accurate review (vendors' stated terms versus actual terms) is often available only within the paid invoice files (back in the payable department), unless management is willing to accept the extra costs of duplicate file maintenance.

5. The approving authority is often overqualified, and the responsibility for approval consequently receives a relatively low priority within the daily workload.

    - If responsibility for approval within the purchasing department is assigned to a person in a clerical position, the training required for this function could more properly be given to an individual in the accounts payable operation.

6. Approval may well become routine, with little actual effectiveness.

There is one other factor—the human element—that in and of itself should eliminate Payable by Approval procedures. Within the paid invoice files of most companies using such procedures, we often find notations on numerous invoices such as, "Pay as invoiced—the $37.50 is too small to contest." This type of "approval" notation is sometimes found to have been placed on invoices of sizeable amounts by the buyers to whom they have been returned for approval. Buyers who place millions of dollars worth of orders in any given period of time mistakenly believe that any corrections to invoices in error are a costly process. But, the notation to pay $37.50 which is not owed is directed to employees in accounts payable departments who are often found to be receiving close to entry-level wages and may have just been denied wage increases by their supervisors. What may be unimportant and lacking in materiality to one person, may well be most material and important to another.

The "if they don't care, why should I?" attitude can become inevitable in systems using Payable by Approval procedures. As a consequence, the very personnel charged with controlling transactions (at least on the surface) may well abandon their responsibilities.

In spite of all these recognizable faults, based on observation, it is probable that at least 50% of the major corporations in North America use Payable by Approval procedures. In our experience, this control weakness often goes unnoted by both internal and external auditors.

The solution:

PAYABLE BY DIRECT PURCHASE ORDER CONTROL

In systems within this category, the purchase order terms are directly applied by the accounts payable department in the processing and payment of vendor and other transaction-related documents, using the *Best of Terms* concept. This procedure is so effective that we find no reason to use any other, unless we accept and tolerate purchase orders issued with imprecise (or outright incorrect) terms.

INTERNAL AUDITORS

The requirements for exercising control of transactions (see the flowchart in Figure 3.3) through the direct applications of purchase order terms are both minimal and reasonable. These requirements

1. Provide for the clear and concise presentation of all prices, terms, and conditions on all purchase orders when written.
2. Provide the accounts payable department with a complete control copy of each purchase order upon issuance.
3. Route receiving documentation directly to accounts payable for matching with purchase order control copies and invoices, for audit and payment processing.
4. Enable the accounts payable department to apply directly the terms and conditions of the purchase orders, without reference to any outside authority. Here, the "best of terms" should be used: purchase order, invoiced, or otherwise established terms.

In item 4 of the preceding list is the phrase "otherwise established terms." During a review of the paid invoice files in a medium-size health care institution, we observed two rather overall and sharp reductions in the prices charged for products from an individual supplier. The associate conducting the review found a note from the CEO of the health care institution attached to an invoice and the accompanying purchase order copy.

Addressed to the purchasing director, the note was accompanied by a photocopy of a magazine article that discussed and charted the high, low, and average prices paid for this product line by all similar institutions in the region. The note, dated just prior to the first price reduction, simply asked, "How do we stand? Are our prices in line?"

The institution's five-year agreement to purchase the product line was negotiated at prices that were approximately 20% more than the highest prices being paid by others, according to the magazine article. This discovery triggered a meeting with the vendor's salesperson. She immediately, on her own authority, reduced the prices on the agreement by this 20% figure, adding a notation that a further reduction would be forthcoming from her company's corporate headquarters. The second general price reduction was based on authority received in a letter from the supplier's corporate headquarters.

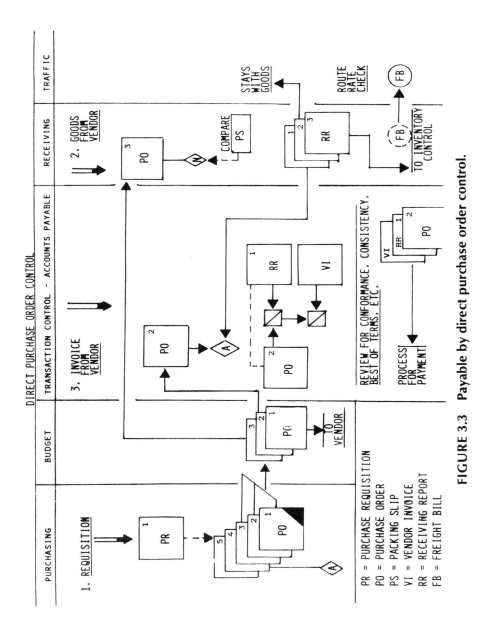

FIGURE 3.3 Payable by direct purchase order control.

THE BEST OF TERMS

As the five-year agreement had been in effect for a two-year period, our associate made an observation and an accompanying recommendation:

- The sharp reduction in prices (made so quickly without argument by the salesperson and confirmed by the subsequent reduction made by her company) was, in fact, an admission that the institution had been overcharged for at least two years of the existing contract.
- It was recommended that a chargeback be created to recover the estimated overpayments.

The final settlement after negotiation was in excess of $100,000. This incident is a perfect illustration of "otherwise established terms."

The principal argument against directly applying purchase order terms at the accounts payable level is the possibility of disturbing vendor-purchaser relationships. This is generally fallacious. Vendor-purchaser relationships are more likely to be the result of the rapport between the respective purchasing, sales, and engineering and technical staffs of the two parties.

At worst, the direct application method of control may cause initial confrontation between the financial divisions of the two organizations. Usually such confrontations can be amicably settled through negotiations by the sales and purchasing departments of the respective organizations.

Directly applying purchase order terms to vendor documents yields several benefits:

1. When any vendor contests deductions made as the result of the interpretation of terms by the accounts payable department, the purchasing department can review the established purchase order terms and their interpretation and application by the accounts payable department. If either is found to be in error, a simple reversal can be effected by issuing an appropriate purchase order change notice.
2. Transactions are conducted in full daylight. The inherent checks and balances have caused the contested transactions to

INTERNAL AUDITORS

be exposed to the vendor's financial and marketing divisions, as well as to the purchasing and financial divisions of the purchaser.

3. Each transaction can be appraised in its entirety at any time by directly referencing the control copies of the purchase orders, receiving documents and related freight charges, and the vendor's invoices and history of similar transactions.

All of the above are readily at hand in the vendor's paid invoice file or as work-in-process.

Once you completely understand the control procedures used by your company, you can identify those transactions for which either Payable by Authorization or Payable By Approval procedures are used. Without exception, wherever either is used, losses are sure to occur in almost every element of the transactions.

THE BEST OF TERMS

To provide effective and positive controls over purchase transactions, disciplines must be based on a *Best of Terms* concept. Many companies have systems designed to function with the use of Direct Purchase Order Control procedures. However, for some reason, their purchasing departments are often found to have a complete lack of confidence in their own purchase orders. Consequently, soon after Direct Purchase Order Control procedures have been implemented, amendments to the policies and procedures manual follow. The resulting modifications almost always produce Payable by Approval procedures.

Keep the overall procurement process in mind for a moment. Usually it is initiated by a user department's request for material. The purchasing department subsequently selects a vendor and issues an appropriate purchase order, which is sent to the vendor. Under Direct Purchase Order Control procedures, a *mirror image of this purchase order* is sent as a control copy to the financial division.

THE BEST OF TERMS

Premise for Best of Terms Concept

Presumably, the vendor reads the purchase orders prior to making shipments. Thus, any shipments and invoicing that are contradictory to terms and conditions provided on the orders must, consequently, be due to some error on the part of the vendor's personnel or system.

When a vendor fails to read customers' purchase orders and advise them of any errors in pricing, terms, conditions, and so forth, prior to shipping, administrative costs are transferred from the vendor to the purchasers.

The mere fact that a vendor ships an order does not necessarily prove his *acceptance* of the terms and conditions of the purchase order. At best, shipment and invoicing in a manner contradictory to a purchaser's stated conditions merely negates the transaction without any obligation, if the purchaser so desires.

Another presumption is that the vendor should *expect* that the purchaser will make all payments in accordance with the prices, terms, and conditions on the purchase orders. The vendor has been placed on notice by the purchase order as to those prices, terms, and conditions that the purchaser understands to be in effect. Any hidden losses or inconveniences to the vendor resulting from the vendor's failure to read the purchase orders are most appropriate.

Best of Terms Disciplines

Contrary to casual first impressions, the direct disciplines of purchase order terms are not based on the enforcement of all the terms and conditions of purchase. Instead, they involve the straightforward and direct application of the purchase order terms in the processing of payments to vendors. Application of the Best of Terms concept requires only that

1. Those initiating purchase orders do so with the knowledge that payments are going to be made accordingly. In essence, we should know what we are buying, as well as the terms and conditions of purchase.
2. Control copies of purchase orders should carry all of the terms of purchase, such as the following:

INTERNAL AUDITORS

- Price
- Freight terms
- Shipping point
- Return privileges, consignments
- Credit and financial discount terms

3. The accounts payable department, acting as the focal point of control—and using interpretations of all terms and conditions of purchase that are the most favorable to the purchaser—makes all payments as follows:

- Paying the lesser of invoice versus purchase order prices
- Using the most favorable credit and financial discount terms established for a given vendor from various possible sources
- Deducting from payments any unauthorized freight charges, whatever the source
- Directly disciplining all special allowances, rebates, trade discounts, and so forth, whatever the source.

Best of Terms disciplines merely shift back to the vendors those administrative expenses that are properly theirs.

Another benefit to management is a built-in procedure for improvement in the quality of the purchase orders being issued. Such improvement directly results when charges (such as for pallets, setup costs, and so on) not provided for by purchase orders appear on vendor invoices. Under the proper applications of Best of Terms, the accounts payable department deducts any such charges when paying the invoices. If, in fact, the charges were appropriate, a debit memo will most likely be received from the vendor to collect the amounts deducted. This debit memo is routed to the purchasing department. Accompanying the debit memo is a request for a Purchase Order Change Notice (POCN), if appropriate. Upon receipt of the POCN, the accounts payable department can process the vendor's debit memo for payment.

Too often, we find continuing invoices from the principal suppliers to our clients that have pallet charges, for instance, against

THE BEST OF TERMS

purchase orders, but none providing for the charges. After one or more debit memos from a principal supplier, resulting from the application by accounts payable of Best of Terms, the buyers see the light and, where appropriate, specifically provide for the charges.

Without the application of Best of Terms, the exact opposite can result. Minor charges receive routine acceptance and payment. During the energy crisis in the 1970s, one vendor arbitrarily applied an "energy surcharge" to each and every invoice issued. The charge was a standard $4.90, regardless of the total amount of the invoice—an amount that was just under the typical $5.00 figure used by many purchasers as a tolerance (see Chapter 6 for a discussion of tolerances). A typical purchaser from this wholesaler to industry was found to have received two shipments per week from the supplier. Each shipment consisted of three or more invoices against individual purchase orders. Although each "energy surcharge" was incidental, the total of the surcharges during the year for this purchaser exceeded $1,500.

When one of our industrial clients moved to recover these inappropriate charges, the wholesaler suggested that the client institute a similar charge on his billings to his customers. The phrase "It works, hardly anyone catches it" was used during the conversation.

Best of Terms applications are in management's best interest and should, therefore, be mandated. They should be used by all personnel who process vendor transaction-related documents for payment. The financial division should be given no choice in this area, because it is an easy "out" for the controller to be able to say, "It had the buyer's signature approving payment, so we paid it as directed."

It is not in management's best interest to have the financial division personnel, who are responsible for maintaining the integrity of the transactions, receive action decisions from those individuals (usually in the purchasing department) who are deeply involved in the transactions themselves. What if the action decision received from the purchasing department as a result of using the Payable by Approval routing appears to be improper? If this decision appears to the financial division to result from some impropriety on the part of the decision maker, what action can the company management expect the division to take? If the financial division (through its accounts

INTERNAL AUDITORS

payable department) questions the "approval," the very question itself may be inferred as a charge of impropriety. Any further action by accounts payable personnel will result in a strained relationship between those in the purchasing and payable departments.

In one review performed for a major industrial client, we found a point-of-sale advertising credit in a vendor's paid invoice file. The credit was for the fourth quarter of a previous year, based on a percentage of purchases. As no other similar credits could be found in the vendor's file, we instituted, on behalf of our client, a chargeback for a two-year period, less the credit for the quarter of one year that had been found in the files.

Under the client's Payable by Approval procedures then in effect, the chargeback went to purchasing for approval prior to processing. The chargeback was rejected by the buyer, who stated that a price concession had been obtained in lieu of the advertising allowance. An analysis of pricing over the period in question disputed this stand, and the chargeback was applied to the vendor's account in spite of this rejection. The vendor very quickly produced cancelled checks made out to a dummy company for the amounts in question. During this rather awkward procedure, the buyer drew his vacation pay and departed.

In this situation the financial division ultimately had to go out on a limb. It would have been safer to accept the authorized signature rejecting the chargeback. This would have been in complete accord with the Payable by Approval procedures then in place.

Under Best of Terms concepts, such conflicts never occur. The unveiling of the credit would automatically trigger the chargeback, with advice to purchasing that it had been initiated and charged. Then, if for some reason the chargeback itself was found to be in error, it could easily be reversed. The principal advantage is that by management's mandating that Best of Terms disciplines be used, any conflicts between departments are avoided. The accounts payable department is doing only what management has mandated.

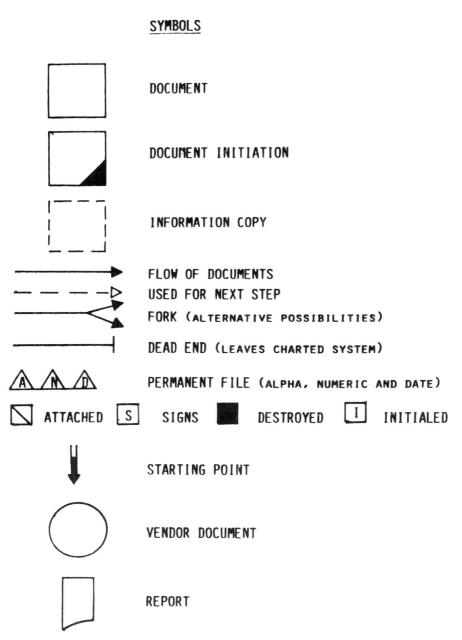

FIGURE 3.4 Identification of symbols used in Figures 3.1, 3.2 and 3.3.

AUDIT GUIDE: Review of the Procurement Process

I. INTRODUCTION

These audit guides are intended as a summary of the major audit points covered in the preceding chapters. In some instances the guides suggest specific audit actions that can be taken; in others, questions regarding individual aspects of the subject area are asked. Unlike some lists (such as internal control questionnaires) that relate to audit actions, the questions are not intended to elicit simply a yes or no response. Rather, they are meant to spark a critical review of the individual subject raised, with the goal of bettering the operation in some manner.

II. PREPARATORY ACTIVITIES

Familiarization with existing procedures and processes that relate to the framework for internal control of vendor transactions is especially important.

III. ORGANIZATIONAL FACTORS

Requisitioning departments authorize transactions to procure goods and services for an organization. The purchasing department approves and processes the requisitions. Once the goods or services have been received, the responsibility for controlling the transac-

AUDIT GUIDE

tions should rest with the accounts payable department. Otherwise, fiscal checks and balances are minimized.

IV. PROCESSING INVOICES FOR PAYMENT

A. Review the flow of transaction-related documents to determine exactly what happens at each step in the process.

Which type of controls are in use?

1. Payable by Authorization (This category of control should be used only for expense reports, dues, subscription fees, and the like.)

   a. Does the user or purchasing department receive and match the invoice to the purchase order?

   b. Does the user or purchasing department discipline the terms (price, freight, discounts, and so on) for the transaction?

   c. Does the user or purchasing department authorize the payment for the transaction?

   Note: If the review determines the answer to the above three questions to be yes, Payable by Authorization is the category in use.

2. Payable by Approval (This category of control is comparable to that of Payable by Authorization, but masks its deficiencies.)

   a. Does the accounts payable department receive invoices directly from the mail room and prepare the invoices for payment?

   b. Is the accounts payable department provided with control copies of all purchase orders as issued?

   c. Are receiving documents routed by the receiving department directly to the accounts payable department?

   d. Are questions involving invoices with apparent purchase order violations sent to purchasing (or other initiating authority) for direction and approval prior to final processing for payment?

AUDIT GUIDE

Note: If the review determines the answer to the above four questions to be yes, Payable by Approval is the category in use.

3. Payable by Direct Purchase Order Control (The effective category of control.)

   If the answers to a, b, and c in 2 (above) are determined to be yes, and if the accounts payable department directly applies the terms and conditions of the purchase orders to vendor invoices, without reference to any outside authority, the category of in use is Payable by Direct Purchase Order Control.

V. THE BEST OF TERMS DISCIPLINES

1. Do all of the control copies of purchase orders carry all of the terms and conditions of purchase?
2. Does the accounts payable department
   a. Pay the lesser of invoice versus purchase order prices?
   b. Use the most favorable credit and financial discount terms that are established for each vendor?
   c. Deduct from payments any charges not specifically authorized by purchase orders?
   d. Directly discipline all special allowances, rebates, trade discounts, and the like?
3. Is there a written policy that mandates the use of the Best of Terms concept?

PART II

CONTROLLING ADJUSTMENTS TO VENDOR ACCOUNTS

4

VENDOR CREDIT INVOICES VERSUS CHARGEBACKS (DEBIT MEMOS)

Auditors experience the first real measure of control effectiveness when they identify who is actually in charge of their company's fiscal policies and bookkeeping practices. This can usually be determined by a glance into the paid invoice files to determine how returns and adjustments to vendor accounts have been initiated and effected. For example, do the files contain the vendor credit documents as the primary sources for making the adjustments? Or are adjustments initiated and effected through established procedures for routinely initiating chargebacks (debit memos) to vendor accounts?

Let us say that the principal source documents for adjustments to vendor accounts are found to be credit invoices issued by the vendors. In this case, the conclusion may be that the company accomplishes returns and other adjustments to vendor accounts by seeking "credit invoices" from the vendors. This generally evolves from an acceptance of the boilerplate that appears on most vendor invoices: "No returns accepted without prior authorization. All returns and adjustments must carry our Return Goods Authorization number." When such instructions are accepted by the purchasers, the vendors are actually setting fiscal policy for their customers.

Substantial losses usually occur when "requests for credit" are regularly used to make claims back to suppliers. The resulting credit invoices, as issued by the suppliers, rarely favor the purchaser. The

VENDOR CREDIT INVOICES VERSUS CHARGEBACKS

use of this adjustment procedure generally indicates a need for more positive controls and the institution of firm policies for handling adjustment transactions.

A classic example of such a loss (actually, losses) resulting from the use of credits issued by the vendor was discovered buried in the paid invoice files of one of our early clients. The client, a Fortune 500 company, had purchased a certain piece of equipment with a purchase price of $10,000, stipulating "one each." The manufacturer subsequently sent five separate shipments of the item, against this purchase order that called for but one. All five were shipped freight "collect," in accordance with the terms of the purchase order. The four redundant pieces of equipment were returned using the "request for credit" procedure. In effecting the return, our client concisely followed the instructions provided on the vendor's Return Goods Authorization. Each return shipment was made prepaid in accordance with the vendor's instructions. The resulting credits issued by the vendor failed to reimburse our client for either the inbound or the return freight. To add insult as well as further injury, the vendor added a 15% restocking charge when issuing the credits. The net loss to our client exceeded $8,000 for this one $10,000 transaction.

The following represent the common hidden losses resulting from the acceptance of credit memos as issued by the vendors:

1. Handling charge deductions. (These are never appropriate if the adjustments are due to vendor error.)
2. The likelihood that vendors will fail to reimburse purchasers for freight costs incurred in the original receipts and the subsequent returns of purchased materials that are returned owing to vendor errors. This situation is most common when original shipments are made "collect" to the purchaser, and most certain when returns are made via UPS or parcel post, the charges for which are ordinarily paid by the shipper.
3. Interest expense. The vendor has the use of monies until a number of sequential, time-consuming events occur, such as

    - The requests for credit are made and the Return Goods Authorization is received from the vendor.

VENDOR CREDIT INVOICES VERSUS CHARGEBACKS

- The return shipment is made and the materials are received by the vendor. Only then will vendors issue the required credits.

Moreover, after the vendor issues the credit, the credit document itself must be received by the purchaser and processed through the payable operation to provide for a deduction to be made from the next check issued to the vendor. Only then does the purchaser recover the funds due for the adjustments.

4. The recovery from vendors of deposits made for pallets, oxygen tanks, and so forth are most difficult to control when solely dependent upon vendor credits.
5. The excessive administrative costs of maintaining effective suspense file disciplines to assure recovery of the monies due.
6. Potential *losses of entire credit amounts* due which can occur as the result of the complexities of the system.

Corporate controllers are always concerned when their company is found to have a debit balance with a supplier—a situation wherein the vendor owes the customer. Debit balances with vendors can be a consequence of the normal delays in recovering monies due from them under the "request for credit" procedure.

A series of debit balances with vendors resulted in one of our more interesting consulting reviews. We were called into a major defense contracting company by its director of internal audit. The parent company had been advised that there was a strong possibility that the ratings on its bonds could be lowered because of the slow payment practices of one of its divisions. As the organization had no cash flow problems, we were called in to review the division's accounts payable procedures.

We found the slow payments to be a direct result of the division's use of the "request for credit" method to effect returns to vendors. A sizeable portion of the materials purchased routinely failed to meet existing quality control standards, resulting in continuing returns to vendors. Over a period of time, several of the division's suppliers declared bankruptcy. As their accounts had debit balances (attributable to credits that had been issued for returns), the division suffered direct losses in the amounts of those debit balances.

VENDOR CREDIT INVOICES VERSUS CHARGEBACKS

In an endeavor to prevent such losses in the future, the division's chief executive had mandated that no invoices be paid until the materials were inspected and released by the quality control department. A severe backlog in the inspection process occurred, with direct effects on the processing of invoices for payment through the accounts payable department.

Our recommended solution was simple. A chargeback (debit memo) procedure, as outlined in the following chapter, was instituted. Rather than delaying the recoveries due from vendors for the materials rejected and returned, the use of the direct chargeback procedure kept such recoveries current. Debit balances with vendors were drastically reduced.

In situations wherein continuing purchases are being made from established suppliers, quality control inspections do not necessarily have to be a step in the payable process. It can be accepted that, because of the continuing flow of incoming materials from individual suppliers, the purchaser will generally be found to be continually in debt to the suppliers. As long as there is a procedure at hand that provides a method for the more immediate recoveries of monies due for returns, any risks resulting from conducting quality control inspections apart from the payable process are reduced to an acceptable level.

During this same evaluation of the division's payable process, a number of ancillary losses were discovered, all directly related to its "request for credit" return procedure. While most returns to vendors of rejected materials were shipped back to them "collect" via common carriers, some were returned on the division's own trucks. As can be expected, the credits issued by the vendors failed to reimburse our client for this transportation cost. Nor did any of the credits reimburse the client for the freight costs of the original inbound freight. Losses in these areas, over a two year period, approached $100,000.

Any errors occurring under "requests for credit" procedures, are almost always in favor of the vendors. These losses, resulting from a lack of positive control over adjustment transactions, are *hidden* and show up only through a biased audit.

A word of caution: We find many clients who have a debit memo form but misuse it. Rather than creating the actual debit against the vendor for the return or adjustment, client debit memos are often used to initiate the request for the desired credit actions. Then, copies

VENDOR CREDIT INVOICES VERSUS CHARGEBACKS

are held in either the purchasing department or accounts payable suspense files awaiting the receipt of the appropriate credits from the vendors.

Under normal circumstances, vendor credit documentation should serve no purpose other than to support the purchaser's debit memo. The purchaser's debit memo is the document that should have been posted to the purchaser's books long before the credit document is ever received from the vendor.

There are acceptable exceptions to this situation. In some instances when the vendor is performing some special accommodation (repurchasing an overstocked condition, for example) it is only politic to await the receipt of the credit memo before posting to the vendor's account.

5

CHARGEBACK (DEBIT MEMO) PROCEDURE

If a company is using a debit memo procedure, it should be reviewed for (1) format and (2) the policies and procedures established for its use. Of course, if there is no debit memo (chargeback) procedure in use, one should be recommended for immediate implementation. More trivial (but cumulative and preventable) losses are incurred in this area than in almost any other in industry.

First, let us examine policies and procedures regarding returns and adjustments. These fall into two principal categories:

- Vendor responsibility—owing to an error on the part of the vendor
- Vendor accommodation—the repurchase of products ordered in error, for instance

Any charges to vendors for materials returns, special allowances due the company, rebates, overcharges, and corrections of any other purchase order violations should always be initiated through chargebacks (debit memos) and their direct application to vendor accounts.

Too often, when reviewing our clients' policies and procedures covering returns and adjustments to vendor accounts, we find they have been issued by the purchasing department. As a result, the actual procedures are not primarily based on the necessity of protecting the assets of the company, but rather designed to comply with those conditions established by their vendors. We recommend that

CHARGEBACK (DEBIT MEMO) PROCEDURE

all policies and procedures in effect be reviewed to determine whether the following pertinent points are included:

POLICY HIGHLIGHTS

1. Any and all returns and adjustments to vendor accounts shall be initiated by use of the company chargeback form (debit memo). (See recommended format, Figure 5.1.)
2. No materials are to leave the premises without carrying an authorization copy of the chargeback form. One copy of the chargeback is to be used as a waybill to accompany the shipments.
3. All costs resulting from and associated with materials rejected, scrapped, or returned to vendors (owing to their errors) shall be fully recovered. These include

   - Inbound and/or outbound freight
   - Special packing, pallet charges, and so on
   - Import duties
   - Brokerage fees
   - Demurrage charges
   - Special order charges
   - Set-up charges
   - Any other such charges

4. The responsibility for recoveries relating to returns and other adjustment transactions shall be assigned to the accounts payable department. It has the required information at hand in the paid invoice files.

PROCEDURAL HIGHLIGHTS

1. Chargebacks must clearly indicate the reason for any returns (vendor responsibility versus vendor accommodation).

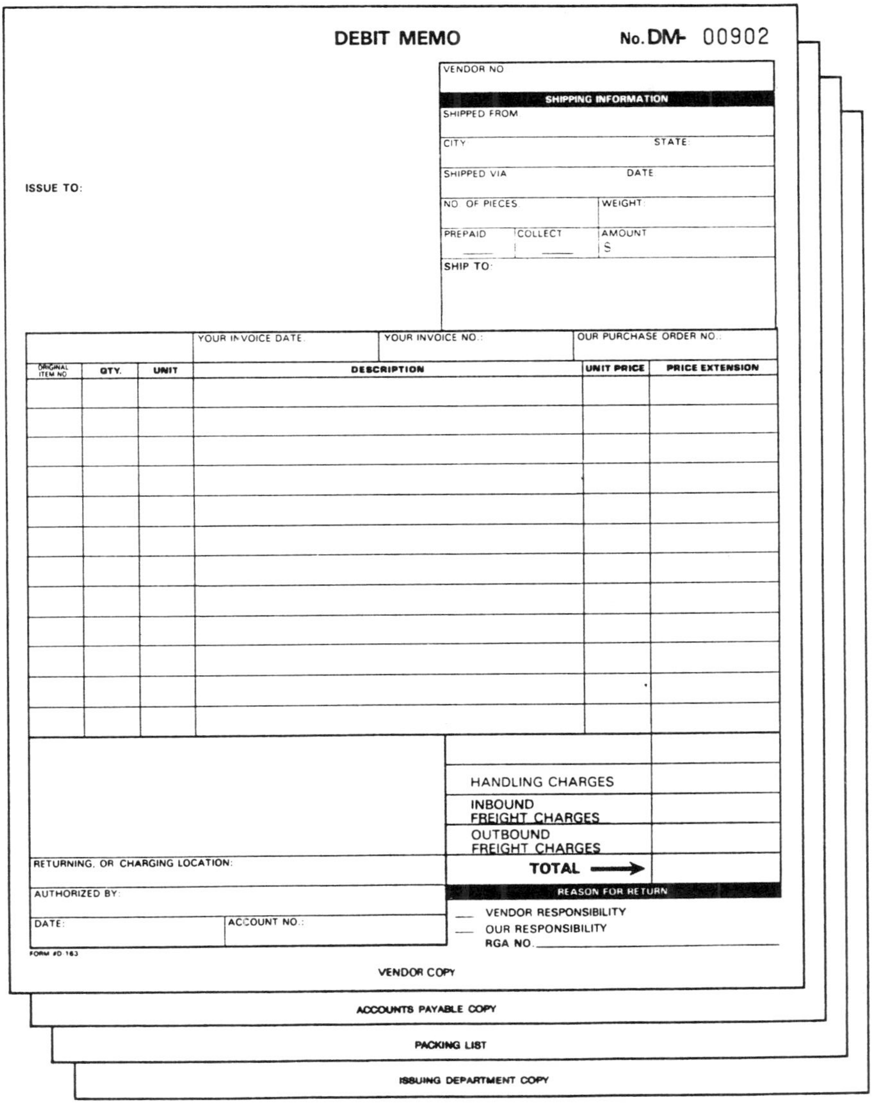

DEBIT MEMO No. DM- 00902

VENDOR NO

SHIPPING INFORMATION

SHIPPED FROM

CITY STATE

SHIPPED VIA DATE

NO. OF PIECES WEIGHT

PREPAID COLLECT AMOUNT $

SHIP TO:

ISSUE TO:

	YOUR INVOICE DATE	YOUR INVOICE NO.:	OUR PURCHASE ORDER NO.:		
ORIGINAL ITEM NO.	QTY.	UNIT	DESCRIPTION	UNIT PRICE	PRICE EXTENSION

HANDLING CHARGES

INBOUND FREIGHT CHARGES

OUTBOUND FREIGHT CHARGES

TOTAL

RETURNING, OR CHARGING LOCATION:

AUTHORIZED BY:

DATE: ACCOUNT NO.:

REASON FOR RETURN

___ VENDOR RESPONSIBILITY

___ OUR RESPONSIBILITY

RGA NO. ___

FORM #D 163

VENDOR COPY

ACCOUNTS PAYABLE COPY

PACKING LIST

ISSUING DEPARTMENT COPY

FIGURE 5.1 **Recommended debit memo format.**

CHARGEBACK (DEBIT MEMO) PROCEDURE

2. Shipments for returns owing to vendor responsibility are to be made "collect" to the vendor. If prepaid (via UPS, parcel post, and so forth), the costs of the prepaid shipment are to be recovered on the chargeback.
3. Shipments for returns owing to vendor accommodation should be prepaid, unless otherwise provided on the face of the chargeback document.
4. Chargebacks are to receive the highest priority processing at all levels

- Initiating department
- Shipping department
- Accounts payable department

Chargebacks remain non-interest bearing assets until deducted.

5. Chargebacks are to be posted to the vendor accounts at face value, with no financial discount consideration.

The recommended posting of chargebacks to vendor accounts at face value, with no financial discount consideration, is primarily based on the fact that purchasers vary as to their realizations of financial discounts when paying for the original transactions. Some financial discount payment dates are missed, so discounts are not taken. Or, if the discounts are taken, they may be subsequently repaid if charged back by the vendor as "unearned" at a later date.

In addition, few organizations wish to incur the administrative cost of the research necessary to determine, when posting credits, whether the original discount was realized. Consequently, to assure against possible loss, they establish policies directing that all credits, received from vendors, and debits against vendor accounts be taken at face value.

The vendors themselves are faced with the reverse of this situation. To minimize their own administrative expense, they forgo the research necessary to determine whether original documents were discounted when paid. Instead, when issuing their credits they take one of two courses of action:

PROCEDURAL HIGHLIGHTS

1. Issue all credits without showing any terms
2. Show their terms and discounting on all credit documents without regard to whether the original documents were discounted when paid.

Even when the second approach is used, vendors will most often accept, without question, the deduction of the face value of credit items.

A supplemental foundation for *not initiating the return of financial discounts* to vendors is the recognition that a preponderance of adjustments to vendor accounts results from vendor errors. In such instances, even if the financial discounts for the original shipments were earned and taken when paid, the discounts were based on the prompt payments of monies due. However, there is generally a period between the time of the initial payment, the discovery of defective (or incorrect) material, and its return, and the subsequent recovery of the monies, during which the vendor has had the use of the purchaser's monies while the purchaser has had nothing of value in return.

Vendor errors, discovered by the purchaser, can in actuality be a transference of quality control costs to the purchaser that are more properly those of the supplier. As a consequence, the purchaser has incurred the costs of receiving and inspecting the original shipment. Other cost items include the investment in inventory and operational disruptions, as well as the expenses of transaction and document processing.

In light of these facts, there is ample justification for establishing a policy against posting financial discounts when accepting either vendor credits or debits made against vendors' accounts.

In addition to not returning financial discounts, many clients are now imposing handling charges on returns and adjustments attributable to vendor responsibility.

The chargeback (debit memo) procedure eliminates the need for complicated suspending mechanisms. Returns and adjustments become immediate.

The recommended chargeback should be a prenumbered and controlled document. Any document that allows a company asset to

CHARGEBACK (DEBIT MEMO) PROCEDURE

be removed from the premises should be subject to control—and to subsequent audit.

Document flow is to be that which is provided on the accompanying Debit Transaction Flow Chart (Figure 5.2). The Material Inspection Report (MIR) procedure generally would apply only to those vendors for which highly technical quality control information is required.

It is important that chargebacks be restricted to vendor-related transactions. We find too many instances in which, in the name of forms reduction, a catch-all "trash can" form is used as a debit memo. The same form is also used for a variety of tasks, from sending typewriters out for repair to sending the company president's golf shoes to Palm Springs. For items sent out for repair or replacement that will remain the property of the company, we recommend that a separate "off-premises asset" form be devised.

Because of contractual agreements, a company may agree to accept vendors' credit invoices for a few "select" vendors. *Such agreements should be executed only in coordination with the financial division*, and *such arrangements should be severely limited*. Several of our clients require that such vendors issue credits against the clients' chargebacks (by number) within five days of the date of the returns or adjustments. Otherwise, the clients will automatically apply their chargebacks to the accounts.

A recent experience with a major manufacturing client both reinforces and proves the viability of using the chargeback (debit memo) procedure for making adjustments to vendor accounts. Our review was conducted at five separate plant locations. Each was found to be using the "request for credit" procedure to recover monies due from their vendors. Similar overpayments to suppliers were discovered throughout the five locations.

As a result of our recommendations, four of the plants adopted the chargeback (debit memo) procedure to initiate recovery of the overpayments. Recovery of the monies due in those four locations was effected quickly, reflecting an 85% percent acceptance of the chargebacks without contest on the part of the vendors. The fifth division used the chargebacks as "request for credit" documents. A letter was sent to each vendor, which asked, in essence, "Do you owe us the

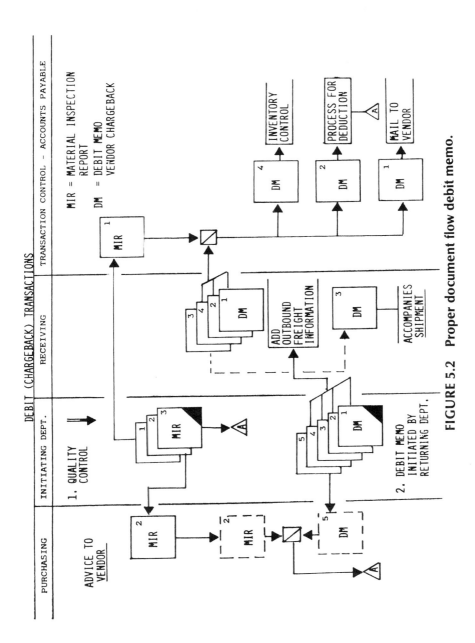

FIGURE 5.2 Proper document flow debit memo.

CHARGEBACK (DEBIT MEMO) PROCEDURE

amounts shown on the attached?" Nine months later, this plant had still not resolved the issues. It continued to experience delay in the recovery of overpayments, totaling in excess of $60,000, which were, in many cases, identical to those of the other plants.

Based on this experience, our client's corporate headquarters is in the process of issuing stringent policies to assure that positive chargeback procedures are used throughout the organization.

6

TOLERANCES

The term *tolerance* and its various applications require detailed discussion. Within different organizations, it can have various meanings according to where and how it is being used. Too often, its correct usage for one department is not the norm in other departments, resulting in losses that, although not hidden, are considered acceptable.

The first and only really acceptable "tolerance" relates directly to the purchasing of certain types of products or bulk commodities. A classic example can be found in the printing industry. Almost without exception, as an industry standard within the printing industry, the vendor is allowed a plus or minus 5% variance (tolerance) from the quantities ordered when filling orders.

Seldom does one find the resulting shipments to fall below *the ordered quantity.*

An unacceptable tolerance is a printer's invoicing for 10,000 printed forms, but shipping only 9,700. The purchase tolerance standard should not be applied. The vendor is entitled to payment only for the number of forms actually received, even though the shortage falls within the 5% industry tolerance.

Sizeable losses can be incurred when receiving tolerances are allowed in companies that purchase large quantities in bulk, receiving truckload and tank car shipments. One client, with three separate plant locations, had been been experiencing inventory shortages at one of the locations. This plant was constantly running out of raw materials while its inventory records indicated otherwise. Then it

TOLERANCES

was discovered that the quantities invoiced by the vendor were being input into the plant's inventory control records. However, a perusal of the receiving documents indicated that only about 85% of the quantities invoiced were actually unloaded from the tank trucks and physically placed into the inventory. Corrective action was taken. Only those quantities actually received were entered into the inventory control system. However, the accounts payable department continued to pay for the *invoiced* quantities. When questioned by our associate who was conducting the review, the answer from the individual in the payables department was, "That's an industry tolerance. We've been told that it is OK." The overpayments recovered from the vendor in this instance were in excess of $50,000. Our review of two other plant locations that purchased and received the identical raw material revealed that, counter to the practice in the first location, they both paid only for the quantities actually received.

Any form of *receiving* tolerance should be unacceptable. Payments should never be made for quantities other than those actually received. Any tolerance in this area should be completely unacceptable.

Companies using Payable by Approval procedures (see Chapter 3), in order to reduce the excessive routing of documents that occurs as a direct consequence of the system, will create an "allowed tolerance." This provides a "pay as invoiced" policy if any errors or violations of purchase orders result in overcharges that fall within certain limits. Any "allowed tolerance" policy is generally based on the premise that it is more costly to make minor adjustments than it is to absorb the excessive charges. *This is a fallacious assumption.* The real expense has already occurred: the administrative expense of determining that errors exist, whether major or minor. Once errors are discovered, the preliminary audit has placed all of the necessary information at hand.

The following chapter discusses in detail procedures for making minor adjustments without incurring excessive administrative expense.

7

ADJUSTMENTS TO VENDOR ACCOUNTS

The auditor should review accounts payable department procedures to determine whether excessive administrative costs are being incurred when adjustments to vendor invoices become necessary. Any excessive administrative costs related to the making of adjustments to vendor accounts can easily be eliminated. This simply requires that the posture taken by the accounts payable department is a positive one. The direct application of Best of Terms concepts during document processing through the accounts payable department can put a completely new face on the concept of adjustments to vendor accounts.

This positive attitude is critical to the effectiveness of the controls exercised during the processing of documents relating to vendor transactions. *The more positive and direct the approach to the payable operation, the more efficient and economical the result.* This is particularly certain in adjustments to vendor accounts.

Continuing variances between the records and balances shown on vendors' books, as well as on those of purchasers, are a normal occurrence in business. There are no strong guidelines in accounting to indicate that either set of books is more correct. In actuality, the more persistent party usually prevails. Vendors' credit department personnel receive continuing training in sophisticated collection tactics. Few accounts payable personnel (up to and including management) receive comparable training. This situation leaves a wide disparity between the abilities of the department staffs. It can be left to the reader as to which department is more likely to prevail.

ADJUSTMENTS TO VENDOR ACCOUNTS

A strong and efficient accounts payable department will not concern itself with adjusting its records to conform with those of its vendors, no matter how persistent the vendors, unless such variances are found to be the result of the purchasers' errors.

Adjustments to vendor accounts are necessary for various reasons. Sometimes they may be discerned during the processing of the original documents relating to the transactions. In other instances, adjustments may be required subsequent to this processing. Both fall into the following categories:

1. Violations of the purchase order terms relating to

   - Price
   - Quantity
   - Financial discount and credit terms
   - Trade/volume discounts
   - Freight allowances
   - Other considerations

2. Arithmetic errors on invoices
3. Returns or other adjustments because of vendor error, in such areas as

   - Quantity
   - Quality
   - Shipments of incorrect items
   - Duplicate shipments
   - Early or late shipments

4. Returns or adjustments because of vendor accommodation, in such cases as when

   - Vendor accepts (buys back) returns of items purchased in error
   - Vendor buys back excessive inventories or discontinued items

ADJUSTMENTS TO VENDOR ACCOUNTS

In categories 1 and 2 (violations of purchase order terms and invoice errors), the necessary adjustments are usually evident when the original invoices and related documents are being processed for payment. In category 3 (returns because of vendor error), the resulting returns and adjustments may be initiated after the original documents have been processed and input for payment.

Requests for credit, if used at all, should be used only for those adjustments included in category 4 (returns because of vendor accommodation), in those cases in which the vendor is doing a favor for the purchaser.

All adjustments in categories 1, 2, and 3, when accomplished *after* the processing of the original documents, should always be initiated by the purchaser through the execution of chargebacks (debit memos) to be deducted directly from the vendors' accounts upon issuance. (See "Chargeback Procedure," Chapter 5.)

The discovery of any overcharges falling within categories 1 or 2, *during* the original document-processing procedure, commonly results in any of several possible actions.

1. *Allowed Tolerance.* Some organizations have a "pay as invoiced" policy if the error, or violation of the purchase order, results in an overcharge that falls within certain limits.

   - This policy is generally based on the premise that it is more costly to make minor adjustments than it is to absorb excessive charges. *This is a fallacious assumption.* As noted earlier, the real expense has already occurred, that is, the administrative expense of determining that errors exist, whether major or minor. By discovering errors, the preliminary audit has placed all necessary information at hand, and the adjustment can be made with little additional expense.
   - Many vendors have "allowed tolerances" for any minor underpayments that they may receive. Any use of tolerances by purchasers may well preempt the similar policy in vendors' receivable departments. By establishing tolerances, purchasers thus assure that they will almost always be the losers.

ADJUSTMENTS TO VENDOR ACCOUNTS

2. *Hold, or Return Invoice.* (Awaiting a corrected invoice from the vendor).

   - This procedure requires establishing a suspense file that must be maintained while awaiting the receipt of correcting credits or the return of a corrected invoice. Such suspense files require accompanying disciplines and associated administrative expenses.
   - The corrections that must be made are not normally within the province of the vendor's credit and receivables department. The required adjustments are usually issued by either the vendor's marketing or warehouse department. Therefore, withholding such invoices from payment may well generate extensive correspondence or communications with the vendor's credit department as to why the invoice in question has not been paid.
   - There are increased processing costs because the accounts payable department has to handle transactions at least twice.
   - The only possible benefit is the interest income resulting from the withholding of the entire payment. However, the benefit is not really worth the distortions of the general ledger accounts while the items are being withheld from payment.

3. *Debit Memo.* (Pay as invoiced and execute a chargeback (debit memo) to be processed coincidental with the payment). This procedure is preferable to the previous two. However, it requires the additional steps of creating the chargeback (debit memo) and processing it as an additional transaction.

4. *Direct Adjustment.* (Correct any overcharges or other errors directly on the face of the invoice). In making a direct adjustment, the processor should process the corrected document for payment in the proper amount. Coincident with making the correction, the vendor should be notified regarding the adjustment. Such notification can be very simple, providing the vendor with the invoice number, the reason for the adjustment, and the amount by which the invoice is adjusted.

ADJUSTMENTS TO VENDOR ACCOUNTS

In previous chapters much has been said about the disadvantages to the purchaser resulting from the use of "request for credit" routines. They are most prevalent when corrective action is preempted by the company's purchasing department. Not realizing the effects of their actions, buyers may, when applying the purchase order price, call or write the vendor requesting a price-correcting credit. At the same time, buyers may be instructing the accounts payable department to withhold the invoices from payment while awaiting the requested credits.

Although the reasons for the instructions to withhold incorrect invoices from payment may be seen to have merit by buyers, they fail to recognize the problems that result. In this situation, a buyer is dealing with his or her counterpart in the vendor's marketing department. Once invoices are issued, however, their collection becomes the responsibility of the vendor's credit department.

Good intentions do not always result in good accounting or business procedures, particularly when the use of "request for credit" procedures is coupled with attempts to accommodate a vendor's accounting procedures. The following scenario can be the result:

- First, the buyer uses the "request for credit" procedure to obtain a corrected invoice.
- If no credit is immediately forthcoming, follow-up letters are sent. Eventually the follow-up letters that contain threats of direct action. Then, in order to recover funds due from the vendor, some sort of debit against the vendor's account is effected.

During this period (which may be quite lengthy), the vendor's accounts receivable department is unconcerned about the problem that has arisen between its marketing department and the customer's purchasing department. All it knows is receivables: an invoice is on its books that some deadbeat has not paid. In addition, the collection routines in major concerns are rather automatic, often without regard to any conflicts or adjustments that may be in progress.

Classic losses that are discovered during our reviews of client procedures include late-payment service charges applied by vendors because of late payments of invoices (with glaring errors) that have

ADJUSTMENTS TO VENDOR ACCOUNTS

been withheld from payment while the purchaser is awaiting a correcting credit.

It is always in the best interest of the purchaser to *initiate* all adjustments to vendor accounts in a straightforward and positive manner. It is not always necessary to initiate chargebacks (debit memos) to effect adjustments to vendor accounts, as we recommended earlier in this chapter. The previously described situation would be more efficiently addressed through a direct adjustment procedure.

In manual payable operations, the simplest and most direct method of making adjustments coincidental with document processing is to issue a simple notification to the vendor. See Figure 7.1 for a typical adjustment notification letter.

Care should be taken to ensure that administrative expenses, that is, vendor expenses, are not transferred to the purchaser. There is no real need to prepare lengthy explanations or schedules to demonstrate that the vendor is in error in his invoiced charges. The vendor has at hand (or should have) the following documentation:

- A copy of the purchaser's order containing all of the terms and conditions of the purchase
- A copy of the invoice
- A record of the method of shipping

By using a vendor adjustment notification letter, either inserted with checks to vendors or sent to them under separate cover, minor adjustments are made without incurring involved or expensive procedures. Any burden of contest lies with the vendors.

A similar process can be incorporated into most modern computer payable programs. The reason for the adjustment then appears directly on the remittance advice, thus eliminating the need for manual preparation of the letter. Incorporating this procedure, one client discontinued all "allowed tolerances" and was able to make minor adjustments on payments of all invoices found to be incorrect, including some in amounts of hundreds of thousands of dollars, resulting in this client saving almost $100,000 in the first month.

VENDOR DEDUCTION NOTIFICATION

Date:

_____

_____

_____

ATTENTION: Accounts Receivable Department

SUBJECT: Your Invoice No. _____ Invoice Date _____

Our Purchase Order No. _____ Amount $_____

Gentlemen:

Please note that the amount paid differs from your invoice by

$_____ for the following reasons:

☐ Extension error. Please correct your records.

☐ Discount Terms do not agree with invoice.

☐ Freight Terms do not agree with our Purchase Order.

☐ Other _____

☐ Invoice Item price(s) do not agree with our Purchase Order.

ITEM NO.	INVOICE PRICE	P.O. PRICE

If you have any questions, please contact our Purchasing Department at (555) 467-8924.

FIGURE 7.1   Notification to vendor when invoice amount is adjusted.

AUDIT GUIDE
Review of Procedures for Adjusting Vendor Accounts

I. INTRODUCTION

This audit guide is intended as a summary of the major audit points contained in Part II. In some instances the guide suggests specific audit actions that can be taken; in others, questions regarding individual aspects of the subject area will be asked. Unlike some lists (such as internal control questionnaires) that relate to audit actions, the questions are not intended to elicit simply a yes or no response. Use them instead to think critically about the subject that is raised, so that it can be related to the operation in a worthwhile manner.

II. PREPARATORY ACTIVITIES

Knowledge of the business activities that result in the necessity for adjustments to vendor accounts is most important. Therefore, familiarization with existing procedures for making adjustments to vendor accounts is essential.

III. ORGANIZATIONAL FACTORS

Any department may determine the need to return goods to a vendor. However, the accounts payable department is responsible for the recovery of any monies due as a result of the return. It is also respon-

AUDIT GUIDE

sible for making necessary adjustments to vendor accounts for other reasons.

IV. VENDOR CREDIT INVOICES VERSUS CHARGEBACKS (DEBIT MEMOS)

A. Which of the following is the principal source of documentation for adjustments to vendor accounts?
   1. Vendor credit memos
   2. Corporate debit memos (chargebacks)
B. If a vendor issues a credit memo to correct a vendor error, these are questions one must consider:
   1. Does the credit memo provide any allowances for in-bound or out-bound freight that may have been initially charged to the purchaser?
   2. Is it free of handling charges?
   3. Does it allow for credit in the full amount of the purchase, without regard to financial discounts?
   4. Does all material leaving the premises carry an authorization copy of the debit memo form?
   5. Are all costs resulting from and associated with materials that are rejected, scrapped, or returned to vendors (owing to vendor error) fully recovered?
C. Chargeback procedures
   1. Is the responsibility for recoveries assigned to the accounts payable department?
   2. Do the chargeback (debit memo) forms clearly indicate the cause for the return of the goods?
   3. Are shipments for returns owing to vendor responsibility made on a "collect" basis (or, if prepaid, are the charges recovered)?
   4. Are chargebacks given the highest priority for processing in the initiating department? in the shipping department? in the accounts payable department?

AUDIT GUIDE

5. Are chargebacks posted to vendor accounts at face value?
6. Is the chargeback form prenumbered and controlled?

D. Other adjustments to vendor accounts
   1. Does the accounts payable department make direct adjustments (short pay) to invoices that are found to be in error (including arithmetic errors or violations of purchase order terms)?
   2. Does the accounts payable department hold (or return to the vendor) an invoice while awaiting a correction from the vendor?
   3. When direct adjustments are made to correct vendor invoices, are proper notifications made to advise the vendors of the reasons for the adjustments?
   4. Is there a policy that prohibits the use of "tolerances" for quantity, freight, and price variances with purchase order terms and conditions that may appear on invoices?

PART III

POLICIES, PROCEDURES, AND PRACTICES

8

FINANCIAL DISCOUNTING AND PAYMENT PRACTICES

Auditors should not assume that a simple comparison between the financial payment terms on the purchase orders and/or invoices and the due dates and discounts applied during the payment process is an adequate reconciliation of payment disciplines and practices. Any or all of these may be in error.

A common fault is the promiscuous use of Net 30 terms by those creating the purchase orders. You should first check to see whether any financial terms on purchase orders are less favorable than those provided on the vendors' invoices.

For example, some *purchase orders* may carry terms of Net 30, while the *vendors' invoices* carry 2% 10 or other terms more favorable than the Net 30 shown on the orders. If this occurs frequently, it may indicate that the purchasing department may not be assigning sufficient importance to the negotiations of beneficial cash flow and financial discount availability from vendors.

If the purchase order formats used by a company fail to provide for the display of any payment and financial discount terms, then the auditor can be assured that losses are being incurred in this area. The very failure to include such a display is an indication of the lack of importance assigned to cash flow negotiations.

The second check should be to determine whether the realization of beneficial payment and discount terms has been made a definite responsibility of the accounts payable department. Is the department actually disciplining this element of transactions? We can almost guarantee that somewhere in the company's paid invoice

FINANCIAL DISCOUNTING AND PAYMENT PRACTICES

files will be repeated invoices from a regular supplier with erratic terms offerings. For invoices containing the same line items, one invoice may be at Net 30, another at 2% 10, and subsequent invoices with similar variations. If the accounts payable department is actually *disciplining* the financial terms, all of the payments to this vendor will have been processed under the 2% 10 terms. If the payments have been processed as invoiced, then there are no real disciplines in place for beneficial payment and financial discount realization.

All purchase order terms should be strictly enforced in a positive and straightforward manner, using the Best of Terms concept. Effective control can best be effected by using the accounts payable department as the focal point of control. However, in order to do so, there must be a complete understanding and awareness of the proper applications of the specific payment and financial discount terms used in various industries. The following is an abbreviated glossary of financial discount terms and their proper applications:

- *POR*—Payment upon receipt.
- *Net 30*—Payment in full 30 days from invoice date.
- *Net 10th*—Payment in full on the 10th of the month following invoice date.
- *1% 10, Net 30*—A 1% discount may be deducted if payment is made within 10 days of invoice or date of receipt. Otherwise, net payment is to be made 30 days after such date.

  Note: Other percentages may be used and the number of days for both discounting and net payment may also vary.

- *1% 10 ADF*—A discount of 1% (after deducting any freight charges) may be taken if paid within 10 days. The freight charges may be built into the price and so indicated in the invoice. This is a standard practice in the lumber industry.
- *1% 10th, Net 30*—A 1% deduction may be made if paid by the 10th of the month following invoice date. Otherwise, payable on the 10th of the second month following the invoice date. (See additional detail on proximo terms following the glossary.) These terms may also be stated as 1% 10th Prox.
- *1% 10 ROG*—A 1% discount is earned if paid within 10 days of receipt of goods.

FINANCIAL DISCOUNTING AND PAYMENT PRACTICES

- *1% 10th & 25th*—A 1% discount is earned as follows:
  - Invoices dated from the 25th to the 10th of the next month, payable with discount on the 25th.
  - Those dated from the 10th to the 25th of any month, payable with discount on the 10th of the following month.

Of course, there are many variations and combinations of these financial terms. The percentages, number of days, and datings often vary.

Care must be taken in the development of any such glossary with its accompanying instructions for applications of the varying terms. A number of years ago, during the period when the prime interest rate hit the high teens and low twenties, we noted one division of a major corporation whose accounts payable department was processing documents with terms of ½% 10, Net 30, for payment in 10 days without discounting.

In answer to our query regarding this obviously detrimental practice, we were shown a letter from corporate headquarters regarding ½% 10 days terms. The letter advised that "due to the high cost of monies, no longer are ½% 10 days terms to be applied during the processing of documents for payment." Consequently, the department was not taking the ½%. Yet it continued to pay within 10 days. A telephone call to our contact at corporate headquarters caused the issuance of a clarifying letter of instruction.

Misunderstandings about some industry terms can generate early payments and associated missed discounts. Classic misunderstandings of financial discount and payment terms are constantly being found in applications of financial discounts and due dates under proximo terms.

Proximo should by no means be interpreted as meaning "approximately." For accounting purposes, it specifically indicates *the next month*. But, in common use, this meaning does not always hold. Proximo ("Prox") terms have evolved from the days when most all credit purchases were paid upon receipt and reconciliation of the vendors' monthly statements. Those offering discounts for prompt payments generally had several legends at the bottom of their statements, such as

FINANCIAL DISCOUNTING AND PAYMENT PRACTICES

- If the above current items are paid within 10 days of the receipt of this statement, a 2% discount may be taken.
- No payments received by us, nor items invoiced after the 25th of the month are shown above—such will appear as current items on your next statement.

Under Prox terms items invoiced prior to the 26th of any month are discountable if paid by the 10th of the following month. Any that are invoiced on the 26th or later are discountable if paid by the 10th of the second month following the invoice date.

The misunderstandings and incorrect applications of, for instance, 2% 10th, Net 30, terms usually occur on invoices dated from the 26th to the end of the month. The first errors are usually due to what is incorrectly thought to be late processing, coupled with incorrect computation of discountable due dates.

Next, because of someone's thinking that the discount date has been missed, a due date is assigned for payment on the next check issued, without discounting, as in the following example:

Invoice—dated 06/27/90
Invoice Payment Terms: 2% 10th, Net 31
Invoice amount $10,000
Processed through the Accounts Payable Department on 07/15/90
Paid by check issued on 07/15/90
No discount taken

Under the 2% 10th Prox terms, with payment being made on or before the 10th of the month *following the month in which the invoice was issued*, a $200 discount was earned, but not taken. If a discounted payment is not made on the 10th of the appropriate month following the invoiced date, then the net payment should not be made until the 10th of the following month. In the foregoing example, the payment of the full $10,000 invoice amount should not have been made until September 10.

A simple way of checking to see whether there is complete understanding of Prox terms is to make an appraisal of the number of checks issued to a Prox vendor during one year. Such a vendor should receive only 12 checks per year. The only exception would be

FINANCIAL DISCOUNTING AND PAYMENT PRACTICES

a check issued to cover a long-past-due item missed during regular processing.

One multibillion dollar industrial client was found to have issued 13 checks to a Prox discount vendor in the month of January. The discounts earned, but not taken, from this one vendor exceeded $25,000. More important than the losses from the missed discounts (which were later recovered from the vendor), was that our discovery led to a complete review of the glossary of payment terms being used throughout the company. Along with the creation of more concise glossaries, a greater corporate-wide emphasis was placed on negotiations of payment terms with vendors. As a result of both the improved sophistication in application of payment terms and improved terms negotiations, the client realized an improvement in cash flow, averaging an additional 19 days in extended payments to vendors during the following year. On the slightly less than one billion dollars in purchase transactions with vendors, this 19-day improvement resulted in cash-flow benefits in excess of well over $2,000,000. *We frequently encounter vendors who offer but do not fully understand Prox terms.*

Accounts payable departmental policies should be completely reviewed, comparing the actual circumstances discovered through reviews of the paid invoice files with the stated policies and established procedures of the department. A key item to be checked is the departmental policy regarding the taking of financial discounts when payments of invoices being processed will fall past the discount-available dates. Is the decision about discounting left to the discretion of the departmental personnel? If so, they are being given the privilege of adjusting their own workload. By not taking the discounts, they can, in effect, make sure that they do not get any vendor correspondence that requires their further action. Their solution can easily be the practice of paying vendors whatever amount is invoiced as quickly as possible without applying disciplines. If this is done, very little will be heard from vendors' accounts receivable departments.

The more sophisticated of our clients are found to have a firm accounts payable policy of taking all financial discounts, whenever paid. When we first encountered a policy of this type, we naturally

FINANCIAL DISCOUNTING AND PAYMENT PRACTICES

questioned the ethics of such an approach. After many years of experience, we have found much that justifies and validates this policy.

The justifications for corporate policies requiring the taking of all financial discounts, whenever paid, are vendors' receivable practices and the potential for errors in their invoices that cause delays in invoice processing by the purchasers.

The large majority of vendors do accept late discounted payments that are received in a *reasonable* time past the stated periods. In addition, we find that the payments of invoices past discount due dates are often the result of delays in accounts payable processing *owing to vendor errors in shipping and/or invoicing*, as follows:

- Failure to include correct purchase order number
- Incorrect pricing on invoices
- Disparities between quantities invoiced and quantities received
- Invoiced payment terms contrary to contractual agreements
- Invoicing of unauthorized charges
- Receipts of invoices substantially past the actual invoice dates
- Freight charges and/or shipment routings that are contrary to those established

When any of these errors occur, delays in processing of documents through accounts payable will result.

With credit, financial and trade discounts, freight, and most other allowances being considered a function of pricing, many vendors have set very definite criteria for their billing and credit departments in this regard. And, with few exceptions, the established criteria are found to be for periods of time greater than those stated on the vendors' invoices and statements. Thus, the criteria disciplined by the vendors become their actual terms, as opposed to their stated terms.

It is important to keep in mind that this is a fluid situation, subject to the pressures of the marketplace, today's rapidly fluctuating interest rates, and their resulting effects on vendors' cash-flow situations. Yesterday's experience may have no relation to today's circumstances in dealing with the same vendor.

FINANCIAL DISCOUNTING AND PAYMENT PRACTICES

It is impractical for most corporate financial divisions to be continuously aware of each vendor's criteria for enforcement of financial discount terms. *Individual judgments in this regard should never be left to the personnel in the accounts payable department.* The practical solution is to:

1. Make every effort to pay all vendor documents when due.
2. Take all financial discounts, whenever paid. Allow the vendor to determine whether the payments fall within the established criteria of terms disciplines—the vendor's actual terms. Important to this concept is the recognition that the purchaser is entitled to the vendor's best terms, whether actual or stated.
3. When late discounted payments result in claims from the vendors for return of the discounts, they may be gracefully refunded.

A further evaluation of accounts payable departmental procedures should be made to determine whether certain processing priorities have been established.

To keep to a minimum the missed discounts resulting from late payment processing, departmental administrative disciplines should be in place. These should assure that a "first-in, first-out" philosophy is not used in the accounts payable department. Documents should be processed according to an established priority schedule, taking into account

1. Company debit and vendor credit memos (non-interest-bearing assets until deducted). This minimizes the potential for incurring debit balances with vendors.
2. High discount, short term
3. Low discount, short term
4. Medium and longer term, according to available discount
5. Net documents

These priorities should apply to all work-in-house, regardless of when received.

FINANCIAL DISCOUNTING AND PAYMENT PRACTICES

Auditors should be aware of another critical area as they search through the paid invoice files. Vendors—some without thought, others with possibly a high degree of sophistication—may attempt to adjust a price through notices directed to their customers' accounts payable departments. See the XYZ Corporation letter of June 1, 1991, and invoice of July 3 in Figures 8.1 and 8.2. This letter, addressed to the accounts payable department of XYZ's customer, advises that its terms are to change to Net 30 Days. It fails to state that the payment terms being changed were originally 2% 30 Days.

As the due dates did not change, this notification was, no matter how you look at it, a notification of an across-the-board 2% price increase.

An accounts payable department should ignore any correspondence directed to it that attempts to change terms or any other conditions of purchase. Such correspondence should be addressed to the purchasing departments of vendors' customers. The decision regarding whether to accept the price increase should be made *knowingly* by those responsible for initiating purchase orders, not by accounts payable.

During our review of the client who received the XYZ Corporation's letter, we found that the company's accounts payable person not only accepted the notification, but actually enforced it. The illustrated invoice, dated after the effective date of July 1, carried the established 2% 30 day terms. However, because of the letter, the invoiced terms were crossed out by the accounts payable individual and the lesser Net 30 Day terms were applied when making the payment.

Any dialogue between the financial division (at the payable level) and the company's vendors should be restricted to financial matters only. The department should confine such dialogue to discussion of when the vendor can expect payment, arithmetic errors on invoices or payments, and the like. There should be no conversation at this level concerning prices, terms, or other conditions of purchase.

xyz corp
1520 North Street
Anytown, USA 98741

June 1, 1991

American Corporation
1100 South Street
Anytown, USA

Att: Accounts Payable Department

Please note that our financial discount and payment terms will change to Net 30 Days, effective July 1, 1991.

John Doe
Credit Manager

FIGURE 8.1 Notification of accounts payable of payment terms change should be made to the customer's purchasing department.

xyz corp

1520 North Street
Anytown, USA 98741

Invoice

No. 15996
Date 07/03/91
Shipped To _Same_

Sold To _American Corporation_
- _1100 South Street_
- _Any Town_

Your Order No. 4-220	Our Order No. 66015	Salesman ASE	Terms 2%	30 days	
Date Shipped 7/1/91	Shipped VIA UPS	F.O.B. Dest.			
Quantity Ordered	Quantity Shipped	Stock Number/Description	Price	Per	Amount
250	250	22-1630 Hampers	2 00		500 00

Original / Invoice

FIGURE 8.2

9

TRADE AND VOLUME DISCOUNTS

To effectively conduct an operational audit of their companies' procurement controls, auditors should have at least some general knowledge of the elements of transactions that affect the ultimate costs of purchased items. When making evaluations of individual transactions, the written page (the vendor's invoice) is too often taken as gospel. As long as the prices and terms on purchase orders and invoices are in agreement, they may well be accepted without question. This assumes that the purchase orders are well written.

The purchaser's position in a number of industries will often allow trade and/or volume discount entitlements. However, very few companies are found to have written policies and procedures specifically covering the treatments of purchases made subject to trade discounts and/or volume rebates.

In addition, the purchase orders issued by the various initiating departments seldom carry any information regarding trade or volume discount availability. And even less frequently do we find copies of such agreements in the *financial division*. All major contracts and purchase agreements with suppliers should be considered assets of the corporation and be readily available to the financial division for proper control. We find the lack of such availability to be prevalent throughout corporations, and the only control copies of the agreements to be in the hands of those who negotiated them (purchasing departments).

The consequences of leaving all such trade discount control in the hands of the negotiators can be most costly. During a review of a major health care center, one of our associates discovered that in-

TRADE AND VOLUME DISCOUNTS

voices from the center's principal wholesaler carried a column in its format titled "Disc." (see Figure 9.1). Most of the column was left blank. Intermittently, the letter "N" was found as an entry accompanying specific products.

The natural question was posed to the center's controller: "Are all these items without an 'N' (net) entry entitled to some percentage of discount?" This query triggered a meeting with the pharmacy division. During the meeting, it was determined that the center, based on contracts, was entitled to a 10% trade discount for all non-net items. A search of the paid files revealed that no credits reflecting the receipts of this 10% trade discount had been posted during the past two years.

Further, during the meeting, it was learned that the pharmacy department assumed that the earned trade discounts were being routinely provided on the wholesaler's monthly statements. This assumption reflected a lack of expertise in the center's accounts payable procedures. The center paid by individual invoice, not by monthly statements. In any event, a review of the vendor's monthly statements disproved the assumption. No credits were so provided.

More than $30,000 in trade discounts had gone unrealized by the center in only one year. This loss was due solely to a failure to indicate on the control copy of the purchase order the trade discount availability. Those negotiating the contract had obviously left the realization of the negotiated discount completely in the hands of the vendor.

This finding and recovery led to our associate's conducting very biased audits of all of this vendor's accounts with others of our clients. Of 15 clients within the geographical area served by the vendor, only two were properly disciplining, and subsequently realizing, the negotiated trade discounts.

Trade and volume discount entitlements can be either very simple or complex. The following is a brief description of the basic concepts involved.

TRADE DISCOUNTS

Trade discounts are those deducted from established market or list prices, for which the purchaser is entitled for any of a number of

VOLUME DISCOUNTS

reasons, such as its position in the industry, or in return for the purchaser's performing central purchasing, warehousing, and other similar functions. Such discounts are generally predetermined and provided directly upon invoicing or at payment.

VOLUME DISCOUNTS

Volume discounts are those provided to the customer in consideration of the volume of purchases made (or anticipated) within given periods. Volume discounts may be provided through several avenues:

1. They may be given directly on individual invoices, based on anticipated purchases. If so provided, the vendor may require some reconciliation and adjustment at the end of the buying period. Anticipated volumes are often used by the vendor to extend beneficial pricing to preferred customers. No reconciliation is ever required.
2. The invoices may be issued at list (or established) prices. Then, periodic rebates, based on the volume of purchases during the base periods, are issued through credit memos or in the form of checks made out as the purchaser directs. This second method is most common. Although very easy to apply, such disciplines are most often lacking in payable operations.

Many vendors, in order to induce greater promptness in the payments from their customers, have been noted to convert standard trade and volume discounts to the status of financial discounts. Although we are sure that the credit managers of suppliers do not regard this as a "sharp" business practice, in the real world it can be considered just that.

Under this "trade discount conversion," the face of vendor's invoices will clearly indicate, often on the basis of line item by line item, that the purchaser is entitled to a specific trade discount. Then it is presented in the invoice summary as a *financial discount* related to prompt payment of invoices.

ABEL WHOLESALE CORP.
1200 North Street
Anytown

INVOICE #14228
DATE: 09/09/91

Sold To American Corp.
         1100 South Street
         Anytown

Order No. 25560	FOB: Dest.	Via: UPS	Terms: Net 30		
QTY	Stock No./Description		Price	Disc.	Extension
18	11-119	Cups	22.50	N	405.50
10	18-162	Covers	15.00		150.00
22	22-183	Cloth Wraps	5.50		121.00
24	22-199	Containers	12.50	N	300.00
48	44-160	Trays	18.00		864.00
36	44-175	Tray Covers	12.00		432.00
8	66-100	Carts	48.00		384.00
	Mdse Total: 2656.50		Less Discount:	0.00	
			Pay This Amount		2656.50

FIGURE 9.1 Invoice with most of discount column left blank.

BCD Corporation PURCHASE ORDER: S-51
1100 South Street
Anytown, USA 12345

SUPPLIER: EFG Corporation
1200 North Street
Anytown, USA 12345

Date: 09/04/90	FOB: Destination	Via: UPS	Terms: Net 30
Qty	Stock No./Description	Unit Price	Extension
4 ea.	677019 Film	300.00	1200.00
Account #1410-10		Total	1200.00

FIGURE 9.2 Purchase order reflecting the agreed price (see Fig. 9.3).

TRADE AND VOLUME DISCOUNTS

The complete inappropriateness of the stances taken by some vendors in making this conversion of terms is revealed in the following example:

BCD Corporation Purchase Order S-51, 09/04/90
    Line item–677019 4 ea. @ $300.00 $1200.00

EFG Corporation Invoice #31388, 09/14/90
    Line item–677019 4 ea. @ $450.00   1800.00

Merchandise	1800.00
Sales Tax 6.00%	108.00
Invoice Total	$1908.00

        If account is current
        Disc. $600.00 if paid by 10/13/90

(See Figures 9.2 and 9.3.)

Note: In this instance, the purchaser clearly expects to pay $300 each for the purchased items. No reasonable individual would anticipate or accept the type of penalty the vendor is imposing by converting the trade discount to the status of a financial discount, to be applied for a payment made after the 30-day due date. The "late payment service charge" statement on the invoice (Figure 9.3) already imposes a penalty for any failure to make payments in a timely manner.

When processing this invoice for payment, the invoiced price should have been reduced to that shown on the purchase order, regardless of when payment was to have been made. The invoice should then have been extended properly and *the sales tax refigured.* Then, any appropriate *financial* discount would be in order. The vendor should be given routine notification regarding the adjustment.

Regardless of the vendor's stance in regard to such conversion, we recommend that it be completely unacceptable to the sophisticated purchaser. Corporate policies should reflect this position.

To place this "conversion" of discounts into a proper perspective requires the recognition that most purchasers are fully departmentalized. In the example provided, a number of factors are evident:

EFG Corporation
1200 North Street
Anytown

BCD Corporation
110 South Street
Anytown

INVOICE

No.: 31388
Date: 09/14/90

PURCHASE ORDER NO.	SALESPERSON'S NO.	TERMS	SHIP VIA
S-51	Hse Acct	N-30	OT

QTY	ITEM NO.	DESCRIPTION	UNIT PRICE	EXTENSION
4	677019	X-5 FILM	450.00	1800.00

Invoices paid after net due date are subject to a service charge of 18% per annum, or the maximum allowed by applicable law, whichever is lower. All discounts must be taken at the time of payment, or said discount would be considered void and forfeited.

	MERCHANDISE	1800.00
	SALES TAX 6.00%	108.00
	TOTAL	1908.00

* IF ACCOUNT IS CURRENT *
DEDUCT   600.00   IF PAID BY 09/24/90

FIGURE 9.3

TRADE AND VOLUME DISCOUNTS

- The purchasing department has selected the vendor on the basis that, among other possible considerations, the company is to get a trade or volume discount on the items purchased.
- The summary section of the invoice inappropriately "converts" the trade discount to a financial discount.

It is inconceivable that those in charge of purchasing products would accept the fact that even a one-day delay in the processing and payment of any invoice could result in an approximate 30% increase in the price paid for goods or services. Allowing the vendor to apply this type of conversion could destroy any viable departmental budget control. If the vendor's materials constituted a major cost-of-goods increment, minor delays in processing invoices for payment could prove to be most costly and damaging to the company.

The company has presumably established the prices to be charged to its own customers based on the cost of materials as at least one of the criteria. If, in times of financial stress or backlog of work in the accounts payable department, the company's major supplier's invoices were paid late (by only a day or so), the annual budget for materials could be completely used up by the end of August owing to a hidden 30% increase in the cost of materials as a result of acceptance of the conversion by accounts payable. If allowed to do so, the accounts payable individual, when processing invoices for payment, can actually (although inadvertently) affect the company's cost of goods.

Without strong disciplines in place in the purchaser's accounts payable processing procedures, the vendor ends up in an enviable position. The vendor's marketing department provides the customer's procurement people with excellent pricing through a trade discount provision. Then the vendor's financial division raises the price back to list for myriads of customers through misdirection in invoicing. Thus the vendor is able to promise the customer anything—and end up giving nothing.

Another subtle result of this kind of conversion is that it can cause any sales taxes, or other items based on a percentage of invoiced price, to be overstated. In a number of states the sales and use tax laws require such taxes to be assessed on the total amount invoiced for products, rather than on the net amount paid.

10

FREIGHT CONTROL ANALYSIS

The most frequent errors that occur in purchase transactions are vendor violations of established freight terms. When reviewing the efficiency of the disciplines for controlling freight charges, the auditor should include an analysis of the frequency of corrective actions taken by the accounts payable department. These actions are reflected in the paid invoice files. If frequent adjustments are not present in the files, an in-depth evaluation of existing freight controls is in order.

During this analysis, the auditor should determine, solely from information in the paid invoice files, certain facts pertinent to effective controls over possible freight violations by vendors. The analysis should determine whether

1. Paid invoices are consistently supported by receiving information regarding the method of receipt, such as

    - Carrier waybill/probill number
    - Shipping point
    - How received—prepaid or collect
    - Cost of freight related to the shipment—whether prepaid or collect
    - Shipment weight, number of containers, cartons, and so on
    - Number of pallets (if palletized)
    - Shipment over or short, and any damage information, clearly presented

FREIGHT CONTROL ANALYSIS

2. Control copies of the purchase orders relating to the shipments against paid vendor invoices are readily at hand in the paid files. Moreover, do these control copies carry sufficient information on freight terms for direct disciplines? This information should include the following:

- FOB point—the point at which the title to the materials passes from the supplier to the purchaser
- Whether this is a delivered price—or exactly who absorbs what portion of the freight costs, and from what point
- Point from which the purchaser intends the materials to be shipped by the vendor
- Amount of specific freight allowances, if any are to be earned
- Demurrage—under what conditions they are allowable or not allowed
- Pallet or container charges—should be acceptable only if authorized by the purchase order

From the information at hand in the paid invoice files, and without having to reference any outside sources, the auditor should be able to reconcile completely both the propriety and the correctness of the amounts of incurred freight costs relating to each invoiced shipment. Such reconciliations should include these classic violations of freight terms that most frequently occur:

- Shipments made collect, but invoiced as prepaid, with freight charges added to invoices.
- Shipments made collect from warehouses or production points other than those from which purchased.
- Backorder shipments. Freight on such shipments should be absorbed by the suppliers, regardless of freight terms, if partial shipments are made at the vendors' convenience.
- Excessive freight charges added to invoices, under freight prepaid and added terms.
- Shipments made collect when purchase orders and established terms provide for full freight allowances.

DEFICIT FREIGHT

- Freight equalization arrangements, whereby one vendor, located farther away from the purchaser than another vendor, will equalize freight costs to the purchaser in order to be competitive.
- Deficit freight—excessive freight costs owing to vendor's failure to fully load trucks or other carriers.
- Improper pallet or container charges.
- Demurrage resulting from vendor shipping prior to due dates, causing excessive charges owing to shipments arriving prior to expected and scheduled dates.

Some of these typical freight violations are discussed in greater detail in the following section.

The auditor should determine both the exactitude and the level of sophistication of current freight controls. This determination should question whether the company is aware of some of the more subtle hidden freight losses that may be occurring. Such losses may include the following:

DEFICIT FREIGHT

Losses resulting from deficit freight charges are most typically found with shipments of raw materials against large blanket orders, when the purchaser is responsible for freight costs. These losses occur when, *against orders for truckload quantities*, the vendor fails to fill trucks or carriers completely to capacity. The freight rates per hundredweight (per cwt) are much higher for "less than truckload" (LTL) shipments than the rates for entire truckloads (TL).

The rates for a given commodity, for shipments between two geographical locations, generally follow a graduated pattern. For example, a small shipment of up to 3,000 pounds might have a rate of as much as $5.50 per cwt. Then, in graduated weight increments, the rate per cwt decreases, with a truckload shipment of 40,000 pounds paying but $1.97 per cwt.

This incremental rate structure creates circumstances under which it is advantageous for the shipper to pay the carrier the trans-

FREIGHT CONTROL ANALYSIS

portation costs for an entire truckload, even when the actual shipment falls somewhat short in volume. The resulting freight bill will be for the established truckload weight in order to qualify for the lower rate—such as 36,000 pounds, billed as 40,000 pounds.

The following example, taken from a series of invoices for a bulk purchase order, clearly illustrates the losses that can occur as a result of deficit freight charges.

BLANKET PURCHASE ORDER

Order #4288
    400,000 lbs. bulk @ 1.50/lb. $600,000.00
       To be shipped in truckload quantities
       weekly until complete.
    Freight terms: "Collect"

INVOICE

Invoice #1666
    38,000 lbs. bulk @ 1.50/lb. $57,000.00
    Less: Deficit freight (2,000 lbs.)   39.40
        Total $56,961.40

Pro Bill #899999
    38,000 lbs. bulk
    Shipped as 40,000 lbs. (TL) @ 1.97/cwt   788.00

INVOICE

Invoice #1690
    37,000 lbs. bulk @ 1.50/lb. $55,500.00
        Total $55,500.00

LOADED FREIGHT CHARGES

Pro Bill #7666999
    37,000 lbs.   bulk
    Shipped as 40,000 lbs. (TL) @ 1.97/cwt   788.00

In invoice #1690 the supplier's billing clerk failed to include the deficit freight credit as a line item. In effect, the purchaser ended up paying freight charges for 3,000 pounds of air at a cost of $1.97 per cwt.

Vendors should be held responsible for assuring that carriers are loaded to capacity for orders specifying truckload quantities. In the consulting engagement from which these examples were taken, it was found that our client paid in excess of $3,000 in freight charges for product that was not received.

BACK ORDER FREIGHT

Repeated partial shipments of individual orders, when made at the vendor's convenience, can create excessive freight costs to the purchaser. In instances of back-ordered partial shipments, made at the vendor's convenience, all freight charges for such shipments should be borne by the vendor.

A company policy regarding back-order freight should be clearly established. If there is such a policy in effect, a review (again in the paid invoice files) of the effectiveness of any disciplines is in order.

LOADED FREIGHT CHARGES (Prepay and Add Terms)

Operating in a highly competitive environment, it has become common practice for freight carriers to substantially discount published rates in order to receive "preferred carrier status" from their customers. When shipments are made under "prepay and add to invoice freight terms," some vendors have been found to add to their in-

FREIGHT CONTROL ANALYSIS

voices freight charges at the published rates, rather than at the discounted rates actually paid to the carriers. With these discounts ranging from 30% to 60%, those vendors who fail to properly pass them on to their customers can realize real profits on their freight charges.

This practice is quite common. In fact, we estimate that well over 50% of prepaid and added freight charges are "loaded" and require discipline. In order to so discipline, receiving documents must include the dollar amounts of freight charges, whether shipments are received on a prepaid or collect basis.

FREIGHT EQUALIZATION (Freight Basing Point)

Freight equalization is a standard practice in bulk chemical, steel, and other similar industries. Freight charges are based on those costs that would be incurred if the materials were shipped from the closest production facility, regardless of the actual shipping point used by the vendor.

The losses found in this area are generally due to failures on the part of the vendor's billing department to (1) include the proper allowances on the invoices, or (2) use correct freight rates.

The auditor should not accept as a viable control any procedure that depends solely upon the routing of documents carrying freight charges to the traffic department for approval. Two separate and distinct controls are required for proper disciplines of the freight elements of vendor transactions:

1. Propriety of freight charges

    - Under the terms of the purchase order and/or industry practices (or other conditions), should the vendor absorb the freight costs? Or should the costs be an expense of the purchaser?

2. Quality of the freight charges

FREIGHT EQUALIZATION

- Were the routing directions followed?
- Does the shipment carry the proper description of materials for rate determination?
- Has the proper rate been applied by the carrier?
- Are the computations of applicable rates performed correctly?

With all pertinent freight information included on both purchase orders and receiving documents, the two controls can be assigned to those departments with the best capabilities for the exercise of each control.

1. Propriety—accounts payable should be assigned the responsibility of assuring that any freight charges themselves were in accordance with the terms of the purchase orders.
2. Quality—the traffic department should be concerned solely with the correctness of shipment routing, descriptions used for rate determination, and any other technical aspects of the freight charges.

Through this procedure, the pertinent freight information is properly recorded on the receiving report, and the appropriate receiving log entries are made by the receiving department. Then the freight probills can be separated from the transaction and sent directly to the traffic department for quality appraisal. All the information necessary for evaluation of the propriety of the freight charges (based on purchase orders and/or established terms) should be readily available on the receiving report. This information includes the following:

- Date received
- Quantity (number of cases, pallets, and so forth)
- Shipping point
- Net weight received and unloaded (gross/tare weights)
- How received—prepaid or collect

FREIGHT CONTROL ANALYSIS

- Freight charges—the dollar amounts, whether received on a prepaid or collect basis
- Over/short or damage report—as required.

The freight information carried on the receiving document (Figure 10.1) may then be directly disciplined under the Best of Terms concept against the terms established on the purchase order and/or the established terms for the vendor. The purchase order format provided on Figure 10.1 makes provision for the clear and concise presentation of all terms:

- FOB Point—where title is to pass from supplier to purchaser
- Freight charges—very simply stated, who absorbs the transportation costs: supplier or purchaser?
- Shipping Point
- Routing
- Pallets received

One of our industrial clients, having accidentally discovered that a major shipment had been invoiced as having been prepaid (with the freight added to the invoice) was actually received as a "collect" shipment. A resulting edict was issued by the corporation's president to prevent such occurrences. It required that all invoices, probills, and receiving documents be sent to the traffic department for approval prior to processing for payment through the accounts payable department. The traffic department's personnel strength was subsequently increased from 25 to more than 40 to handle the flood of documentation received. Our review (conducted several years later) disclosed losses in excess of $100,000 attributable to inappropriate freight charges. The traffic department experts appraised the "quality" of the freight charges appearing on the invoices and the "quality" of the freight charges that appeared on the probills. Each had either received minor corrections or had been stamped as reviewed and "approved" by the department. An appraisal of the supporting documentation within the paid invoice files revealed numerous instances in which the approval stamp had been applied to freight charges that, under the terms of the purchase orders, should have been more properly the responsibility of the vendor.

PURCHASE ORDER-RECEIVING COPY

No. 15391

DATE

DATE ACK.

SHIP TO:

V
E
N
D
O
R

PAYMENTS WILL BE MADE IN ACCORDANCE WITH THE PRICES, TERMS AND CONDITIONS ESTABLISHED BY THIS PURCHASE ORDER. IN CASE OF CONFLICT, CONTACT OUR PURCHASING DEPARTMENT PRIOR TO SHIPMENT. PHONE

SHIP TO ARRIVE BY:	FOB	SHIP. POINT	DESTINATION	OTHER:

FREIGHT CHARGES	ACCT. OF BUYER	FROM:	ACCT. OF SELLER

SHIP VIA	PARC POST	UPS	TRUCK	RAIL	AIR	OTHER	ROUTING:

TERMS OF PAYMENT	NET 30 DAYS	% 10TH PROXIMO	% 10 DAYS	OTHER:

ITEM NO.	QUANTITY	UNIT	V. PRODUCT #	DESCRIPTION	UNIT PRICE	AMOUNT

[ ] THIS ORDER IS EXEMPT FROM STATE AND/OR LOCAL SALES & USE TAXES - SEE EXEMPTION CERTIFICATE.

[ ] THIS ORDER IS SUBJECT TO STATE AND/OR LOCAL SALES & USE TAXES.

DATE	ITEM NO.	QUANT.	UNIT	RCVD VIA CARRIER	$ AMOUNT PREPAID	$ AMOUNT COLLECT	WEIGHT	# OF PALLETS	PRO NUMBER	SHIP POINT

RECEIVING DEPARTMENT

FIGURE 10.1 Format provides clear and complete presentation of all terms.

FREIGHT CONTROL ANALYSIS

Moreover, in many instances we found that the freight charges added to an invoice as having been "prepaid" were actually received "collect." In those cases, both the invoices and the probills (or other receiving documentation) all carried the traffic department's stamp of approval for payment.

To properly discipline freight charges, one must have at hand a copy of the purchase order (complete with freight terms), the receiving document and/or probill that discloses the actual method of receipt with the associated charges, and the vendor's invoice. If all of this is to be provided to the traffic department, it might as well function as the accounts payable department and process the document package for payment. Naturally, we recommended moving the freight discipline to the accounts payable department. Given the proper instructions, accounts payable can easily discipline the propriety of freight charges as a routine of the payable process.

Whenever freight controls are conducted in a process separate and apart from the payable routine, we find them to be relatively ineffective.

One of the routines of the internal audit process should be to assure that the information provided on purchase orders and receiving documents is both accurate and concise. Otherwise, costly losses can be incurred. Typical is the situation observed wherein the receiving department of one client considered as "prepaid" all inbound freight shipments that were received as "backhaul" shipments (shipments actually picked up from the vendors and carried on the purchaser's own fleet of trucks), even though it was obvious that all involved transportation was at the client's expense. Only when freight shipments were received on a "collect" probill via common carrier did the receiving documents so indicate.

Analyses of the adequacy and/or the "propriety" of freight charges or allowances can appear to be most complex. However, matters can be simplified by posing two questions:

1. Should we be paying any freight costs related to *this purchase?*
2. If so, how much?

A review of another client that used its corporate truck fleet extensively to make "backhauls" to transport purchased materials revealed more subtle losses that were being incurred.

FREIGHT EQUALIZATION

In recent reviews of various clients' controls over the freight element of their vendor transactions, we found the same old tired players in what is now a brand new ball game. Deregulation of the trucking industry has established new sets of criteria for effective control over the propriety of such costs.

Under past regulations, with established and mandated published rates for the trucking industry, many user corporations assigned all of the decisions and disciplines of freight to their traffic departments. These departments, with their freight technicians, had primary authority for the routing of shipments, the selection of types of carriers (barge, rail, and so on), and the specific carriers to be used.

Then entire sections were developed within traffic departments to conduct compliance reviews of all waybills, probills, and other documents relating to shipments. In some companies, control by these groups was extended to the actual processing of the freight documents for payment. Moreover, many companies turned over the function to outside traffic consultants who actually paid the organization's freight bills.

In light of the deregulation of interstate trucking, the established procedures for freight control may be completely inappropriate. As one expert in freight cost evaluations aptly put it, "The published tariffs are now list prices." Contract haulers are used more frequently. Volume discounts are now offered in return for providing selected carriers with "favored nation" status. Consequently, management must take a new look at established traffic procedures. It is very possible that standard purchase order control procedures may have to be applied to contracts for both inbound and outbound freight agreements with carriers.

There is a new look to the old trucking company probills. Those strips of freight charge bills, each in smudged carbon carrying the bold title "ORIGINAL" and identified with pro numbers of 14 to 20 digits, now can often have an additional line item or, more importantly, may lack an essential line, as illustrated in Figure 10.2.

The first probill carries a volume discount. The second is lacking the discount. Without positive discipline, the omission of the volume discount entitlement on the trucking company's invoice can become extremely costly.

We recommend that the accounts payable individual assigned to payment of the freight bills be given a schedule of such discount

XYZ TRUCKING COMPANY			Probill #: 12457429815	
Consignor: ABC, Inc.	Date: 03/21/92	COL:	X	PPD:
Ship To: RCH Industries 1 Industrial Park Sebring, FL 33870	Ship to Arrive By: 03/30/92 Deliver only between 9 AM - 4 PM			
Units	Description:	Wgt:	Rate:	Extension:
4 Pallets	Product 1	4000 lbs	4.75	190.00
	Total			190.00

XYZ TRUCKING COMPANY			Probill #: 12457430021	
Consignor: ABC, Inc.	Date: 04/22/92	COL:	X	PPD:
Ship To: RCH Industries 1 Industrial Park Sebring, FL 33870	Ship to Arrive By: 04/28/92 Deliver only between 9 AM - 4 PM			
Units	Description:	Wgt:	Rate:	Extension:
4 Pallets	Product 1	4000 lbs	4.75	190.00
	Volume Discount @ 42%			−79.80
	Total			110.20

FIGURE 10.2

FREIGHT EQUALIZATION

entitlements. It is a simple matter to discipline payments in accordance with the established schedule.

Has your internal audit department conducted an operational audit that specifically addressed the effects of the deregulation of the trucking industry on the company's freight controls? If not, it should be done.

11

FILING SYSTEMS

As labor costs and other expenses have increased severely, numerous and varied ways to reduce clerical expenses have been tried by corporate America. Most of these have been related to the more mundane tasks such as the filing and storage of paid invoices, purchase orders, and receiving documents. Of course, these savings are realized by reducing costs in the lower end of the corporate pay scale. Such reductions are often found to be "penny-wise and dollar-foolish."

The most prevalent method used to achieve administrative savings in the accounts payable department area is the adoption of "batch-in-which-paid" filing systems. Such a system allows for the filing of documents merely in the order in which processed through the department. Although this system makes for ease of filing, extensive cross-referencing of register, invoice, purchase order, and similar document numbers is necessary to tie together those related to individual transactions.

There are various versions of "batch-in-which-paid" filing systems. All use a simple numerical filing sequence, such as by check number, voucher or register number, or other document number. The cost of initial file maintenance is reduced, but this is achieved only through certain sacrifices and compromises of efficiency; in particular, sacrifices in fiscal control over transactions.

Disciplines of vendor compliance with established terms and conditions of purchase must be almost perfect during the initial document process using this system. Once documents are filed in a "batch" system, a number of appraisals recommended earlier become impractical.

FILING SYSTEMS

1. Consistency of terms on vendor's invoices

   - If the vendor's invoice provides 2% 10th Prox, whereas the purchase order is written at Net 30, a review of previous paid invoices is in order, but most difficult.
   - The appearance of a freight allowance on a vendor's invoice not substantiated by purchase order terms merits a general review of all previously processed documents for the vendor to assure that all previously processed invoices provided the freight allowance.

2. Quality of disciplines applied by the accounts payable department during the processing of transaction-related documents is likewise impractical. Once they are filed, management oversight of certain disciplines becomes so cumbersome as to be almost impossible

Most important of all, *management* soon discovers that questions that ought to be asked regarding past transactions with the various vendors, or regarding certain categories of purchases, cannot be answered easily without assigning a task force to pull the required documents from their random locations in the files.

Batch filing converts files from their function as tools to aid and enhance productivity, to a graveyard for documents best left undisturbed.

The use of "batch-in-which-paid" filing systems prevents any real or meaningful reviews of individual vendor billing practices. Documents for individual vendors are filed out of context with each other. Therefore, the sole control for terms disciplines becomes completely dependent on each individual purchase order. Any errors or omissions on purchase orders can result in the possibility of overpayments being made on a continuing basis. Once the paid documents are filed (or "buried") in a batch system, review of the accuracy of payments to individual vendors becomes impractical. Thus, there is a necessary presumption, when using a batch-filing system, that adequate controls exist through the simple matching of terms and conditions of purchase orders with invoices and receiving documents during the payment process itself.

FILING SYSTEMS

One of our associates, reviewing transaction controls in a major manufacturing concern where paid invoices were filed in a batch system, discovered a remittance advice (check copy) with 10 invoices for the same product. No purchase order control copies were attached. All 10 invoices, even though appearing on the same remittance advice, had been processed for payment independent of each other, according to the regular payable routine. Normally, invoices to the vendor concerned were paid on individual checks throughout the year. A review of the 10 invoices (all in sequence) revealed unexplained pricing fluctuations.

This discovery triggered a complete review of all invoices paid to this vendor during the previous year. Because of the "batch-in-which-paid" filing mode, the mere pulling of the invoices was most tedious and time-consuming. A list of the 70 or more invoices paid to the vendor had to be taken from a check register. This register identified the vendor and the location of the batch in which each of the required invoices could be found. In this instance, the search produced dividends. It was found that although price fluctuations for the product were themselves a normal occurrence, the prices actually paid were in error. A recovery from the supplier for overpayments in the amount of $139,000 resulted.

This specific search through the batch files produced excellent results; however, many other equally tedious and time-consuming searches proved to be fruitless. If this client's files were maintained in an "alpha-by-vendor" system, reviews of this nature could have been conducted with little effort. The client, as a result of these and other findings, has not only reverted to the "alpha-by-vendor" filing system, but now requires regular reviews of major vendor-paid invoice files by the internal audit department during scheduled audits, as well as by accounts payable department supervisory personnel.

The principal argument of proponents of the "batch-in-which-paid" filing system is that the number of references to the files is minimal. They also think that they should not have to bear additional filing expense as a convenience to auditors.

However, there are benefits directly derived from the use of "alpha-by-vendor" filing systems that are impossible to attain in any

FILING SYSTEMS

of the "batch" file modes—principally, the recoveries of ancillary costs associated with returns and adjustments to vendor accounts. These functions can be more properly performed by the accounts payable department that has access to paid invoice files that are maintained "alpha, by vendor."

- Accounts payable should be given the routine assignment of completing all chargebacks to vendors for returns and other adjustments.
- Part of the routine includes referencing the paid invoice files to assure proper pricing on the chargeback and to determine whether any ancillary costs need recovery.

Similar recoveries, when files are maintained in the "batch" mode, are so involved as to be virtually impossible. The capability of making such recoveries can more than pay for any increased clerical cost required for "alpha" file maintenance.

12

ACCOUNTS PAYABLE DEPARTMENT ANALYSIS

Critical to any appraisal of the effectiveness of controls over vendor transactions is an evaluation of the accounts payable department's structure, assigned duties, and responsibilities. Several questions must be resolved by those making this audit:

1. Are those personnel directly involved in the payment process allowed to affect their own workload? How much latitude is allowed the individuals within the accounts payable department in the disciplines of any vendor errors that might be discerned during the payment process? Application of disciplines by the personnel who process documents for payment may well invite vendor correspondence, thus increasing the workload.
2. Is due dating of payments and financial discounting left to the general discretion of those actually processing transaction-related documents? Vendors may contest aggressive discounting. In addition, this practice may increase the correspondence and workload of the individual concerned.
3. Are tolerances established that allow minor overpayments to be made to reduce administrative costs?
4. Do those individuals who process a specific vendor's documents for payment also receive vendor correspondence or phone calls regarding the account?

ACCOUNTS PAYABLE DEPARTMENT ANALYSIS

If a "wrong" answer to any of these questions is given, and if there is a preponderance of vendor credit memos in the paid invoice files, the auditor is looking at a potentially ineffective system of control over vendor transactions.

Although the reasoning behind most of these questions is relatively transparent, question 4 may merit some explanation. A sophisticated accounts payable department does not refer calls from vendors to the personnel responsible for paying the vendor. Rather, all calls should be directed to someone trained to handle vendor inquiries.

Not all departments are so sophisticated. We observe far too many in which accounts payable personnel are on a first-name basis with their accounts receivable counterparts and vendors' receivable personnel feel free to call the payable desk directly. In this situation, a personal—and often costly—relationship can evolve whereby individuals have a natural desire to be helpful and to do the "right" thing for their friends.

Then there is the "squeaking wheel" approach. A certain major pharmaceutical and chemical manufacturer has to be admired. The receivable personnel know their payable counterparts on a first-name basis. And although the calls are pleasant, their requests for payment are both firm and constant. This persistence pays off, with their documents getting priority processing for payment by the accounts payable personnel—just to eliminate the calls.

Allowing this direct relationship between the accounts payable personnel and their assigned vendors can result in even more costly results. In one client review for a major health care institution, we found an accounts payable person who was taking bribes from a vendor in the amount of $100 to $150 per week by paying that vendor's invoices, not on time, but from 25 to 30 days past the individual invoice discount-due dates.

During this period, the client was experiencing cash flow problems and was taking extreme advantage of vendors' credit terms and paying all invoices no sooner than 90 days—some as late as 180 days past the invoice due dates. Because our client had no barriers in place between the vendor representatives and the accounts payable department, this vendor had ready access to the individual responsible for due dating and processing the invoices for payment. This vendor's payment terms were 2% 30 days. Not wishing to wait as long as

ACCOUNTS PAYABLE DEPARTMENT ANALYSIS

120 to 180 days for payment, it was but a short step to an arrangement whereby the vendor would pay the accounts payable individual a 2% kickback for all invoices paid within 60 days. Our review disclosed this pattern of early payments.

The solution was simple: the client established a vendor inquiry desk. The personnel assigned to the desk were knowledgeable in all aspects of the payable system. More important, they were trained to answer vendor inquiries in a gracious manner, while at the same time firmly applying our client's corporate policies and procedures. The solution also provided several ancillary benefits:

- An expense reduction resulted when 20 or more telephones were removed from the accounts payable department.
- A measurable department-wide improvement in production resulted. Relieved of their constant involvement in phone conversations with vendors, the accounts payable personnel devoted all of their energies and time to processing transaction-related documents.
- Many of the inquiries (50% or more) being received from vendors did not properly fall within the province of the accounts payable department. The trained personnel at the vendor inquiry desk directed those calls to the proper departments.
- An overall staff reduction from 26 to 19 in the accounts payable department resulted in increased efficiency.

The creation of the vendor inquiry desk provided an additional benefit. Prior to its establishment, the organization's various department heads and buyers wandered in and out of the accounts payable department at will. They would go directly to the individual payable personnel with questions regarding invoices, receiving documents, and the cost accounts against which shipments had been applied. As those posing the questions invariably outranked the accounts payable individuals within the organization, there were constant disruptions.

Firm policies were established that eliminated direct access to both the accounts payable personnel and the paid invoice files. All contact with the department is now made through the vendor inquiry desk. Responses to questions regarding transactions are now

ACCOUNTS PAYABLE DEPARTMENT ANALYSIS

made in an orderly manner. Also eliminated was the undue influence that, in some cases, was being exercised by buyers over the payable personnel. As a result, the checks and balances necessary to maintain the financial integrity of transactions with vendors were enhanced. In essence, *the financial division gained control over its own personnel*, something it had not experienced under the previous setup.

There is another sophisticated aspect that the auditor might wish to address when analyzing an accounts payable department's efficiency and effectiveness of control. This is maybe of particular interest if the department is sizeable (with five or more people).

In most accounts payable departments reviewed, we find the standard breakdown of assignments for those processing documents for payment to be designated alphabetically by vendor. This structure results, for example, in one individual's being assigned the duty of processing documents for all companies whose names start with "AAA" through "DD."

This is counter to the manner in which similar job assignments are made in the same company's purchasing department. Almost never can one find buyers purchasing from vendors whose names range alphabetically from "A" through "D." Instead, buyers are generally responsible for the procurement of various categories of material. One or more buyers are assigned to purchase raw materials such as steel or chemicals, and another to purchase office and janitorial supplies.

Accounts payable departments should be similarly structured. This practice recognizes that many industries have specific terms and conditions of purchase and industry practices that must be disciplined. It is impractical to even attempt to train each one of 10 or more accounts payable people to discipline effectively the various elements of transactions for all of the industries from which purchases are made.

A typical department structure may have two or three individuals (one of them senior) processing chemical invoices for payment. They would be organized into what might be best termed the "chemical desk." This "desk" would receive instruction in all of the various elements of transactions with chemical vendors and their proper applications. Among others, these would include

ACCOUNTS PAYABLE DEPARTMENT ANALYSIS

- Freight equalization arrangements—how to appraise and reconcile the freight allowances given on the invoices
- Receiving documents—how to reconcile and discipline the differences that normally occur between the bulk quantities invoiced and the quantities actually unloaded
- Price equalization provisions—determination of whether or not the several vendors were meeting competitors' prices under the agreements

A number of interesting questions can result from organizing the accounts payable department in this manner. A typical question might be, "Why, when ABC Chemical Company has agreed to meet its competitor's price, do we not get 2% 30 day payment terms from ABC, as we do from the XYZ Chemical Company?" In a payable department organized in an alphabetical-by-vendor system, this question is rarely asked.

The suggested structure provides an ancillary benefit. New employees assigned to the "desk" can receive the necessary training from their peers.

AUDIT GUIDE:
Review of Policies, Procedures, and Practices

I. INTRODUCTION

These audit guides are intended as a summary of the major audit points which are contained in the chapters of Part III. In some instances the guides suggest specific audit actions which can be taken; in others, questions regarding individual aspects of the subject area will be asked. Unlike some lists (such as internal control questionnaires) which relate to audit actions, the questions are not intended to elicit simply a "yes" or "no" response. Rather, the questions are meant to cause a critical review of the question raised, with the goal of bettering the operation in some worthwhile manner.

II. PREPARATORY ACTIVITIES

The auditor should initially complete whatever study and research is necessary for familiarization with the following subjects:

- Purchase order format and preparation
- Financial, volume, and trade discounts
- General business payment practices
- Freight control

AUDIT GUIDE

- Administration of accounts payable departments
- The nature of the filing system used for paid invoices

III. ORGANIZATIONAL FACTORS

A search of the paid invoice files can be most effective in detecting deficiencies in policies, procedures, and practices used by organizations to process documents when paying vendor invoices. The focal point of control should rest with the accounts payable department.

IV. VENDOR DISCOUNTING

A. Financial payment terms disciplines
   1. Is there a preponderance of an individual vendor's invoices that show more favorable financial discount and payment terms than the corresponding purchase orders?
   2. Do the purchase order formats provide for the display of financial discount and payment terms? Are they consistently and correctly filled in by those initiating orders?
   3. Is the accounts payable department clearly responsible for the realization of beneficial financial discount and payment terms?
   4. Are all purchase order terms strictly enforced by using the Best of Terms concept?
   5. Is there a comprehensive glossary of financial discount terms readily available in both the purchasing and accounts payable departments?
   6. Do accounts payable personnel clearly understand the correct applications of all of the various payment terms (such as the term *proximo*)?
   7. Were there more than 12 checks issued to any individual "Prox" term vendor during the past year? If so, explain.
B. Accounts payable departmental policy relative to financial discounts

AUDIT GUIDE

1. Is the policy specific as to the timing of payments of vendor invoices with financial discounts?
2. Are all financial discounts taken regardless of when the vendor invoices are paid?
3. Is there a priority schedule for document processing in accounts payable?
4. Are all changes to terms and/or any other conditions of purchase channeled through the purchasing department?

C. Trade and volume discounts
  1. Do purchase orders show appropriate trade and/or volume discounts?
  2. Do vendors attempt to convert trade and volume discounts to the status of financial discounts and payment terms?

D. Freight control
  1. Are the paid invoices in the files always supported by receiving information regarding facts relating to the method of shipment and accompanying freight charges?
  2. Do the control copies of purchase orders carry sufficient information on freight terms so as to allow the accounts payable department to discipline the appropriateness of any freight charges? Has the accounts payable department been assigned this responsibility?
  3. Are control copies of the purchase orders that relate to the individual shipments against paid vendor invoices readily available in the paid invoice files?
  4. Have any "collect" shipments been invoiced as "prepaid," with freight charges added to the invoices?
  5. Have any "collect" shipments been made from warehouses or production points other than those from which purchased?
  6. Have freight charges been paid for shipments of goods that were back-ordered at the vendor's convenience?
  7. Have the volume freight discounts that the carriers allowed the vendors been passed on to the purchaser?

AUDIT GUIDE

    8. Have the proper freight equalization allowances been provided by the vendors?

    9. Are payments being made for truckload freight charges for truckload shipments in those instances when the vendor failed to load the carriers fully as called for by purchase orders? Have the deficit freight costs been noted and recovered?

   10. Have charges been disciplined for any improper pallet or container costs that may have been applied by vendors?

   11. Are excessive demurrage charges being incurred owing to shipments arriving prior to expected and scheduled dates?

   12. Has the Best of Terms concept been consistently applied against those freight terms established by purchase order or the vendors' standard terms?

E. Filing systems

    1. Does each paid invoice file contain the original vendor invoice, a control copy of the purchase order, a copy of the receiving report, and full freight documentation?

    2. Are paid invoices filed "alpha by vendor"?

F. The accounts payable department structure, assigned duties and responsibilities

    1. Are accounts payable personnel permitted to routinely discipline vendor errors during the processing of invoices for payment?

    2. Is the realization of financial discounts and due dating of payments left to the general discretion of those actually doing the document processing?

    3. Are tolerances established that allow for overpayments (price, freight, and so on) in an endeavor to reduce administrative costs?

    4. Do those individuals who process documents for specific vendors' accounts also receive the correspondence or telephone calls from these vendors regarding the accounts?

    5. Are the vendor assignments to accounts payable department personnel made according to industry and category of purchased material?

APPENDIX

SAMPLE POLICIES AND PROCEDURES FOR IMPLEMENTING PROCUREMENT CONTROLS

AMERICAN CORP
POLICIES & PROCEDURES—PROCUREMENT

SUBJECT: RESPONSIBILITY/AUTHORITY	SECTION: I PAGE 1 of 4

A. *Financial*

1. The Treasury Department shall determine the frequency of disbursing funds based upon the Corporate philosophy of paying vendors in strict accordance with contracts, vendor and industry practices, cash management decisions and marketplace credibility.

2. General Accounting shall maintain adequate records and controls to ensure the proper accounting of transactions with vendors.

3. Vendor Accounting (Accounts Payable) shall process vendor and related documents for payments in accordance with established contracts/purchase orders and shall monitor that vendors are using agreed-upon terms and/or established vendor and industry practices.

4. Generally two methods of disbursement control are to be utilized in the performance of the Vendor Accounting function: (1) payments upon appropriate authorizations and (2) payments through the direct application of purchase order terms.

   The latter method provides a more positive fiscal control over the procurement process due to the improved documentations of the terms and conditions of the agreements (purchase orders/contracts), their acceptance by the vendors (acknowledgments and/or receipts of goods), and the final payments as processed. It provides for certain checks and balances through the separation of the payment authority from that of the authority to negotiate and purchase.

   Situations do arise where payments by authorization are required because the use of the purchase order procedure would be inappropriate. Such situations shall be kept to the minimum, and only as approved and directed by management.

ORIGINATING DEPT	DATE ISSUED:	EFFECTIVE DATE:
	SUPERCEDES No.:	DATED:

AMERICAN CORP
POLICIES & PROCEDURES—PROCUREMENT

| SUBJECT: | SECTION: I |
| RESPONSIBILITY/AUTHORITY | PAGE 2 of 4 |

B. *Purchasing*

1. All purchases (regardless of the initiating authority) shall be made in accordance with the best interest of Corporation as outlined in these Purchasing Policy and Procedure Directives. Such shall include those purchases initiated by:

   - Food Service
   - Health Services
   - General Stores
   - Maintenance
   - Construction/Engineering

2. The Purchasing Department shall ensure that the terms and conditions of all purchase orders will allow for a reasonable length of time after the receipts of materials and invoices to permit routine processing with the realization of allowed financial discounts.

3. After issuance of the contract/purchase orders and receipts of goods and invoices, Vendor Accounting shall have the responsibility and authority for the monitoring for vendor compliance.

   Documents shall be processed for payments in accordance with the "best of terms" as indicated on invoices vs. purchase orders vs. established vendor and/or industry practices.

4. When any contests are received from vendors resulting from payments made in accordance with "best of terms," all such contests with the exception of those involving financial discounts shall be forwarded directly to the Purchasing Department for resolution. Honoring of the vendor contests shall be accomplished by the initiation of appropriate Purchase Order Change Notices.

| ORIGINATING DEPT: | DATE ISSUED: | EFFECTIVE DATE: |
| | SUPERCEDES No.: | DATED: |

AMERICAN CORP
POLICIES & PROCEDURES—PROCUREMENT

| SUBJECT: | SECTION: I |
| RESPONSIBILITY/AUTHORITY | PAGE 3 of 4 |

- Purchase Order Change Notices (regardless of the dollar amount involved) shall be subject to the same routings and approvals required of the original purchase orders.

C. *Operational*—Receiving Function

1. The Receiving Department shall record *all* receipts so as to provide the capability for correlation with the appropriate contracts/purchase orders. Any overages, shortages, or damages that are apparent at the time of receipt shall be so recorded on the receiving documentation to allow Vendor Accounting to properly adjust subsequent payments.

2. The following information is to be recorded on all receiving documents and forwarded to Vendor Accounting on a timely basis:

   a) Vendor
   b) Receiving record number
   c) Purchase order number
   d) Shipping point
   e) How received—prepaid or collect?
   f) Amount of freight charges—whether prepaid or collect
   g) Quantity and/or weight
   h) Date received
   i) Carrier
   j) Pro number/waybill number
   k) Remarks—over/short/apparent damage

| ORIGINATING DEPT: | DATE ISSUED: | EFFECTIVE DATE: |
| | SUPERCEDES No.: | DATED: |

AMERICAN CORP
POLICIES & PROCEDURES—PROCUREMENT

SUBJECT:	SECTION: I
RESPONSIBILITY/AUTHORITY	PAGE 4 of 4

3. The Receiving Department shall expedite the shipment of such materials that are sent to them for return to vendors. (Such materials remain non-interest bearing assets of the Corporation until the returns are effected and the accompanying debit memos are deducted from vendor accounts.
4. Return goods shall be shipped in accordance with the Corporation's established policy:

   a) Returns due to a Vendor Accommodation: to be shipped prepaid, unless otherwise so directed on the body of the chargeback.

   b) Returns due to Vendor Responsibility: to be shipped *collect*.

   - For those shipments made where "collect" methods are impractical or impossible (via parcel post, UPS, etc.), the amount of the prepaid freight shall be clearly indicated on the chargeback.

   c) The freight section of the Debit Memo (Chargeback) shall be completed in full for every return.

ORIGINATING DEPT:	DATE ISSUED:	EFFECTIVE DATE:
	SUPERCEDES No.:	DATED:

AMERICAN CORP
POLICIES & PROCEDURES—PROCUREMENT

SUBJECT:	SECTION: II
DELINEATION OF AUTHORITY/RESPONSIBILITY	PAGE 1 of 5

The following procurement control policies are provided so as to delineate specific areas of authority and as a basis for Purchasing, Vendor Accounting, Treasury, and Operational Departments to prepare more detailed procedures and assign control responsibilities.

A. *Purchasing*

1. The Purchasing Department shall, in coordination with User Departments, have the prime responsibility for, and authority over:

    a) Selection of vendors.

    b) Negotiations of prices, terms and conditions of purchase.

    c) Maintenance of vendor relations.

    d) Purchase order issuance

    - including the issuance of Purchase Order Change Notices, as required.

    e) Acceptance and retention of overshipped quantities

    - through the issuance of POCNs.

    f) Returns to vendors of materials.

2. The Purchasing Department shall, in coordination with General Accounting and Vendor Accounting, have the responsibility and authority for ensuring that all purchase orders are issued in compliance with the policies and directives that have been established to provide for effective controls over the procurement process.

ORIGINATING DEPT:	DATE ISSUED:	EFFECTIVE DATE:
	SUPERCEDES No.:	DATED:

AMERICAN CORP
POLICIES & PROCEDURES—PROCUREMENT

SUBJECT:	SECTION: II
DELINEATION OF AUTHORITY/RESPONSIBILITY	PAGE 2 of 5

    a) *Purchase Orders*

        Each individual or blanket order shall carry all those terms and conditions of purchase that have been negotiated, or are established by vendor or industry practices:

- credit terms
- financial discounts
- trade discounts
- pricing
- freight terms
- earned volume rebates, etc.
- return privileges and conditions
- price protection

    b) Negotiations with vendors shall be based upon obtaining the vendors' best financial discounts, trade discounts, freight and other terms at all times.

- All purchase agreements foregoing any of the above shall clearly so state on the body of the contracts/purchase orders.

B. *Vendor Accounting*

Shall have the prime responsibility and authority for:

1. Verifying new vendors for authenticity.
2. Maintaining the lists of authorized signatures for disbursement requests, invoices (without purchase orders) and expense reports.
3. Ensuring that any payments are authorized.

ORIGINATING DEPT:	DATE ISSUED:	EFFECTIVE DATE:
	SUPERCEDES No.:	DATED:

AMERICAN CORP
POLICIES & PROCEDURES—PROCUREMENT

| SUBJECT: | SECTION: II |
| DELINEATION OF AUTHORITY/RESPONSIBILITY | PAGE 3 of 5 |

    a) Authorization can be in the form of a purchase order or an authorized signature (for those purchases and expenditures not requiring purchase orders).

    b) Specific approval procedures shall be established for the processing of documents that are not the originals, i.e., when replacement copies are used in the payable process.

4. Verify that receipts correspond in type and quantity with that which was ordered.

- Such verification may be that afforded by the receiving documentation.

Payments for receipts that depart from the ordered materials and/or services shall be supported by Purchase Order Change Notices.

5. Shall compare transaction-related documents (invoices, receiving documents, chargebacks to vendors, etc.) with the purchase orders and vendor and industry practices for:

    a) price

    b) extensions

    c) propriety of freight charges

    d) applicable trade discounts

    e) financial discounts

    f) appropriateness of any ancillary charges

- pallet or packing charges
- minimum order charges
- etc.

Documents to be processed in accordance with the "best of terms," invoiced vs. purchase order and established vendor and industry practices.

ORIGINATING DEPT:	DATE ISSUED:	EFFECTIVE DATE:
	SUPERCEDES No.:	DATED:

AMERICAN CORP
POLICIES & PROCEDURES—PROCUREMENT

| SUBJECT: | SECTION: II |
| DELINEATION OF AUTHORITY/RESPONSIBILITY | PAGE 4 of 5 |

6. Make every effort to make timely payments of all invoices. However, take all financial discounts, no matter when paid.

7. Upon any contests by vendors that result in the refunding of unearned discounts, such shall be posted to a Missed Discount Account.

   Any such refunds shall require financial management authorization.

8. Have the prime responsibility for the capture of all rebates based upon any agreements that may call for volume and/or preferential vendor status rebates.

9. Ensure that cost distributions are made to the proper accounts as established by General Accounting and *so provided on purchase orders.*

C. *Treasury Department*—Payment and Check Distribution Control

   A separation of duties is to be emphasized in this area. The size of the operation at any given time shall determine the extent to which separation of duties can be applied. During extensive operations the Treasury or Disbursement Department may control signature and disbursement. At other times, only individuals may be involved.

   1. Vendor Accounting

      a) Maintains controls

      b) Approves check registers

      c) Controls preparation of checks

   2. Treasury/Disbursement Department, or a designated individual *not* associated with the Vendor Accounting function

      a) Ensures that the printed checks agree with the check register.

      b) Accounts for all checks.

| ORIGINATING DEPT: | DATE ISSUED: | EFFECTIVE DATE: |
| | SUPERCEDES No.: | DATED: |

AMERICAN CORP
POLICIES & PROCEDURES—PROCUREMENT

SUBJECT: DELINEATION OF AUTHORITY/RESPONSIBILITY	SECTION: II PAGE 5 of 5

    c) Signs checks and maintains control over the number of the checks signed.

    d) Assures that the checks signed out for processing are all accounted for.

    e) Segregates checks for executive audit and assures that any required authorizations are on all checks prior to distribution.

    f) Mails or otherwise ensures the distribution of checks direct to the payees.

ORIGINATING DEPT:	DATE ISSUED:	EFFECTIVE DATE:
	SUPERCEDES No.:	DATED:

AMERICAN CORP
POLICIES & PROCEDURES—PROCUREMENT

SUBJECT: INTERNAL CONTROLS	SECTION: III PAGE 1 of 5

The following controls are to be in effect to ensure the integrity of the procurement, payable, and fiscal functions.

A. *Procurement*

1. The Purchasing Department shall make every effort to ensure that *all* of the terms and conditions (all of the elements) of each transaction are clearly and concisely displayed on each contract/purchase order when issued.

2. Appropriate control copies of purchase orders shall be expedited to the departments concerned (Vendor Accounting, Receiving, Stores, Quality Control, etc.).

3. The transaction control copy (that copy provided to Vendor Accounting) shall display all those authorizations required for the initial release of the contract/purchase order.

    Such authorizations are those that may from time to time be established by directives and based upon:

    - the size of the order
    - the type of order (capital expenditure, specific restricted cost accounts, etc.)

4. Any changes in the contract/purchase order terms and/or conditions shall be accomplished solely through the issuance of a Purchase Order Change Notice (POCN) by the Purchasing Department.

5. All Purchase Order Change Notices shall be required to carry the same authorizations and follow the routings identical to those specified for the release of the initial orders (Internal Controls, Section III, A-3).

    - POCNs may be issued at any time during the transaction, or may be retroactive if so required.

ORIGINATING DEPT:	DATE ISSUED:	EFFECTIVE DATE:
	SUPERCEDES No.:	DATED:

AMERICAN CORP
POLICIES & PROCEDURES—PROCUREMENT

SUBJECT: INTERNAL CONTROLS	SECTION: III PAGE 2 of 5

B. *Vendor Accounting*

1. The Vendor Accounting Department shall have the sole responsibility for the processing of payments to vendors. This action shall be conducted independently, *without recourse to any outside authority or department.*

2. Payments shall be established, upon the receipt of the necessary supporting documents, by directly using the Best of Terms at hand from:

    - purchase orders
    - invoices
    - receiving documents
    - industry practices
    - the vendor's history—developed from prior transactions

    All applications of terms shall be based upon those interpretations that prove to be most favorable to the Corporation.

3. Payments are to be made in a timely manner (when due).

    Measures shall be established to ensure against the early payments of monies due without specific authorizations from the management.

4. Any contests from vendors regarding payments shall be reconciled according to the category of the contest:

    a) Financial discounts and other payment terms—the responsibility of the financial division.

    b) Price, freight terms, and all other elements of transactions shall be referred directly to the Purchasing Department for reconciliation.

ORIGINATING DEPT:	DATE ISSUED:	EFFECTIVE DATE:
	SUPERCEDES No.:	DATED:

AMERICAN CORP
POLICIES & PROCEDURES—PROCUREMENT

SUBJECT:	SECTION: III
INTERNAL CONTROLS	PAGE 3 of 5

5. To the extent possible, it shall be the Corporation's policy that in the reconciliation of any contests regarding terms and conditions, any discussions and negotiations should be conducted with the appropriate departments—of the vendor as well as the Corporation.

    Calls from vendors' credit or accounts receivable departments regarding deductions from payments taken because of terms and conditions of purchase are inappropriate. Such calls should be taken by the Purchasing Department only when the source is the vendors' sales or marketing department.

6. Vendor Accounting shall notify the Purchasing Department of any major deductions taken due to discrepancies between those terms and conditions invoiced by vendors and those established by contracts/purchase orders.

    a) Notification to Purchasing of discrepancies shall *not* preclude Vendor Accounting's taking of independent action by applying the "best of terms" during the document processing.

    Notification shall be coincidental with these disciplines.

    b) The Purchasing Department shall be *advised* of any actions taken that may have an affect upon vendor relations.

C. *Treasury Department*

The Treasury/Disbursement Department, or designated individual, shall have custody of all blank checks and be responsible for all checks released and returned. This department/individual shall also be responsible for the control of signing checks, either by signature plate or manual means.

ORIGINATING DEPT:	DATE ISSUED:	EFFECTIVE DATE:
	SUPERCEDES No.:	DATED:

AMERICAN CORP
POLICIES & PROCEDURES—PROCUREMENT

| SUBJECT: | SECTION: III |
| INTERNAL CONTROLS | PAGE 4 of 5 |

1. The following controls serve to provide custodial responsibility of blank checks:

    a) Provide security storage and control.

    b) Release blank checks to authorized personnel only.

    c) Maintain a control log indicating the date that checks were released for processing, to whom the checks were released, first and last check numbers, and the checks returned.

2. Signature controls will consist of the following:

    a) An authorized manual signture only will be issued.

    b) Facsimile signature plates should be stored in a secure area and used only by the Treasury/Disbursement Department, or designated individual, to sign the checks.

    Keys to the check-signing machine to be controlled by this department/individual.

D. *Executive Verification Procedure*

Management shall, from time to time, by directives determine those disbursement amounts that are to receive predisbursement verification.

The designated executive shall:

1. Review the signed check and all supporting detail for the correctness of the disbursement.

2. Initial, or otherwise authorize the check after determining the correctness of the disbursement.

3. Return the checks to the Treasury/Disbursement Department or designated individual for distribution to the payees.

E. *Operations*—Receiving

In order to assure a certain degree of independent control over transactions with vendors, the Receiving Department shall maintain a log of all receipts of materials (Section I, D), assign to each receipt a receiving number, and prepare receiving documentation.

ORIGINATING DEPT:	DATE ISSUED:	EFFECTIVE DATE:
	SUPERCEDES No.:	DATED:

AMERICAN CORP
POLICIES & PROCEDURES—PROCUREMENT

SUBJECT: INTERNAL CONTROLS	SECTION: III PAGE 5 of 5
 1. The Transaction Control Copy of this Receiver shall be routed *directly* to the Vendor Accounting Department. F. *Document Cancellation and Retention* 1. Documents supporting disbursement shall be cancelled to preclude their duplicate payment processing. Cancellation may be accomplished by stamping or perforating the "paid" document, or by any other systems or manual procedures that assure that documents cannot be processed again in error. 2. Retention of the documents shall be in accordance with Corporate policy. G. *Reconciliation of Vendor Accounting Bank Account* The reconciliation of the Vendor Accounting Bank Account shall be accomplished by a department or a designated individual that is *not* associated with the Vendor Accounting function. 	

ORIGINATING DEPT:	DATE ISSUED:	EFFECTIVE DATE:
	SUPERCEDES No.:	DATED:

AMERICAN CORP
POLICIES & PROCEDURES—PROCUREMENT

SUBJECT:	SECTION: IV
DOCUMENT PROCESSING—VENDOR ACCOUNTING	PAGE 1 of 3

A. *Priority Processing*

Documents should be processed using priorities that are most advantageous to the Corporation. Before commencing each day's activities, all documents in-house should be sorted for processing in the following order of priority:

1. Credit memos/Corporate debit memos.
2. Transactions with discounts—by due dates.
3. Net invoices.

B. *Verification/Disciplines*

1. All vendor invoices shall be checked against supporting and related documentation (purchase orders/contracts, receiving documents, established vendor terms, etc.) for the following:

    a) The vendor to be paid agrees with the vendor provided for upon the contract/purchase order.

    b) Invoiced terms agree with those on purchase order, or otherwise established:

    - propriety of freight charges—allowances.
    - financial discounts and credit terms.
    - appropriate trade discounts.
    - correct pricing.
    - quantities agree—ordered/received/invoiced.
    - extensions correct.
    - footings/totals are correct.

    c) Proper approvals are at hand for those invoices covering engineering, consulting, services, etc., to ensure that the items have been received or completed to the Corporation's satisfaction.

ORIGINATING DEPT:	DATE ISSUED:	EFFECTIVE DATE:
	SUPERCEDES No.:	DATED:

AMERICAN CORP
POLICIES & PROCEDURES—PROCUREMENT

SUBJECT:	SECTION: IV
DOCUMENT PROCESSING—VENDOR ACCOUNTING	PAGE 2 of 3

2. Documents shall be processed for payment *when due* according to the "best of terms" concept—invoiced vs. purchase order and established terms and conditions of purchase.

3. In those instances where discrepancies occur between the terms and conditions of the purchase order/contract and those invoiced by the vendor, Vendor Accounting shall directly apply those most advantageous to the Corporation, without reference to any outside authority, and in the following manner.

    a) Directly adjust the invoice to properly reflect:

    - invoiced prices found to be greater than those provided by purchase order.
    - corrections of arithmetic errors occurring on invoices.
    - recaptures of improper freight charges due to the inappropriate shipping procedures or improper freight charges on invoices.
    - applications of trade discounts, etc., that are properly due to the Corporation, but not displayed on the vendor's invoice.

    b) Pay only those amounts properly due to the vendor.

4. Coincidental to the making of any adjustments to vendor invoices under the Best of Terms concept, Vendor Accounting shall:

    a) Advise the vendor of the adjustment and the reason for it, using an appropriate form of notification.

    b) Advise the Purchasing Department in those cases where substantial adjustments are being made.

5. Where the terms and conditions of purchase, as reflected by the vendor's actions, invoices, etc., are more favorable than those presented on the purchase orders/contracts, Vendor Accounting shall so advise the Purchasing Department.

ORIGINATING DEPT:	DATE ISSUED:	EFFECTIVE DATE:
	SUPERCEDES No.:	DATED:

AMERICAN CORP
POLICIES & PROCEDURES—PROCUREMENT

SUBJECT:	SECTION: IV
DOCUMENT PROCESSING—VENDOR ACCOUNTING	PAGE 3 of 3

- Payments under the above will not result in any advisory to the vendors as the invoiced amounts are being applied.
- Purpose of the advisory—to assure that future orders reflect the vendor's best terms.

ORIGINATING DEPT:	DATE ISSUED:	EFFECTIVE DATE:
	SUPERCEDES No.:	DATED:

AMERICAN CORP
POLICIES & PROCEDURES—PROCUREMENT

SUBJECT:	SECTION: V
VENDOR INQUIRIES	PAGE 1 of 2

As the Corporation has in effect the direct discipline of purchase order and established vendor and industry terms in the processing of vendor and related documents for payment, the following is presented so as to establish policies for the resolution of inquiries and contests received from vendors.

A. *Vendor Monthly (Regular) Statements*

   Statements from vendors shall receive Vendor Accounting supervisory review for outstanding invoices (those in material amounts only) that are in excess of 90 days old.

   1. Invoices (in material dollar amounts), 90 to 120 days old, shall be thoroughly reviewed and resolved.

      Where it is deemed necessary, vendor to be contacted for proof of delivery.

   2. Debit memos for such items as late payment/finance charges or the vendor's failure to accept the Corporate's routine payment adjustments (based upon Best of Terms) *shall not normally receive any consideration* in the reviews of vendor's monthly statements.

      All such items to be handled on an individual basis, and only upon specific inquiry from vendors.

   3. Purchasing to be kept advised of any material (major) debit items that remain unresolved.

      - The criteria for each vendor in the determination of materiality should be established in coordination with the Purchasing Department.

B. *Contests*

   The following are presented as criteria for the establishment of procedures under which to reconcile contests from vendors relating to contracts/purchase orders.

ORIGINATING DEPT:	DATE ISSUED:	EFFECTIVE DATE:
	SUPERCEDES No.:	DATED:

AMERICAN CORP
POLICIES & PROCEDURES—PROCUREMENT

SUBJECT:	
VENDOR INQUIRIES	SECTION: V PAGE 2 of 2

1. Financial—contests relating to the taking of financial discounts and extensions of payment terms shall be routinely reconciled by Vendor Accounting.

2. All other contests—those regarding established or negotiated elements of the transactions shall be referred directly to the Purchasing Department for reconciliation with the sales and/or marketing departments of the vendors. Such shall include:

   - pricing
   - freight terms
   - trade discounts
   - special allowances
   - etc.

3. Acceptances of the vendors' postures in such contests shall be reflected by the issuance of appropriate POCNs by the Purchasing Department.

   - The resulting POCNs to follow the same routing for release as that required for the issuance of the original purchase order—regardless of the size of the adjustment.

4. Subject to normal management review, nothing in this section shall be construed so as to preempt the Purchasing Department's prime responsibility and authority over vendor relations and its consequent final authority for such reconciliations.

C. *Late Payment/Finance Charges*

1. Late payment/finance charges shall be honored by the Corporation only when properly charged against late payments of invoices subject to signed "Truth in Lending" notifications and acknowledgements.

2. Authority for the acceptance of "Truth in Lending" agreements is specifically reserved to the financial division.

ORIGINATING DEPT:	DATE ISSUED:	EFFECTIVE DATE:
	SUPERCEDES No.:	DATED:

AMERICAN CORP
POLICIES & PROCEDURES—PROCUREMENT

SUBJECT:	SECTION: VI
OVER, SHORT, OR DAMAGED MATERIALS	PAGE 1 of 2

The disposition of receipts constituting overshipments, shortages, and damaged goods against contracts/purchase orders remains the province of the Purchasing Department in coordination with the User Departments.

A. *Overshipments*

  1. Upon determination from receiving documents that overshipments have been received, Vendor Accounting shall:

      a) Withhold the payment processing of the related documents.

      b) Notify the Purchasing Department of the overshipment.

  2. The Purchasing Department, in coordination with the User Department, shall make the determination as to whether the excess quantities are to be retained or returned to vendors.

      a) Retention—accomplished through the execution of appropriate POCNs.

      b) Return—through the initiation of an appropriate chargeback (debit memo).

  3. Upon receipt of POCN/Chargeback, Vendor Accounting to process all related documents for payment.

B. *Shortages*

  Shortages in this concept shall be the receipts of materials in quantities less than those *invoiced* by the vendors.

  1. Vendor Accounting to directly adjust vendors' invoices to reflect the proper quantities (as indicated on the receiving documents) and process for payments accordingly.

  2. Notify the vendor of the adjustment and the reason, with an accompanying advice to the Purchasing Department.

ORIGINATING DEPT:	DATE ISSUED:	EFFECTIVE DATE:
	SUPERCEDES No.:	DATED:

AMERICAN CORP
POLICIES & PROCEDURES—PROCUREMENT

| SUBJECT: | SECTION: VI |
| OVER, SHORT, OR DAMAGED MATERIALS | PAGE 2 of 2 |

C. *Damages*

Receipts of damaged materials fall into two categories: (1) where the resulting claims are to be made against the carriers, and (2) where claims and/or adjustments are the responsibility of the vendors.

1. For damaged materials received due to the responsibility of the carrier, Vendor Accounting shall:

    a) Notify the Purchasing Department for the initiation of appropriate claims against the responsible carrier.

    b) Process the related vendor documents as though the materials were received in good order.

2. For those instances where the damages are the responsibility of the vendors, Vendor Accounting shall:

    a) Notify the Purchasing Department and withhold payment processing.

    b) Upon receipt and payment processing of the appropriate chargebacks (debit memos) for the return or adjustment resulting from the damaged materials, shall process the original transaction documents for payment.

| ORIGINATING DEPT: | DATE ISSUED: | EFFECTIVE DATE: |
| | SUPERCEDES No.: | DATED: |

AMERICAN CORP
POLICIES & PROCEDURES—PROCUREMENT

SUBJECT:	SECTION: VII
RETURNS AND ADJUSTMENTS	PAGE 1 of 5

The following is to establish policies and procedures for the returns and/or adjustments of purchased materials or services. Upon initiation of any returns and adjustments by the Purchasing Department in coordination with the User Departments, the prime responsibility for the control of the resulting transactions shall be that of the Vendor Accounting Department.

All returns and/or adjustments shall be deemed to fall into one of two categories: (1) Vendor Responsibility or (2) a Vendor Accommodation.

All related documents shall clearly indicate whether returns/adjustments are being made due to Vendor Responsibility or a Vendor Accommodation. The resulting procedures shall be based upon the category of the return/adjustment.

A. *Vendor Responsibility*

   1. This category is to be used for all returns and/or adjustments made due to vendor errors in the filling of contracts/purchase orders (i.e., rejections due to quality, not as ordered, and any violations of the terms of purchase) that are discovery after the processing of the original transaction-related documents.

   2. All returns and/or adjustments made due to Vendor Responsibility shall be made in such a manner as to assure that the Corporation does not incur any ancillary losses due to the purchased materials or services being rejected or returned due to the vendors' errors.

   3. The following procedure shall be used for returns and/or adjustments due to Vendor Responsibility:

      a) The User Department initiating the return or adjustment, after notifying the Purchasing Department, shall execute a Vendor Chargeback (Debit Memo) which shall carry the following information:

         - Name of the vendor (vendor number).

ORIGINATING DEPT:	DATE ISSUED:	EFFECTIVE DATE:
	SUPERCEDES No.:	DATED:

AMERICAN CORP
POLICIES & PROCEDURES—PROCUREMENT

SUBJECT:	SECTION: VII
RETURNS AND ADJUSTMENTS	PAGE 2 of 5

- Reason for the return/adjustment—Vendor Responsibility.
- Material description—stock number, etc.
- Quantity of material involved—including any that may have been scrapped.
- Disposition—(scrapped, or ship to information).

b) For adjustment chargebacks (where there is no return of materials involved):
- Initiating department retains one copy of the chargeback.
- Forwards information copy to the Purchasing Department.
- Forwards the 1st and 2nd copies to Vendor Accounting.

c) For chargebacks generating the returns of materials to suppliers:
- The initiating (User) department retains one copy of the chargeback—to reconcile the missing material or asset.
- Forwards the information copy to the Purchasing Department:
- Sends the materials to be returned and the 1st, 2nd, and 4th copies of the chargeback to the Receiving Department for return to the vendor.

d) Receiving Department shall:
- Verify the quantities indicated as those being returned.
- As the returns are due to Vendor Responsibility, make the return shipments on a "collect" basis, or
- If a collect shipment is inappropriate (via parcel post, UPS, etc.), ship prepaid and enter the freight cost in the shipping information section on the chargeback.

ORIGINATING DEPT:	DATE ISSUED:	EFFECTIVE DATE:
	SUPERCEDES No.:	DATED:

AMERICAN CORP
POLICIES & PROCEDURES—PROCUREMENT

SUBJECT:	SECTION: VII
RETURNS AND ADJUSTMENTS	PAGE 3 of 5

- Enter shipping information on the chargeback
    - date of shipment—method and carrier
    - quantity/weight
    - freight charges—for shipments prepaid
- Include 4th copy of chargeback in the shipment as a waybill.
- Forward 1st and 2nd copies to Vendor Accounting.

e) Vendor Accounting, through reference to the vendor's paid invoice file, shall:

- Determine, and enter on the chargeback, the prices of the returned materials.
- Determine the method of the original manner of receipt of the materials that are being returned.
- Determine from the shipping information provided by Receiving under the shipping information section of the chargeback, whether the return was made on a "prepaid" or "collect" basis.
- Extend and complete the chargeback, including charges to the vendor for the recapture of any and all costs incurred by the Corporation for the receipt and the return of the materials.
    - any materials scrapped coincidental to the discovery of the vendor error.
    - any inbound freight costs incurred by the Corporation.
    - related packing charges, pallet costs, etc.—both inbound and return.

ORIGINATING DEPT:	DATE ISSUED:	EFFECTIVE DATE:
	SUPERCEDES No.:	DATED:

AMERICAN CORP
POLICIES & PROCEDURES—PROCUREMENT

SUBJECT:	SECTION: VII
RETURNS AND ADJUSTMENTS	PAGE 4 of 5

- Assign chargebacks a high departmental processing priority.
  — chargebacks to be considered as noninterest bearing assets until deducted.
- Post to the vendor's account for immediate deduction.
- Mail the original copy of the chargeback to the vendor as substantiation for the deduction from the next payment to the vendor.

  Or, to act as an invoice and establish the receivable in the case of "one time" vendors.
- File the control copy and all supporting documentation (quality control reports, etc.) in the vendor's paid invoice file.

f) Vendor Accounting to post *all* chargebacks at face value, without any financial discount consideration.

B. *Vendor Accommodation*

1. This category to be used in those circumstances where the vendor is making an accommodation to the Corporation, (the buying back of improperly ordered materials, quantities held in excess of the Corporation's inventory requirements, etc.) and will usually result from separate negotiations (requests for credits) on the part of the Purchasing Department.

2. The return procedure shall remain the same as under (A) with but the following exceptions:

   a) Where so required, the return of materials will await the receipt of the vendor's return goods authorization.

   b) Shipments may be made on either a prepaid or collect basis—as directed by the return authorization.

ORIGINATING DEPT:	DATE ISSUED:	EFFECTIVE DATE:
	SUPERCEDES No.:	DATED:

AMERICAN CORP
POLICIES & PROCEDURES—PROCUREMENT

SUBJECT:	SECTION: VII
RETURNS AND ADJUSTMENTS	PAGE 5 of 5

    c) Agreed-upon handling charges are acceptable—as directed by the Purchasing Department.

    d) Recoveries of ancillary costs are *not* in order.

ORIGINATING DEPT:	DATE ISSUED:	EFFECTIVE DATE:
	SUPERCEDES No.:	DATED:

AMERICAN CORP
POLICIES & PROCEDURES—PROCUREMENT

SUBJECT:	SECTION: VIII
PURCHASE ORDERS/CONTRACTS	PAGE 1 of 2

Purchase orders/contracts shall be executed in such a manner and upon such formats as to ensure that proper disciplines of all of the terms and conditions of purchase may be effected within the established control and payments procedures.

A. *Purchases/Negotiations*

1. All purchases shall be negotiated within the framework of the vendors' *best* established terms and conditions regarding transactions:

    a) financial discount and credit terms

    b) freight terms and allowances

    c) trade discounts

    d) earned volume rebates and discounts

    e) price protection

    f) return privileges/consignment provisions

    g) general pricing

    h) etc.

2. Any exceptions to #1 (above) shall be valid only when specifically so provided on the body of the purchase orders. Such exceptions to be confined to:

    a) Special buys—from a regular vendor.

    b) Individual and special circumstances—subject to management review.

B. *Purchase Order/Contract Formats*

The purchase order/contract formats shall consist of two principal sections:

1. Heading—with provisions for the adequate display of the following information:

ORIGINATING DEPT:	DATE ISSUED:	EFFECTIVE DATE:
	SUPERCEDES No.:	DATED:

AMERICAN CORP
POLICIES & PROCEDURES—PROCUREMENT

SUBJECT:	SECTION: VIII
PURCHASE ORDERS/CONTRACTS	PAGE 2 of 2

    a) Vendor—name, address, and number.

    b) Available payment terms and financial discounts.

    c) Freight terms and allowances.

    d) Intended point from which it is anticipated that shipments are to be made.

2. Body—with provisions for the display of the following information:

    a) Descriptions of materials ordered—identification.

    b) Quantities.

    c) Prices.

    d) Applicable trade, volume or other discounts.

    e) Price protection provisions.

    f) Return privileges/consignment provisions.

ORIGINATING DEPT:	DATE ISSUED:	EFFECTIVE DATE:
	SUPERCEDES No.:	DATED:

AMERICAN CORP
POLICIES & PROCEDURES—PROCUREMENT

SUBJECT:	SECTION: IX
FINANCIAL TERMS	PAGE 1 of 2

The following policies are established in order to provide for the proper determinations and realizations of earned financial discounts and related payment terms in transactions with vendors.

While the original negotiations to determine vendor's financial terms and payment provisions shall be the province of the Purchasing Department, purchases are to be subject to the vendors' best available terms.

The final determination of such "best" terms shall be the responsibility of Vendor Accounting.

A. *Payment Date/Due Date*

   1. Payments are to be made *when* due. Early payments should not be made.

   2. In calculating the due date, the latest of the shipping, bill of lading, or invoice date should be used.

B. *Financial Discounts*

   1. The determination of the availability of financial discounts should be made from the terms negotiated and indicated upon the purchase orders/contracts and from those provided on vendors' price lists, catalogues, and invoices.

      - *the best of these terms shall be used.*

      In those instances where the financial discounts determined from vendor sources exceed those indicated on purchase orders, Vendor Accounting is to so notify the Purchasing Department so as to assure the upgrading of the vendors' terms on future orders.

   2. Every effort will be made to pay invoices when due. Regardless, Vendor Accounting is to take all financial discounts, no matter when payments are made.

ORIGINATING DEPT:	DATE ISSUED:	EFFECTIVE DATE:
	SUPERCEDES No.:	DATED:

AMERICAN CORP
POLICIES & PROCEDURES—PROCUREMENT

SUBJECT:	SECTION: IX
FINANCIAL TERMS	PAGE 2 of 2

    a) Any missed discounts will then result only from vendor disallowances, based upon vendor criteria of late payment and/or circumstances created by the vendor causing a late payment to result.

    b) *Repayments* of any unearned financial discounts shall be charged against a missed discount account, providing a record of such missed discounts.

ORIGINATING DEPT:	DATE ISSUED:	EFFECTIVE DATE:
	SUPERCEDES No.:	DATED:

AMERICAN CORP
POLICIES & PROCEDURES—PROCUREMENT

| SUBJECT: | SECTION: X |
| FREIGHT TERMS | PAGE 1 of 1 |

The disciplines of the *propriety* of freight charges shall be the responsibility of the Vendor Accounting Department.

1. The following information shall be provided to Vendor Accounting for the discipline of vendors' compliance with established freight terms:

    a) Purchase Orders—shall clearly state the freight terms of purchase.

    b) Receiving Document—shall clearly provide that information required for the proper discipline of the established freight terms:

    - method of receipt—"prepaid" or "collect."
    - amount of freight charges—whether received "prepaid" or "collect".
    - shipping point.
    - carrier.
    - probill number.

2. Vendor Accounting shall compare freight charges or freight allowances provided on vendor invoices with the terms established for the vendor and the inbound freight information provided on the receiving documents.

3. Vendor Accounting shall, when violations on the part of vendors of the established freight terms are discerned, deduct from the payments to the vendors any improper costs to the Corporation that so result.

| ORIGINATING DEPT: | DATE ISSUED: | EFFECTIVE DATE: |
| | SUPERCEDES No.: | DATED: |

INDEX

Accountability, procurement funds and, 9–10
Accounting practices, vendor/purchaser variances, 51
Accounts payable department:
　Best of Terms concept and, 25
　filing systems and, 100
　financial discounting and payment practices, 65–66, 69
　impropriety and, 26–27
　internal auditor and, 11
　Payable by Approval category and, 13, 17
　Payable by Direct Purchase Order category and, 19, 20
　personnel training in, 51
　vendor account adjustments and, 51
Accounts payable department analysis, 101–105
　audit guide:
　　policies, 108–109
　　structure, 110
　questions involved in, 101–102
　structural factors, 104–105
　vendor inquiries and, 102–103
Adjustments:
　chargebacks (debit memos) and, 41, 42
　vendor account adjustments and, 52, 53
　vendor credit invoices versus chargebacks (debit memos), 35–39
Administrative expenses:
　Payable by Approval category and, 18
　vendor account adjustments and, 51
Allowed tolerance:
　Payable by Approval category and, 50
　vendor account adjustments and, 53
"Alpha-by-vendor" systems, described, 99–100

Audit guide:
　policy, procedure, and practices review, 107–110
　　accounts payable department policy, 108–109
　　accounts payable department structure, 110
　　filing systems, 110
　　financial payment terms disciplines, 108
　　freight control, 109–110
　　introduction, 107
　　organizational factors, 108
　　preparations, 107–108
　　trade and volume discounts, 109
　procurement process review, 29–31
　　Best of Terms disciplines, 31
　　introduction, 29
　　invoice processing, 30–31
　　organizational factors, 29–30
　　preparations, 29
　vendor account adjustments, 59–61
　　introduction, 59
　　organizational factors, 59–60
　　preparations, 59
　　vendor credit invoice versus chargeback (debit memo) procedure, 60–61
Audits:
　freight control analysis, 83–95. *See also* Freight control analysis
　retailing industry and, 3–4
　trade and volume discounts, 75
Authorizing signature, internal auditor and, 11–12

Back order freight charges, freight control analysis and, 87

145

INDEX

"Batch-in-which-paid" systems, described, 97–99
Best of Terms concept, 23–27
  audit guide and, 31
  described, 23
  disciplines in, 24–27
  freight control analysis and, 90
  Payable by Direct Purchase Order category and, 19–23
  premises for, 24
Bid requirements, internal auditor and, 11
Buyers:
  controls and, 6
  Payable by Approval category and, 18
  vendor relationships with, 6–8, 19

Cash flow, accounts payable department analysis, vendor inquiries and, 102–103
Chargeback (debit memo) procedure, 41–48
  audit guide, 60–61
  Best of Terms concept and, 25, 26
  filing systems and, 100
  format recommended for, 43
  overview of, 41–42
  policy highlights, 42
  procedural highlights, 42–48
  vendor account adjustments and, 54
  vendor credit invoices versus, 35–39
Clerical expenses, containment of, 97
Competitive bid requirements, internal auditor and, 11
Control:
  document routing and, 3
  retailing industry lesson for, 5–6
Corporate control, *see* Control
Corporate structure:
  accounts payable department analysis, 104–105
  cost reductions and, 3
  trade and volume discounts and, 75–76
Cost control:
  buyer/vendor relationships, 6–8
  corporate structure and, 3
  filing systems and, 97
  transaction controls, 9–10
  vendor account adjustments and, 51
Credit, buyer/vendor relationships, 6–8
Credit department, *see* Vendor credit department
Credit invoices, *see* Vendor credit invoices

Credits, chargebacks (debit memos) and, 44, 45

Debit balances, vendor credit invoices versus chargebacks (debit memos), 37
Debit memo, *see* Chargeback (debit memo) procedure
Debit Transaction Flow Chart, chargebacks (debit memos) and, 46, 47
Deficit freight charges, freight control analysis and, 85–87
Deregulation, of trucking industry, freight control analysis and, 93
Direct adjustment, vendor account adjustments and, 54
Direct Purchase Order category, *see* Payable by Direct Purchase Order category
Discounts:
  freight control analysis and, 93, 95
  Payable by Approval category and, 18
  preferred carrier status, freight control analysis and, 87–88
Document routing:
  Best of Terms concept and, 24–25
  chargebacks (debit memos) eliminate, 46
  freight control analysis and, 88–89
  impropriety and, 26–27
  Payable by Approval category and, 18
  Payable by Direct Purchase Order category and, 20
  retailing industry and, 3–4
  streamlining procedures for, 3
Downsizing, *see* Rightsizing
Due dating, accounts payable department analysis, 101

Early retirement programs, rightsizing and, 3
Energy surcharge, Best of Terms concept and, 26
Error, vendor account adjustments and, 52, 53
Ethics, financial discounting and payment practices, 69

Filing systems, 97–100
  "alpha-by-vendor" systems, 99–100
  "batch-in-which-paid" systems, 97–99
  cost containment and, 97
Financial discounting and payment

INDEX

practices, 65–73
  accounts payable department and, 65–66, 69
  audit guide, 108
  enforcement of purchase order terms, 66–67
  filing systems and, 98
  misunderstandings and, 67–69
  Net 30 and, 65, 66
  policy recommendations for, 70–71, 74
  trade and volume discounts and, 77, 80, 82
Fiscal control, *see* Control
Foreign Corrupt Practices Act, 9
Fraud:
  internal auditor and, 11–12
  Payable by Approval category and, 17
Freight basing point (freight equalization), freight control analysis and, 88–95
Freight control analysis, 83–95
  audit guide, 109–110
  back order freight charges and, 87
  deficit freight charges and, 85–87
  determinations in, 83–84
  freight equalization (freight basing point) and, 88–95
  loaded freight charges (prepay and add terms), 87–88
  reconciliations in, 84–85
  vendor violations of terms, 83
Freight costs:
  chargebacks (debit memos) and, 44
  filing systems and, 98
  vendor credit invoices versus chargebacks (debit memos), 36, 38
Freight equalization (freight basing point), freight control analysis and, 88–95

Handling charges, vendor credit invoices versus chargebacks (debit memos), 36
Hold invoice, vendor account adjustments and, 54

Interest expenses:
  financial discounting and payment practices, 67, 70
  vendor credit invoices versus chargebacks (debit memos), 36
Internal auditor, 11–27
  accounts payable department focus recommendation, 11–12

Best of Terms concept, 23–27
  Payable by Approval category and, 13, 15, 17–19
  Payable by Authorization category and, 12–13, 14
  Payable by Direct Purchase Order category and, 16, 19–23
  traditional approach of, 11
Internal Revenue Service, 17
Invoice:
  consistency of terms on, filing systems and, 98
  freight control analysis and, 83, 90, 92
  Net 30 and, 65, 66
  Payable by Approval category and, 13, 17
  Payable by Authorization procedures and, 12–13
  processing of, audit guide and, 30–31
  vendor account adjustments and, 52, 53, 54
  volume discounts and, 77

Kickbacks, Payable by Approval category and, 17

Late fees, vendor account adjustments and, 55–56
Loaded freight charges (prepay and add terms), freight control analysis and, 87–88

Material Inspection Report (MIR), chargebacks (debit memos) and, 46

Net 30, financial discounting and payment practices, 65, 66

Organizational factors, audit guide and, 29–30
Otherwise established terms, Payable by Direct Purchase Order category and, 20
Overcharges, vendor account adjustments and, 53

Payable by Approval category:
  allowed tolerance and, 50
  audit guide and, 30–31
  impropriety and, 26–27
  internal auditor and, 13, 15, 17–19

INDEX

Payable by Authorization category:
   audit guide and, 30
   internal auditor and, 12-13, 14
Payable by Direct Purchase Order category:
   audit guide and, 31
   Best of Terms concept and, 23
   internal auditor and, 16, 19-23
Payment practices, *see* Financial discounting and payment practices
Payment schedules, trade and volume discounts and, 77, 82
Policy and procedure manuals:
   accounts payable department analysis, 103-104
   freight control analysis and, 87
   Payable by Approval category and, 17-18
   samples of, for procurement control implementation, 111-143
   sources for, 4
   trade and volume discounts, 75
Preferred carrier status, freight control analysis and, 87-88
Prepay and add terms (loaded freight charges), freight control analysis and, 87-88
Procurement funds, accountability and, 9-10
Propriety, freight control analysis and, 88, 89, 92
Proximo, financial discounting and payment practices, 67-69
Purchase order:
   Best of Terms concept and, 24-25
   enforcement of terms of, 66-67
   freight control analysis and, 84, 90, 91, 92
   Net 30 and, 65, 66
   Payable by Approval category and, 13, 17
   Payable by Authorization procedures and, 12-13
   Payable by Direct Purchase Order category and, 16, 19-23
   vendor account adjustments and, 52, 53
Purchase Order Change Notice (POCN), Best of Terms concept and, 25
Purchase tolerance, *see* Tolerance
Purchasing department, chargebacks (debit memos) and, 41

Quality:
   filing systems and, 98
   freight control analysis and, 88, 89

Request for credit procedures, vendor account adjustments and, 55
Retailing industry:
   corporate control lesson from, 5-6
   document routing and, 3-4
Return invoice, vendor account adjustments and, 54
Returns:
   chargebacks (debit memos) and, 41, 42
   vendor account adjustments and, 52, 53
   vendor credit invoices versus chargebacks (debit memos), 35-39
Rightsizing, early retirement programs and, 3
Routing, *see* Document routing

Sales tax, trade discount conversion and, 82
Signature, *see* Authorizing signature
Suspensing mechanism, chargebacks (debit memos) eliminate, 45
Symbol identification chart, 21

Taxation, sales tax, trade discount conversion and, 82
Tolerance, 49-50
   accounts payable department analysis, 101
   definitions of, 49
   internal auditor and, 11
   vendor account adjustments and, 53
Trade and volume discounts, 75-82
   audit guide, 109
   auditor knowledge of, 75
   corporate structure and, 75-76
   financial discounting and payment practices and, 77, 80, 82
   trade discounts defined, 76-77
   volume discounts defined, 77
Trade discount conversion, trade and volume discounts conversion to financial discounting and payment practices, 77, 80, 82
Transaction controls:
   described, 9-10
   effectiveness evaluation of, 12
Transportation costs, *see* Freight control analysis
Trucking industry, deregulation of, freight

INDEX

control analysis and, 93
2% 10, financial discounting and payment practices, 65, 66

Vendor account adjustments, 51–57
audit guide for, 59–61
circumstances necessitating, 52–53
cost control and, 51
policy recommendations, 53–56
vendor notification form example, 57
Vendor credit department, personnel training in, 51
Vendor credit invoice, *see also* Request for credit procedures
audit guide, 60–61
chargebacks (debit memos) versus, 35–39. *See also* Chargeback (debit memo) procedure
Vendor inquiry desk, accounts payable department analysis, 103
Vendors:
buyer relationships with, 6–8, 19
inquiries from, accounts payable department analysis and, 102–103
retailing industry and, 3–4, 5–6
selection of, internal auditor and, 11
transaction controls and, 9–10
violations of freight terms by, 83
Volume discounts, *see* Trade and volume discounts

Mysterious REALMS

THE DUBIOUS ADVENTURES OF EDDIE AND MICKI

Stephanie Jones

BY STEPHANIE JONES

 FriesenPress

Suite 300 - 990 Fort St
Victoria, BC, V8V 3K2
Canada

www.friesenpress.com

Copyright © 2020 by Stephanie Jones
First Edition — 2020

All rights reserved.

No part of this publication may be reproduced in any form, or by any means, electronic or mechanical, including photocopying, recording, or any information browsing, storage, or retrieval system, without permission in writing from FriesenPress.

ISBN
978-1-5255-6229-7 (Hardcover)
978-1-5255-6230-3 (Paperback)
978-1-5255-6231-0 (eBook)

1. *Fiction, Mystery & Detective*

Distributed to the trade by The Ingram Book Company

DEDICATION

To my brother, and in memory of my father, both of whom inspired my imagination which has engendered these tales of dubious adventures for the young and the young-at-heart.

Mysterious REALMS

THE DUBIOUS ADVENTURES OF
EDDIE AND MICKI

Four short stories:

The Birthday Gift

The Grand Prize

The Gypsy Life

A Winter Tale

THE BIRTHDAY GIFT

ONE DAY, EDDIE BEAR, the old cast-off teddy bear, was *not* in the garden, that was because he was sick in bed fighting the worst head-cold anyone had ever had—at least in his opinion. To make matters worse, it was housemate Micki's birthday today and she was driving Eddie mad. She was waiting very impatiently for the morning post, which she felt sure would bring a mountain of cards and presents.

"Do stop jumping on me every five-minutes, Micki!" complained Eddie, blowing his sore, swollen, nose again, "It's bad enough lying sick in this makeshift bed in the parlour without you jumping up on me every two minutes to look out the window."

"But I'm expecting lots and lots of mail today. Mrs. Robbins may not be able to fly with such a heavy load, so I want to meet her at the gate and help her carry the post-bag," explained Micki, examining her small, but strong, white paws.

"I've told you a hundred times already, I will let you know as soon as I see the post-lady flying up the garden path. If she has any birthday post for you, she will *bring* it," said Eddie, hardly able to breathe through his stuffed-up nose.

Micki MacVitie was a black and white Highland cat and today was her ninth birthday, at least the ninth of one of her nine cat-lives, (which the young cat hated explaining to humans because they always looked confused at her explanation). So, of course, today was a *very* special day.

"Please go and make us more of that chamomile tea with lots of honey, and I'll shout if I see Mrs. Robbins coming," said Eddie, sniffing miserably, "And don't forget the chocolate-covered digestive biscuits!"

While Micki was busy in the kitchen deciding just how many chocolate-covered digestive biscuits to put on the plate, she heard a croaky shout from the parlour.

"She's flying in, Micki, here she comes!"

Micki raced back into the front parlour and flung open the cottage door just as Mrs. Robbins, the post-lady, was landing on the doorstep.

"Hurray!" yelled Micki, "All my birthday cards and presents!"

"Good morning, Miss MacVitie," chirped Mrs. Robbins in her little voice, "I'm sorry, but there is only one piece of post for you today. Perhaps more will arrive tomorrow?" she said, trying hard to console an obviously crest-fallen Micki. "And, good morning to you, Mr. Bear," said Mrs. Robbins, turning to look at the sick animal languishing in his bed by the window. "How are you feeling? A little better today, I hope?"

"Perhaps a little, thank you," said the very miserable little bear. "I think I might live another day," he said with an enormous sneeze. Eddie often felt sorry for himself, especially when he was feeling as poorly as he was today.

"You must drink lots of honey and chamomile tea!" said the little robin-redbreast. "But remember, no chocolate-covered biscuits for a week!" And with that piece of sound advice, she hurried off on her way again.

Meanwhile, a very disappointed Micki shed a torrent of tears that dripped onto her thick black fur, "Oh, drat! Oh, pooh and fiddlesticks, only one card!" she sobbed, "Nobody cares about my birthday."

"Be thankful you got one card at least!" said Eddie, comforting his little friend. "Open it up and see whom it's from. But…er, don't forget to serve the honeyed tea and choccy-biccies first!"

As the friends sipped the tea and nibbled several biscuits each, Micki opened up the fatter-than-normal envelope with excited expectation.

"Ooooh!" she said, taking out the beautiful birthday card and opening it. "It's from Cousin Tabby who lives in Darkest Outer Pongolia. We always exchange greeting cards, but I've never met him. He's from the stripy side of the family."

"What are those pieces of paper that have just fallen out of the card?" said Eddie, chomping on his third biscuit—just to keep up his strength—and then washing it down with another swig of tea.

"They're plane tickets," said Micki, looking at them in surprise. "Airplane tickets from here in the Inner Hebrides to Darkest Outer Pongolia—one for each of us! Cousin Tabby says he would be 'ever so happy' for us to have a birthday holiday with him at his home in the wilds of Pongolia."

"Hip-hip-hurray!" shouted the two friends. Eddie Bear's cold suddenly felt much better, and Micki was happier than she had been all day. This was going to be a wonderful birthday after all!

❦

A few days later, an ecstatic little cat and a much-recovered little bear, were at the Inner Hebrides airport boarding their plane to far-away Outer Pongolia. What fun this was going to be!

They both wanted the window seat to look down at the view of course, but since it was Micki's birthday, she got the privilege of sitting there. But, being a kind, generous little cat, she let her best friend sit there sometimes too. They 'oooh-ed' and 'aaah-ed' at the wonderful sights below during the whole flight while they took a little light refreshment in the form of a heaping plate of fish-sticks swimming in butter for Micki; and, for Eddie, six cream buns, a dozen hard-boiled eggs, mounds of buttered toast with thick-cut marmalade, a bowlful of stewed cherries with clotted cream, and a large jar of best honey, all washed down with huge mugs of Pongolian yak-milk. This little repast was patiently brought to them by the very tired-looking penguin steward and stewardess who were getting irritated with having to spend the whole flight running back and forth between the galley kitchen and seats 14 A and 14 B.

"Soon be there now," said Eddie after a few hours of uneventful flight. "I expect your cousin will be there to meet us at the airport?"

"Well, he said he would be—if he can get his sled through the snow," said Micki hopefully.

It was a rather bumpy landing in the dead of night in Darkest Outer Pongolia. Eddie was wishing he had not snacked on that last the little bag of peanuts. He now felt that his bloated tummy might burst against his seat belt as the plane, its reverse-thrusters roaring, bounced along the runway to a jolting stop on the snow-packed runway.

Stuffed to the gills and feeling a little green, Eddie and Micki stumbled their way down the gangplank and shivered in the chill evening air of Darkest

Outer Pongolia. Sadly, there was *no* Cousin Tabby to meet them. However, an announcement came over the P.A. system asking would a Micki MacVitie please report to the information desk. There, a telegram from Cousin Tabby was handed to them by a scruffy old parrot that had seen better days. The bird told them the roads from the town to the airport were blocked by the worst snow drifts seen this century. However, the telegram told them not to worry:

> *Dear Cousin Micki and Friend Eddie,*
>
> *Cannot meet you because snowed in STOP Take taxi to luxury Starshine Hotel by airport STOP Will pick you up there when can get sled out of garage and roads are clear STOP*
>
> *LUV,*
>
> *Cousin Tabby*
>
> *P.S. Starshine serves **great food**!*

The two friends groaned at the mention of food, but they made a note of it.

They went to the luggage carousel to get their cases. Their mass of bags and cases soon started to rumble along the conveyor belt. Eddie, being a clever kind of bear, tried to grab two suitcases at once but he wasn't fast enough or strong enough and, before he knew it, he was having the ride of his life. He screamed, and shouted, and struggled to get to his feet, but to no avail. On his third revolution, he was yanked off by a gruff bullmastiff security guard who'd had just about enough of tourist pranks for today.

The badly shaken Eddie was not impressed. "What took you so long to rescue me? I'm black and blue all over. I'll write to the…"

"Don't get smarty-pants with me, Fatso!" snarled the mastiff, grabbing the little bear by the lapels of his winter coat and lifting him off his feet again.

Micki was horrified at the spectacle and spread her front claws in front of the guard's face. "You should be ashamed of yourself bullying a helpless little bear," she said, flexing her claws.

"Sorry, ma'am," said the bullmastiff, looking warily at the sharp little daggers dangerously hovering inches from his snout. He dropped Eddie like a hot potato. The old dog bowed humbly to the two travellers, explaining that it had been a rough day.

Their luggage finally retrieved, the two buddies made their way across the icy tarmac to a waiting reindeer taxi driven by a man with long, white beard and wearing a red-velvet suit.

"Looks like a jolly sort of fellow," remarked Eddie to his friend as they lifted their cases into the vehicle.

"Yes! And look at the very shiny nose on that front reindeer," said Micki with a smile.

They hopped into the brightly-coloured sleigh and covered themselves with the cozy blankets provided. Then they gave the driver instructions to take them to the Starshine Hotel.

"Get us there as quickly as possible!" commanded Eddie to the driver. "We are very tired and need a good night's sleep!"

"It'll cost you ten 'Iubles' for me to take you there," said the grumpy driver, "Payment in advance!"

The friends thought it expensive but paid the fare. The sleigh slithered speedily along the slippery slope to the hotel where it suddenly stopped. Micki and Eddie looked up at the façade of the grand hotel in awe, bedazzled by its flashing neon sign and twinkling lights that beautifully enhanced the ornate architecture.

"We're going to enjoy it here!" said Eddie, jumping off the sleigh and eagerly lugging his heavy suitcases up the steps to the door…bump, bump, bump…. At the top of the stairs, a concierge was standing with arms folded across his big-bear chest.

"You can't stay here!" said Big Bear Brunovsky in a booming voice. "We're stuffed to the gills with stranded tourists who are stuck because of the snow drifts."

Eddie didn't want to hear about being stuffed to the gills and held his tummy as he groaned.

"But we're stranded tourists too!" cried Eddie, his overfull stomach growling and churning.

"Sorry! No room, I said!" growled the big bear.

"Well then, where can we get a room for the night?" asked Micki, taking her last suitcase off the sleigh.

"Not my problem," said Big Bear Brunovsky, picking up a very large 'NO VACANCY' sign and setting it in plain view at the top of the steps. He then turned and opened the front door and walked into the brightly-lit, cheery-looking hotel lobby and locked and bolted the door behind him leaving the little cat and bear standing flabbergasted on the stone steps in the freezing cold.

"But what will we do? Where can we go?" whined Micki peevishly.

"Well, obviously, he doesn't give a rip, Micki," said Eddie mournfully.

Eddie Bear waved to the driver who was just about to set the reindeer taxi in motion again, "Wait!" he yelled to the red-suited man who was impatient to be on his way to secure another fare. "We can't stay here; this hotel is full. Is there some other hotel you can take us to, please?"

"Depends whether you've been naughty or nice," guffawed the portly old man.

"We're *very* nice people," spoke up Micki proudly.

"Well, there is the old Moonshine Palace further down the road, but no-one stays there if they can help it," muttered the sleigh-driver. "It will cost you 100 lubles extra to have me drive you there".

"A hundred lubles!! Goodness gracious! Positively preposterous price! Highway robbery!" exclaimed Eddie indignantly. "We're not paying you even a fraction of that, my dear fellow! "I'll write a complaint to the Ministry of Transport; you see if I don't!"

"Take it or leave it! Makes no difference to me," gloated the grumpy old man.

"We'll have to pay it, Eddie," said Micki reluctantly. "We have no other choice."

So, they handed over the wad of cash (the sleigh-driver didn't take credit cards) and off they went in the sleigh again, sliding along until the reindeer skidded to a stop outside an old tumble-down mansion enshrouded in misty darkness. The dislodged sign above the door said in faded, hard-to-read letters:

MOONSHINE PALACE

The surly driver left the two weary friends to struggle with their heavy suitcases up the broken wooden steps.

"Not such a jolly fellow when you get to know him, is he, Micki?" said Eddie, watching the driver whipping the reindeer as they sped around the corner out of sight.

"Rather frightful, I'm afraid. I wonder what he had in that big sack?" said Micki with a shudder.

Eddie pulled the bell-rope hanging beside the big oak door. It was a long time before anyone answered the clanging noise within. But, after some minutes, a small peephole in the heavy door was slowly slid open and then suddenly snapped shut with a resounding slap. Moments later, the door creaked open to reveal an immense Rococo-style lobby and with a long, narrow, dimly-lit hallway leading away from it.

Seeing no one about, the two shivering friends nervously stepped over the threshold.

"Hello!" they called out tentatively, "Anyone here?"

"Of course, there is!" said a sharp, snarly voice behind them making them leap into the air, their hearts thumping loudly. "What d'you want?"

The two animals spun around on their heels to see a tall, but very elegantly-dressed black rat behind the door, which he slammed and bolted shut behind them. He turned a massive iron key in the huge brass lock, just for good measure.

"Who are you?" chimed the cat and bear together.

"His Royal Highness, Prince Rat and heir-apparent of the Kingdom of Darkest Outer Pongolia, at your most 'umble service," said the monstrous rat in a gravelly voice as he bowed deeply before them. His colourful, satin-brocade outfit glistened in the candlelight. "Please excuse my not receiving you proper-like, but it's me butler's day off, you see," he said, straightening his powdered wig which had slipped askew as he bowed. "'Ave to do everything me-self wiv 'im gone."

"Oh, …well…no problem, Your Majesty," said Eddie, bowing politely too.

"Pleased to make your acquaintance, Your Royal Highness," said Micki with a little curtsy bob.

"May we have a room for a night or two?" asked Eddie, still feeling a little unsure of things.

"Oh, I'm sure we can find you something," said Prince Rat lifting high an elaborate candelabra which had but one half-consumed candle still burning in it. "Come this way my *friends*."

"Ahem, excuse me, Your Highness, is there a porter to help us with the luggage?" Eddie inquired as amiably as he could.

"Oooh, I'm sure I can find someone—or some*thing*—to take care of that," said the big black rat with a funny look in his beady eyes.

Micki and Eddie followed him apprehensively along the hallway and up the stairs, along another hallway and up another flight of stairs, then along a dark, narrow corridor until they stopped outside a door.

"Number 32!" said the rat with a wicked grin, "and a very good number that is too. You'll be very comfy 'ere."

Eddie and Micki were too tired to ask any more questions and so, went inside without a word. Once within the room, they were very surprised to see their suitcases already there; stacked neatly in a corner of the room. Two huge four-poster beds, hung with blood-red velvet curtains, stood imposingly before them. A large log-fire crackled warmly in the hearth, its leaping flames creating eerie shadows on walls and ceiling.

The door clicked shut behind them, and then they were alone.

Micki slowly and cautiously peeled back the curtain of the nearest bed and peeked into the darkness. "Bring a candle over, Eddie," she said to her friend.

The obliging bear lit the candle that was in a small holder sitting on the mantle above the fireplace. He took it over to where his friend was peeping through the drapery. As the glow from the candle lit up the interior, both animals gasped in surprise. The linens were of the finest white silk and the quilt of the most exquisite, bejewelled, scarlet charmeuse satin. Then they looked into the other bed—it was exactly the same.

Exhausted, they each selected a bed, took off their travel-dusty clothes, and put on their warm pyjamas and night-caps. Tired as they were, they could not resist jumping on the beds to find out just how springy they were. After bouncing up and down as if they were on a trampoline, they climbed up the bed-curtains and swung back and forth with Tarzan-like yells. Then came the pillow-fight, until one pillow burst, sending a cloud of feathers up into the air that then fell like gently-floating snowflakes all around them. Feeling a little guilty and very much exhausted, the two animals snuggled down between the luxurious sheets and slept like logs—until a strange noise woke them both.

Scrrritch, scrrritch, scratch. Scrrritch, scrrritch, scratch. Scrrritch, scrrritch, scratch.

"Do you hear that noise, Eddie?" said Micki nervously, wishing she had left the candle burning.

"It's just mice in the wainscoting," answered Eddie sleepily through the darkness. "Typical in these old buildings."

Micki was quite self-assured around mice, so she settled back down to sleep.

☙

It was morning when they awoke after a good night's uneventful sleep. They yawned and stretched, and Eddie drew back the heavy drapes on the window while Micki tried to get a fire going in the grate using the ample supply of sticks and matches.

"Brrrr…I say, looks jolly cold out there, and it snowed a lot more during the night," remarked the little bear, shivering, despite his woolly pyjamas.

"I'll soon have a good fire going," said Micki. "I'm hungry. Our host didn't mention breakfast arrangements. Should we ring for breakfast to be brought up to our room?"

"Jolly good idea. I'm famished, although, I swore that I would never eat again after yesterday's meal on the airplane," remarked her friend. "The airline caterers really should watch their portion sizes."

Micki, having got a good fire going, went to open one of her suitcases, "Oh, that's strange" she said, fiddling with it. "My case is locked, but I don't have a key—that's why I never lock it." She tried the others, but they were all locked too.

Eddie tried to open his cases. He was very anxious to check on his smuggled supply of chocolate-covered biscuits, only to find the same problem. He went to pick up the phone to call down to the desk—but there *was* no phone. And no bellpull with which to summon the servants—if there were any.

"What kind of a flea-bitten establishment is this? Don't tell me I have to go downstairs to the lobby in my pyjamas to get room-service?" complained

Eddie, "I'll write and give a piece of my mind to the Bureau of Tourism about this, you see if I don't!"

And with that threat, he strode to the door and turned the knob—but the door was locked—from the outside!

"Prisoners!" they both screamed together, and they dashed to the window to open it as a way of escape. But it was painted shut, and no amount of banging and scraping with what they had could loosen it. They banged and yelled at the door too, but it was of no use, no one came. There was complete silence.

In total despair, they sat dejectedly on the hearth rug in front of the fire.

Presently, they heard the little scratching sounds that had awakened them in the night. Thinking it was just mice they ignored them. But then a faint whimpering sound reached Micki's sharp ears.

"Do you hear that, Eddie?" asked Micki, listening; her ears twitching in every direction.

"Hear what? The scratching? Yes, yes, just mice I told you."

"No, a whimpering sound," said his friend.

Eddie listened intently but could hear nothing of the sort.

"I can't hear anything else, Micki. Remember, I'm just an old teddy bear and have only cloth ears, which have never been very efficient," he said a little wistfully, "and as you know, one of them is quite loose."

Micki slunk on four paws, her belly close to the ground and crept noiselessly towards the sound.

"It's coming from in here," she said, peering at the window seat with a puzzled expression on her face. "Let's see if we can lift the lid and look inside."

"Hold on a minute!" said Eddie, picking up the poker from the hearth, "I don't trust anything in this place. If it's an enemy, I'm ready to let it have it!" He took a firm grip on the poker and held it high above his right shoulder ready to swing.

"Just make sure you don't bash me by mistake," said Micki, looking doubtfully at the spectacle above her as she crouched by the window seat. She took a deep breath and *very* slowly and *very* watchfully, inch by inch, lifted the upholstered lid of the window seat and peeked inside.

"Help!" said a tiny voice from within, "Please don't hurt me."

Eddie and Micki looked at the diminutive owner of the sound.

"We won't hurt you," said Micki kindly, "But who are you?"

"I'm Titch," replied the little thing.

"And *what* are you?" added Eddie, looking on in amazement, poker still at the ready.

Micki leaned into the box and lifted the little creature up into her paw.

"Careful, Micki, it might turn vicious!"

"Oh, for heaven's sake, Eddie! Put that ridiculous weapon down before you do some damage!" said Micki.

The two friends looked at the pathetic, trembling, hairy little bundle of nerves that now stood on the carpet in front of the cheery fire.

"What are you?" repeated Eddie again gruffly.

"I'm an Outer Pongolian Boarhound," said the shivering little thing in a squeaky voice.

"You're a DOG! Well, they must have pretty small boars here in Outer Pongolia! You're no bigger than a chihuahua!" growled the bear suspiciously.

"I used to be the biggest and fiercest boarhound in the Kingdom of Darkest Outer Pongolia. I hunted for the king!"

"I thought you hunted for boars?" said Eddie confused.

"I hunted boars *for* the king," explained the diminutive hound, rolling his eyes and clicking his tongue.

"But how did you get to be so small, Titch?" asked Micki with curiosity.

"It's a long story," said the tiny thing, settling onto its haunches, "and a most peculiar one."

"Well, how about you tell it to us while we're trying to find our way out of this prison," said Eddie with mounting impatience.

"Yes, love to hear it," agreed Micki with enthusiasm, "but first, perhaps you can help us find a way out of here. Come to think of it, how did you get *in*?"

"Same way you did," squeaked the hound. "Getting in is easy," he added, scratching a flea.

"We know *that*!" growled Eddie, "We need to know how to get *out*."

"No problem! Easy-peasy!" said the little dog nonchalantly.

"Well Titch, show us the way then, please," said Micki, looking around the room again for a means of escape.

"I suggest you go through the door," said the dog.

"But the door is locked," said Eddie, yanking on the knob again.

"Not *that* door, silly. *That* one's *always* locked. Try the one over there," he said, pointing to a small door in the far corner.

Eddie and Micki looked at the other door in astonishment; they hadn't noticed it before, even though now it was in plain view.

Eddie opened the door and peered warily down the dark passage, not knowing what to expect—nothing in this place was as expected. "We'll need a candle," he said, "There's no light switch."

"But the candle is almost burned out and there are no others," said Micki dismally.

"Why don't you use the LED flashlight?" said Titch.

"What LED flashlight?" said Eddie and Micki in unison, "We don't see one anywhere."

"Look in the nightstand drawer," said the dog.

They dashed over to the nightstand and Eddie yanked the drawer open.

"There it is!" yelled Micki, grabbing it with her paw and pressing the button. A bright light filled the room. "Yay! It even works!"

Eddie took the torch, "Tally-ho!" he cried, brandishing the light above his head and bolting towards the passageway.

The three animals raced along the now brightly-illuminated long passageway at top speed until they were forced to screech to a halt bumping into one another. The way ahead was blocked by a stout-looking door.

They read the sign on it:

Sshhh…. NURSERY…*Quiet Please!*

The three stood and listened to the dreamy lullaby music mixed with soft crooning sounds emanating from within. Then slowly and carefully, Eddie opened the door and they all crept quietly into the softly-lit room.

"Awwww…how cute!" the bear, the cat, and the dog whispered in perfect unison, each clasping folded hands against their chest.

Before them, were two long rows of little cradles covered with pastel pink and blue lace and bedecked with pretty ribbons. In each little bed was a sweet baby rat, fast asleep.

As the threesome approached the nearest cradles, cooing sweet nothings as they bent over the sleeping occupants, they suddenly heard a swooshing sound behind them. They spun around just in time to dodge a vicious blow from a club-wielding humungous nanny-rat with fangs like a sabre-tooth tiger!

"**AAArrrgggghhh....!**" screamed the three friends as they dashed into a nearby cupboard for safety. But it wasn't a cupboard—it was the laundry chute and down, down, down.... they all tumbled into the blackness that ended in the depths of a huge laundry basket in the cellar four storeys below.

They quickly scrambled their way out of a pungent, sticky, heap of dirty, baby-rat diapers and ran for their lives down the dark corridor that led away from the laundry room. They didn't stop until they were sure they were not being pursued.

"Phew! That was a narrow escape!" gasped Eddie, panting heavily. They were all out of breath as they made their way along the winding corridor until they came to a series of ladders, which they climbed up with some difficulty with Titch tucked under Eddie's arm until they came to another corridor which ended with three closed doors, each one a different colour. The sign on the *black* door in front of them said, in big bold letters:

PRIVATE – DO NOT ENTER!

NO ADMITTANCE!

"Better steer clear of *that* place," said Eddie with conviction. The others agreed.

"How about this way?" said Micki, reading the sign on the *red* door to the right which said:

FUN ROOM!

COME ON IN!

They stood and listened outside the red door for a moment, puzzled by the 'moanings' and 'squealings' emanating from within. Micki quickly opened the door and immediately slammed it shut! She stared at Eddie with a look of shock on her angelic face and said, "Did you see what I saw?!"

"I wish I hadn't!" responded Eddie, fanning his face with his hand.

"Guess that's what rats do for fun," said Titch, shrugging his shoulders and scratching his ears.

STEPHANIE JONES

The three friends turned their attention to the *green* door on the left. They looked at the sign:

COMMUNICATIONS ROOM

ALL WELCOME!

They stood and listened for a while to the chattering, beeping, shouting, and laughing that could be heard coming from behind the green door. Eddie took a deep breath and said, "Well, maybe someone in here can communicate to us what we need to do to get out of this rat-hole?" Then he boldly opened the green door and they all went in.

A tangled mass of rats met their stupefied gaze. All manner of rats, on all manner of devices—cellphones, land phones, laptops, tablets, radios, TV's, megaphones, microphones, smartboards, whiteboards, and blackboards. What utter chaos! Surely, no one could hear what anyone else was saying amid the deafening din. No one paid the slightest attention to the three visitors, no matter how frantically the three friends waved their arms and tried to shout above the crowd. Finally, the trio gave up and went back into the corridor, shutting the green door behind them to muffle the hullaballoo. They stood there enjoying the peace and relative quiet.

"Well, now what?" said Eddie, frowning at Titch, "You were so sure you could guide us out of here."

"Yes, Titch," said Micki to the dog who was busily scratching at yet another flea, "Your escape plan doesn't seem to be working too well. D'you have any *more* bright ideas?"

"You haven't tried the *black* door, yet," said Titch, yawning.

"But the sign on *that* one tells us not to go in there," said Eddie, flummoxed.

"What have you got to lose?" said the little pooch, shrugging, "Unless you want to stay trapped in darkness forever."

The cat and the bear certainly didn't want to do that! Besides, they were starving, having not eaten a crumb since they were on the plane. Not even a chocolate biscuit.

Seeing no alternative, they each took a very deep breath and Eddie turned the knob of the black door in front of them. Before pushing the door open, they listened very carefully. There was silence within. He pushed the door open a crack, then waited while nothing happened. He pushed the door open further and popped his head around to peek inside. He opened the door a little wider and stood there in awe.

"WOW!" exclaimed Eddie in wonder.

"What!? What is it, Eddie? What do you see?" said Micki, trying to push past her chubby friend.

Right before their eyes was a beautiful dining-hall of the old-fashioned kind, festooned exquisitely with velvet drapery and ancient tapestries. Enormous crystal chandeliers with blazing lights hung over the massive oak dining table, which was covered with a pure-white, damask tablecloth. The whiteness of the table linen contrasted sharply with the colourful multitude of lavish dishes of the most delicious exotic foods imaginable—and no one else was there!

"Hooray!" shouted Micki and Eddie, suddenly realizing just how famished they were. They ran and sat on the fancy Queen Anne dining chairs and greedily eyed the feast spread before them, quite at a loss as to where to begin.

"I'm for the roast turkey!" said Eddie, picking up the carving knife and fork and lunging at the juicy-looking bird near him. But as he plunged the utensils into the plump bird, the turkey vanished into thin air! Astonished and annoyed, he took a stab at the nearby rack-of-lamb, but before he touched it, it vanished too.

Micki made a grab for a plate of poached salmon in aspic, then a bowl of trifle, then a plate of liver pâté, but all disappeared before her paws could grasp any of it. And so, the crazy charade continued until the two friends gave up and sobbed in despair having not tasted a single morsel of the mouth-watering food.

The two friends hugged to console each other in their sorrow. Tears gushed down their cheeks and soaked their woolly pyjamas.

Tears all spent; they suddenly remembered the tiresome little boarhound—who had gone *very* quiet. They looked around the room and saw him curled up on the hearthrug fast asleep.

"I'm sick of him," pouted Eddie, "I'm sick of him and his useless ideas, sick of dark, scary passages that lead nowhere, sick of weird rat-people that all seem mad."

"I just want to go home," lamented Micki, her innards growling relentlessly, "My tummy hurts so much!" she cried. "A fine birthday gift this has turned out to be!"

They looked over at the miniature dog who was snoring happily.

"Hey, you!" snarled the hungry bear rudely, "Wake up and do something useful to get us out of here!"

Titch opened one eye, and then the other. He looked calmly at the fat bear standing over him. He stretched out his body lazily on the plush carpet and said, "Are you done eating?"

Eddie bared his clenched teeth and looked as if he was going to choke the tiny dog.

"The food kept disappearing before we could eat it," said Micki hurriedly while grabbing Eddie's arm to hold him back from making a big mistake, "We couldn't grasp hold of anything no matter how hard and fast we tried to grab it. We are so tired and hungry."

Titch looked at the young cat and yawned again. "What time is it?" he said, nibbling at a pesky flea that was tickling him at the base of his tail.

"Time you got us out of here!" boomed Eddie at the top of his voice.

"It's too long since we've had any kind of nourishment," explained Micki, trembling with cold and hunger.

"Well, why don't you call for room service?" said Titch, nonplussed.

"Room service!" bellowed the bear. "Have you lost your marbles! How the heck can we do that, pray tell?"

"Easy-peasy," said the boarhound, going over to the intercom on the wall. "Just press the button and place your order. Like this!" He held down the red button and said in a small, clear voice, "A platter of imported cheeses, a loaf of bread, a plate of smoked salmon, a selection of cold meats, a jar of piccalilli chutney, three bottles of ginger beer, a Dundee cake, and a pot of medium-roast coffee…"

"And chocolate-covered digestive biscuits, please," suggested Eddie humbly.

"…and three packages of chocolate-covered digestive biscuits. *Pronto, por favor!*" said Titch, releasing the button.

Eddie and Micki looked at one another speechless. They started to wonder what they had been doing wrong. This little hound just seemed to take everything in his stride and come up with all the solutions.

MYSTERIOUS REALMS

"How d'you do that, dear friend? asked Eddie and Micki.

"Nothing to it, *amigos*," said Titch, whistling a little tune as he took up his position on the hearth rug again.

Presently, a trapdoor opened near them, and several liveried footmen climbed up out of it skillfully carrying up immense trays of the ordered food and setting them on a table near the fireplace.

"Oh, and please build us a big fire, it's pretty chilly in here," commanded Titch.

"Certainly sir," said one of the footmen as he turned his attention to getting a nice blaze going in the great fireplace.

"Will there be anything else, sir?" inquired another footman.

"No, thank you. That'll be all for now," said the little dog, cutting huge chunks of bread and cheese for his friends.

They all ate hungrily as they soaked up the cheery warmth of the crackling fire.

"Perhaps now would be a good time for you to tell us your mysterious story of how you shrunk in size and ended up in this place," suggested Micki, draining her bottle of ginger beer and smacking her lips.

"Good idea!" said Eddie, devouring the last of his pack of biscuits.

"If you insist," said Titch, flicking stray crumbs from his hairy coat. He stretched out on his back in front of the fire and nestled his head into a soft pillow and then began his tale.

"You see, one day, the King ordered me to hunt and kill the biggest and most ferocious boar in the kingdom. '*No problema!*' I said to him, and off I set at top speed. I hunted high and low until I caught the scent. I followed my nose until I saw the great boar just ahead. I dashed forward and flung myself upon him, wrestling him to the ground with hellish snarls. Then, just as I was about to deliver my death bite, he looked at me with the saddest eyes and said,

'Stop! I am an enchanted boar, and if you spare *my* life, I will change *your* life forever and you will live in a magic palace.'

Well, you see, I was getting pretty tired of doing the King's business and chasing stupid boars all over the kingdom. It was a dead-end job. So, I thought, why not have a change, live the good life, free from the fetters of royal demands?" said the little hound with a far-away look in his dreamy eyes. "'Yeah, okay, sounds like a good deal to me,' I said to him as I let him get up," continued Titch.

"Sounds like a scam to me!" said Eddie doubtfully.

"So, then what happened?" asked Micki, eager to hear the rest of the story.

"As soon as he had got on his feet, he said, ''Ere, eat a bit of this,' and handed me a piece of something. 'What is it?' I asked him, knowing I shouldn't eat handouts from strangers.

'Me special magic mushroom,' he said with a wily look glinting in his eye. 'One nibble of this and you'll be changed forever!'"

"Well, he certainly didn't lie," said Micki dolefully.

"So right, my little kitty-friend," agreed Titch. "I changed from being the biggest, fiercest hound to the pathetic little creature you see before you now—and then, he changed too. He showed his true, wicked self—he was none other than the infamous Prince Rat who had shape-shifted into a boar to trap me. I was a fool to have trusted him."

"What did he do then?" asked Eddie, entranced.

"So, then he grabbed me in his filthy paws, took me to his waiting carriage, and shut me in a cage," continued the tiny boarhound. "We drove to his 'magic palace' all right—Moonshine Palace."

"Well, I suppose the rascal did keep his word and delivered what he advertised," said Eddie pragmatically.

"Yeah, guess I should have asked more questions," admitted Titch.

"What happened when you got here, then?" asked Micki.

"At first, I was given the run of the place, but the wicked rat-cook hated me because I persuaded three blind mice to take after her with a carving knife and she had to run for her life. One day, she ordered the hall boy to take me up to Room 32 and shut me in the window seat where I would stay until some kind person came and let me out."

"It's a good thing we came along when we did, or you may have been stuck there a *very* long time," said Micki, wincing at the thought. "You must have been so lonely and afraid."

"Yeah, well, I had a lot of time to think about things," said Titch, scratching at a flea again.

MYSTERIOUS REALMS

"How did you tolerate being shut in a dark box all that time?" asked Eddie, thinking how awful that would be, especially without a supply of choccy-biccies to keep one occupied.

"I admit it was a steep learning curve," said the diminutive dog. "I learned to meditate. Through the practice of mindfulness, I learned to let go of my grasping ways and yield to patience. It's funny, but the more I didn't worry controlling things, the easier life became," said Titch, waxing philosophical and turning to look at his new companions.

But, tired, and with stomachs stuffed with good food, his friends had fallen asleep. The little tyke realized he was pretty sleepy too, and so he turned around and around on the warm rug, then flopped down and fell into a deep, restful sleep.

☙

When they all awoke the next morning, they saw sunlight eagerly edging its way through the gaps in the thick window hangings to ooze blissfully into the chamber.

Eddie pulled back the heavy drapes and let the excited sunbeams do their joyful morning dance around the room.

"Look!" said Eddie, "the snow's all gone!"

Micki went and looked out the window. Sure enough, the warm sunshine had chased away the snowy blanket that had lain so heavily upon the landscape the night before.

"Now, we can go and meet Cousin Tabby at the Starshine Hotel," said Micki, gleefully jumping up and down.

Then she and Eddie remembered that they couldn't do that because they were trapped and had no idea how to get out. They looked hopefully at their little helper.

"Morning guys!" said the little creature, stretching and yawning, "What are you planning to do today?" he asked pleasantly while having a good scratch.

"Well, it *would* be nice to be out in all that lovely sunshine," said Eddie, smiling.

"And, of course, go and meet up with Cousin Tabby as promised, if at all possible," said Micki, feeling quite relaxed for some reason.

"Shouldn't be a problem now," said Titch, "You've learned a lot about how things operate around here since you arrived yesterday."

"We have?" said a skeptical Eddie, throwing a querying glance at Micki.

"Yesterday seems like a lifetime ago now," said Micki pensively. "You know," she said, looking at Eddie, "things seem to work out best when we remain calm and confident as Titch does. He observes the situation quietly and the solution appears—or at least the problem seems not to be there anymore. For him, right things just seem to happen.

"Hmmm…," said Eddie thoughtfully. "You may have a point there my little friend. Maybe we should give it a try."

Micki went over to the intercom and pushed the red button, "May we have our luggage brought down from Room 32 to the lobby, please?" she requested firmly.

"And order a taxi," whispered Eddie loudly to her.

"And a fresh change of clothes," suggested Titch, looking at their shabby, woolly pyjamas.

A little while later, the butler opened the door to the dining room where the now smartly dressed three friends were finishing the scrumptious breakfast that they had ordered through room service. He stood to attention and announced:

"Your luggage and limousine are waiting for you downstairs, sirs and madam," he said with a bow.

"Well, I think we're ready?" said the little boarhound, smiling at Eddie and Micki as they pushed back from the table.

"This way, if you please, then," said the servant. "Just follow me!"

The butler led the way down the elevator and into the long hallway that led to the front lobby. The three friends walked behind him along the corridor, which was lined with tables heavily laden with large platters, each piled high with the most delicious looking cakes, pies, biscuits, and squares. But the animals were still so full of breakfast, and so very eager to leave, that they weren't tempted to stop—well, except for one of them.

They could now see into the lobby and through the open front doors to the welcoming sunshine and the waiting limo that was piled high with all their luggage. Seeing freedom so close, they began to get very excited, and then excitement turned to near panic as the faster they walked, the longer the corridor seemed to become. They started to run, yet no matter how fast they ran, the butler seemed to stay just ahead of them, even though he wasn't walking any quicker than before.

"Come on, hurry!" yelled Micki to her friends, "The doors are closing!"

And sure enough, the big heavy front doors were very slowly, inch by inch, starting to swing shut.

Just as Micki made it into the lobby, she twirled her head around to urge her friends onwards for the final dash. They were just going to make it! Titch was right on her heels, but Eddie was not!

"EDDIEEEE!" screamed Micki and Titch together, "leave all that food, we have to go, NOW!"

Eddie was far back along the immense corridor, busily stuffing his mouth and pockets with chocolate biscuits and all manner of other delicacies.

"Khoming!" he tried to shout with a mouth stuffed beyond full, "Jutht a coupfle more…"

But too late!

The gateway to freedom suddenly slammed shut with a bone-breaking bang, and Micki and Titch spun around to see the butler-rat, now grown huge and dressed as Prince Rat again, stood with his back against the portals with arms and legs outstretched, barring the way.

"Not so fast, me little beauties!" he leered with a nasty grin that bared his yellow fangs. "Not so sure you're ready to leave yet, my little loves," he said with an eerie glint in his beady eyes. And he lunged towards them with a snarl and outspread claws.

"Oh, NO!!!" yelled the little threesome as they turned and fled back down the hallway as fast as their little legs would carry them.

Poor Eddie was so weighed down with all the stashed food he could barely waddle.

"Empty your pockets, Eddie!" yelled Micki as she and Titch grabbed his coat to hurry him along.

Eddie threw the food from his pockets as fast as he could. The squishy mess of biscuits and pastries flying in every direction onto the floor bought them a little time. The pursuing Prince Rat had to slow to a crawl as he fought to stay upright, slipping and sliding on the mushed food under his high-heeled slippers.

The little threesome bolted through the first door they came to and darted up a flight of stairs, they sped along another hallway, leaving startled chambermaids in their wake. Puffing and panting, they clambered up more stairs, then bolted along a curvy-mirrored corridor where they paused at the far end to catch their breath. Eddie held his over-stuffed tummy and bent over. He was on the verge of being sick with all those weird mirror images.

Suddenly, they heard the clattering of their pursuer's shoes along the mirrored corridor where his reflections made it look like a thousand rats were chasing them.

Micki and Titch each grabbed one of the bear's arms and dragged him along the next corridor until they came to a junction of seven passages that led off in all directions.

"Oh, no! Spaghetti Junction!" groaned Eddie.

"Which way shall we go, Titch?" panted Micki.

"I've absolutely no idea!" cried Titch, bewildered.

Micki was afraid she would faint, but then she caught a movement out the corner of her eye. "What's that?" said whispered, pointing at a brightly-sparkling little creature resembling a baby bat that was hovering at the entrance to one of the dark passageways. It was winking at them with big golden eyes.

"Why, it must be Winkerbelle!" yelped Titch in delight, I think she's one of the bats that live in the belfry tower. "She's telling us to follow her!"

So off they sped again with Winkerbelle leading the way. They eventually came to a steep, narrow spiral staircase cut out of stone. Up, up they scrambled still following the glittering little bat with the winking, golden eyes. The steps ended in a little, round room at the top of the tower. They were in complete darkness.

"Stay here!" squeaked the bat, "and bolt the door behind me."

And with that, she flew off down the spiral staircase.

The exhausted friends slammed the door shut and shot the heavy iron bolts. Then they sat down in the darkness and thanked their lucky stars for yet another narrow escape.

"So, what do we do now?" said Micki in a small shaky voice.

"Hello? What's this?" said Eddie, feeling something tickling the top of his head.

Titch reached up and felt around the bear's head. His hand grasped something long, thin, and twisted.

"It's the bell rope! Winkerbelle has brought us to the top of the bell tower!" Titch shouted in glee. "The big bell must be in the open turret above our heads."

"Of course!" exclaimed Eddie with gusto. "We can pull on the rope and ring the bell for help!" And with that, he swung madly back and forth on the end of the rope until the bell clanged loudly above them. Immediately, Micki and Titch yanked him off the rope.

"Stop it!" the other two shouted.

"It may attract a rescue team, *or it may just tell the rats where we are!*" explained Micki sensibly.

"Well, they won't be able to break through that stout, bolted door," said Eddie, a little peeved at the sharp reprimand.

"We'd better think this through carefully, my friends," said Titch.

So, the three sat there in the darkness contemplating their situation.

Presently, Micki and Titch heard a big sniffle coming from their ursine friend.

"It's all right, Eddie," said Micki kindly, putting her paw on his arm, "I'm sorry I snapped at you. I'm sure we'll escape eventually."

"But it's all my fault," sobbed Eddie convulsively, "If I wasn't such a greedy little bear and hadn't stopped to fill my pockets and stuff my mouth, we would have been free in the sunshine now."

"Well, maybe so, Eddie," said Micki thoughtfully, "but I'm no better."

"How so?" said Eddie, blowing his nose noisily.

"Well, I wanted so many things for my birthday, and when I got only *one card*, I ranted and sulked like a spoiled little cat."

"Well," began Titch, "If I hadn't been so greedy and grasping, I wouldn't have ended up in this rat's nest." The little dog paused to wipe a tear that was running down his cheek. "Yes, I didn't know how lucky I was. I had it all when I lived in King Tab's palace. I had such a good life and I threw it all away when I allowed myself to be swayed by false promises. I gave it all up for promised riches I didn't even need."

The others nodded with understanding.

"So, who was this King Tab? Was he a good person?" asked Micki with curiosity.

"He was such a benevolent master," began Titch, gladdening with the memories. "The Great Striped Cat King took great care of me so that I wanted for nothing. His lovely Queen Mab was so kind, and their playful brood of little 'Tablets' and 'Mabkins' would clamber all over me; pulling my ears, swinging on my tail, and making me laugh," said Titch with a wistful look in his dark eyes, which were quite misty with tears.

"So, this king is a tabby cat?" asked Micki with a quizzical look wrinkling the fur between her eyes.

Before Titch could answer, they heard a soft hooting sound outside.

"What's that?" said Eddie, starting to tremble again.

"Sounds like the old hooty owl, hooty-hooting up above," said Titch in surprise, "and it seems to be filling me with an old familiar love!" he crooned.

As they listened, rays of the mid-day sun started to push their way through the chinks in the walls and around the little door that led out onto the parapet.

"Look!" shouted Micki, "There's a door! Perhaps it opens"?

Titch got up, raised the latch on the little door and pushed it open.

There, perched on the castellated parapet was a big, barred owl with huge, beautiful golden eyes. He winked at them. "I believe you are all ready to leave here at last," 'whooed' the big bird with a friendly smile.

The three friends nodded vigorously.

"Then hop onto my back, and let's away!"

Without further delay, the dog, the cat, and the bear eagerly climbed aboard and clung to the silky, striped feathers of their avian rescuer.

Within seconds, they landed safely on the ground by the waiting limousine, which was still piled high with their luggage.

They alighted from the big bird and thanked him. Titch cocked his head on one side and looked deeply into those kind, golden eyes that somehow seemed so familiar. Micki and Eddie could hardly wait to be on their way to meet Cousin Tabby who they hoped was still waiting for them at the Starshine Hotel. But before heading towards the sleek, black car, Eddie and Micki turned and looked at Titch.

"What will you do?" asked Eddie, "Where will you go?"

"You can come with us if you wish," offered Micki, "unless you want to stay here at the Moonshine Palace, that is?

"Are you freakin' kidding me!" said the little boarhound, laughing out loud, "I'm so glad to be out of that rat-infested madhouse!" Then, the little dog hesitated, the wistful look returning to his eyes. "Thanks for the generous offer, guys. I would come with you, but I have a yearning to be back where I truly belong—with my beloved master, with the friends and special family I so wantonly abandoned. If someone would be kind enough to take me back, there?" he added beseechingly.

"Well, maybe we can give you a ride home, if you give us directions," said Micki.

"Whooo?" said the barred owl behind them.

The threesome suddenly remembered their brave rescuer and turned to bid him farewell, but he was no longer there! Instead, there stood a large, splendid, regal tabby-cat with immense, golden eyes.

"I *knew* I had seen you somewhere before!" yelped Titch in delight, bounding up to his old master and throwing himself into his welcoming arms.

Micki and Eddie gasped in shock!

"Are you my mysterious, far-way cousin?" purred a stunned Micki in sheer joy.

"Yes, I am!" said the striped cat. He gave a big wink as he hugged his cousin, "So thrilled to meet you at last! And this must be our dear friend, Eddie?" Cousin Tabby said, receiving a joyful bear-hug from the happy little teddy.

"Well, it's good to say good-bye forever to this horrid place," the freed friends said as they turned to wave a final farewell to the Moonshine Palace from which they had just made their 'Great Escape'—but to their astonishment, *it* wasn't there either—it was just a patch of sandy desert!

"Where did it go?" cried the three friends in amazement.

Cousin Tabby spoke up, "Well, I suppose it's not needed here anymore. It only manifests for those who are obsessed with greediness," he said with another big wink. "Come on, it's time to head off to our *real* palace!" King Tab led the group towards the big car where the patient, fluffy Himalayan cat chauffeur held open the door.

"Wait!" shouted Titch behind them, "Will there be room for me in the car too?"

"Of course, there is room for such a little dog as you," said Eddie over his shoulder as he hurried towards the car.

Micki, following close behind her friend said, "Why would you think there wouldn't be enough room for you?"

"Come on, Titch," said the two buddies together turning to look back at their diminutive friend lagging behind.

But they each got yet another surprise of their life! No longer was Titch a tiny, scruffy little pooch, he had been magically transformed into his former self: a big, magnificent Outer Pongolian Boarhound.

"Certainly, there's room for you, my most loyal and esteemed friend," said Cousin Tabby, walking up to Titch and putting his arm around the noble neck, "Why do you think I brought the stretch-limo!"

The four friends laughed, jostled, and joked as they clambered aboard the limousine and headed for the Grand Palace where King Tab's family and friends were waiting for them.

"Well, that was quite the adventure!" said Eddie, grinning at the others as he snuggled back into the plush seat of the limo.

"Not half!" said Micki, smiling contentedly, "What a great way to start my birthday holiday! And what a lot we have to tell *you*, Cousin Tabby!"

"I think I might already know a little something about all that," said her striped relative with a wink of his smiling, golden eyes!

And off they sped, leaving nothing but the dust to settle behind them.

[THE END]

THE GRAND PRIZE

ONE DAY, EDDIE WAS *not* in the garden and neither was his housemate Micki. That is because it was already winter in the Inner Hebrides where they lived and today was a cold, rainy sort of day. So, Eddie Bear, the caste-off teddy bear, and his friend Micki MacVitie, the Highland cat, were amusing themselves where it was cozy and warm in their snug little cottage by the sea.

While Eddie was busy surfing the Net for all and sundry, Micki was engrossed in filling out a competition entry she had just cut out of a magazine. It promised a grand prize of a stupendous holiday for two at a luxury seaside resort on the Costa Del Sol. Her tongue stuck out the side of her mouth as she focused her attention on writing a 'required explanation' of *why* she and her travel companion would find the offered prize the answer to a life-long dream. Stumped for a good idea, she asked her best friend, Eddie, for a suggestion.

"How would a ten-day holiday on the Costa del Sol fulfill our life-long dream, Eddie?" asked Micki.

"On the costa what?" asked Eddie, cupping his right ear that was coming loose for the umpteenth time.

"The Costa del…a sunny coast somewhere Spain," explained Micki, "I'm submitting a competition essay that has a holiday for two as a grand prize, but I have to write an essay that tells how…."

"Waste of ruddy time!" interrupted the plump bear, munching yet another chocolate-covered digestive biscuit as his brown glassy eyes scanned the colourful images that had suddenly appeared on the computer screen before him. "You're always entering those competitions and you never win anything. Give it up, my friend!" he said.

"Well, it costs nothing but a postage stamp. So, it's worth a try—if only I could think of something...."

"Hey!" yelled Eddie suddenly, "How about *this* offer, online?"

"What offer, Eddie?"

"It says here, 'You have won your dream all-expenses-paid vacation of a lifetime! Enjoy seven glorious days and eight nights on Paradise Island where you will be treated better than royalty. Do not delay, this exclusive offer ends in FIVE minutes!'" read Eddie, his voice quivering and his eyes bulging in excitement.

"What do we have to do to accept?" asked Micki a little skeptically.

"Just click this green button, it says," replied Eddie.

"Are you sure it's safe to do that?" said Micki apprehensively, "I've heard you can't always trust these things."

"Pooh! Stuff and nonsense!" snorted Eddie scornfully, "If it wasn't safe, they would say so. It sure beats mailing off all those silly competition applications you write. And look at all these fantastic photos—blue lagoons, palm trees, sandy beaches, and beautiful people serving you delicious food and drinks, and…. Oh no! It's counting down…we only have TWO minutes left to click on the green button."

"Well, I think we should consider carefully before we act," said Micki, getting up from the table and going over to look at the screen, "What does that tiny print at the bottom say?"

"It says, 'At least one winner must be a REAL animal, one *stuffed* companion per winner okay.' Well, that works for us! Oooh, only ONE minute left, Micki!"

Eddie froze, his paw poised above the button…

"Oh, I don't know Eddie, it does look exciting…but oh, dear, what to do?" said Micki, biting her claws.

Five…four…three…two…one…BAM! Eddie's paw hit the green button in the nick of time! Immediately, there were beeps, and whistles, and flashing lights then something started to rattle out of their printer. Micki grabbed the two sheets of paper as they floated to the floor.

"Holiday resort vouchers for two for a seven-day stay at the Shady Palms Resort on Paradise Island in the Mid-Pacific," read Micki, her paws all a-tremble.

MYSTERIOUS REALMS

"Whooopee!" yelled Eddie leaping from his seat and jumping up and down for joy. "When do we leave?"

"Tomorrow night," said Micki, "We had better start packing right away!"

❦

So, after a mad scramble, a sleepless night, and a hectic of day of doing this and that, the pair were in the security line-up at the Inner Hebrides airport at one minute past midnight the next night.

"Seems like airport security has really beefed-up since our last trip," remarked Eddie to Micki.

"Yes, and I don't like the look of all this weird security machinery," said Micki, glancing around.

Micki placed her carry-on bag on the conveyor belt and watched it disappear into the depths of the X-ray scanner. Then she stepped bare-footed through an 'arch scanner' and then waited to be 'wanded' by a nice guard-lady who smiled kindly while the little cat put her booties back on.

Suddenly, as Micki started to walk to where her cleared baggage was waiting, all hell broke loose behind her! There were beepings, and bangings, and clangings, whistle-blowings, and red lights flashing. Guards with guns raced up to the security 'arch' where the 'wand-waving' security guard was wrestling a very panicked teddy bear to the ground.

"Eddie!" screamed Micki in horror. She stood and faced the guard eye-to-eye, "What are you doing to my friend?" she screeched into the startled orbs of the guard.

"He's stuffed full of something!" said the guard, her eyes almost hanging out of their sockets with the thrill of having caught a smuggler.

"Well, of course he is!" exclaimed the angry cat, "He's a *stuffed* bear! What do you expect?"

"But something inside him set off the security alarms," said the 'wander', still pinning poor Eddie to the ground. "Frisk him!" she commanded to the security police.

Immediately, a terrified Eddie was grabbed by a gazillion rough hands that poked and prodded every inch of his stuffed being—even those parts only his doctor knew about for sure.

"We can feel something strange and unusual in there," growled one of the policemen squeezing the bear's midriff in his huge hand. "Put him through the X-ray scanner!"

And before you could say 'Jack Robinson', Eddie felt himself being lifted onto the conveyor belt where he became wedged between two large pieces of carry-on luggage as the belt moved him forward.

Sad little Eddie had never felt so humiliated in his life—at least not *this* week.

"Thank goodness my friends can't see me now!" he moaned.

But as his aching body neared the black hole of the scanner, a myriad of news reporters appeared from nowhere and set off a clicking lightshow of camera flashes that blinded him until he, with great relief, was engulfed in the dark cavern of the machine. But the peace didn't last long. His stuffed tummy was so high it became jammed in the middle of the machine and the 'Remove Over-Sized Luggage Jam' button began flashing and beeping. It was with much pulling and pushing by all and sundry persons that finally, a very woebegone little bear emerged on the other side with an explosive 'POP!'

"Oh, Eddie! You poor thing!" wailed Micki as she helped him to his feet, "How horribly humiliating!"

"I shall write a letter of complaint to the Ministry of Aviation," said Eddie, straightening his disheveled clothing, "You see if I don't. Appalling treatment of a law-abiding, tax-paying citizen. Just appalling!"

"Yes, yes, Eddie, but quick, put your shoes back on; let's get out of here and board our plane before it leaves!" said his flustered friend.

But before they could make a move, another shock pounced upon them.

"Not so fast young fellow-me-lad, not so fast!" said a uniformed police guard grabbing Eddie by his good ear.

"That scan showed a very fishy-looking lump inside your gut," said the guard.

"Well, I *did* have Finnan Haddie for supper. And perhaps it *was* a larger than average helping," said Eddie, eager to be totally honest.

"Well, we'll just take a closer look, shall we?" said the mean man with a snarl.

And with that, Eddie was frog-marched by two burly policemen off down a hallway to a private room. Micki could only watch helplessly as her dearest companion was ignobly dragged off. She stood there in disbelief and dismay, still holding his little shoes in her paw that hung limply at her side.

Micki sat outside the private room and waited and waited. She counted the tiles in the floor, she asked every official who passed by, "When will my friend be released?" She counted the tiles in the ceiling and waited, and then waited some more.

Finally, after a very long time, a notably indignant little bear was pushed out through the door; his coat over his arm and his shirt undone.

"Eddie!" cried Micki, leaping up and throwing her arms around his neck and kissing his nose. "Are you all right?" she asked, her eyes quizzing his.

"Hummpff!" scoffed her friend, "I wonder what that guy in there tells his wife when she asks him 'How was your day dear?' 'Oh, fine, I had this bear suspect that I had to poke around up inside his…"

"Yes, Eddie, we don't have time to go into the details now, we have missed our flight and have to go sign up for 'standby'," said Micki hurriedly, "Hopefully, we can get the next plane out."

Eddie put on his shoes, and they ran off towards the check-in counter. They presented their travel vouchers to the smart-looking official behind the counter who took her time looking at the Grand Prize documents.

"Is there something wrong?" Micki asked her with trepidation.

"Well no, not really," said the woman, "But the issuers require you to have a microchip installed for security purposes."

Micki and Eddie looked at one another.

"What security purposes?" inquired Micki suspiciously.

"It says here that they like to keep track of their winners in case they get lost," explained the official patiently.

"We are quite smart enough not to get lost," retorted Eddie with a sniff.

"Yes, we've already had enough of security business," said Micki, helping Eddie to readjust the braces on his trousers.

"And they want to make sure you are not imposters," continued the woman, determined to make a point. "You won't be allowed on the plane unless you comply!"

"Oh, well! I guess we don't have a choice then," said Micki, feeling weary and dejected. "Where do we go to get these 'chips'?"

"Down the little corridor across the way, second door on the left," replied the woman, "You'll have to hurry if you want to be on the next flight."

Reluctantly, the two friends made their way to the room and went in. The nurse seemed to be expecting them and stood ready with a very large, threatening-looking needle poised ready for action.

"This won't hurt a bit," she said, "Which one of you is *REAL?*"

Micki looked surprised and said, "I suppose that'll be me, why…" And before the little feline could ask anything else, she was grabbed by the scruff and injected with a microchip.

"What about me?" questioned Eddie.

"Stuffed animals don't matter," said the hard-faced nurse huffily.

"Stuffed animals have rights too!" protested Eddie.

"Don't push your luck, fat-bear!" said the nasty woman with a grin that showed off her crooked, stained teeth.

"Let's leave things be, Eddie," said Micki, feeling sick and tired of all the nonsense, "We don't want any more trouble.

The two animals made a quick exit and headed off to the coffee shop to await their standby call.

Luckily, the cat and the bear were able to get seats together on the very next flight, and never were there two passengers who were more glad to be on their way.

ఌ

They had been flying for some hours when Micki got up to go to the washroom. On her way back from the there, she noticed something odd. As she settled back into her seat, she woke Eddie, who had dozed off again, and spoke quietly to him.

"I tried to chat with the two little rabbits sat behind us, but the nervous creatures had little to say—except that they *also* had won the trip as a grand prize online," said Micki, peeking around the back of her seat at the little lagomorphs.

Eddie's eyes flickered open momentarily, and then closed again.

"Eddie, you know, it's so strange," continued Micki, shaking her companion.

"Uh… uh, what's that?" said the sleepy bear, trying to stretch out his legs in the cramped space.

"I have just noticed that except for two little rabbits in the back seats, we are the only animals on the plane. All the other passengers are human."

"Well, what can I say? I'm not opposed to sharing space with humans," said Eddie, settling down to snooze again.

"But Eddie, they don't seem very pleased to be sharing space with *us*," said Micki, looking askance at the grumpy-countenanced people seated across the aisle. "Maybe it's because they know, from the special big stickers security put on our coats, that we're just prize winners and likely couldn't afford to stay at such an exclusive resort."

"Well, maybe so. Anything is possible," and with that, the bear started to snore.

Micki settled down again and dozed off too but kept one ear and one eye open—just to be safe.

༄

The flight was uneventful and the two exhausted animals, Eddie and Micki, were able to get some shut-eye, but just as both were starting to enter soothing dreams, they were awakened by the intercom chiming: "Hello, holiday passengers, this is your captain speaking. We are beginning our descent onto Paradise Island where the weather is warm and sunny. Thank you for flying with Paradise Airlines. We hope you enjoy your stay."

The sun streamed in at the little window and Eddie and Micki looked out at the view—awestruck! Below, they could see a beautiful island, a tropical paradise of lush greenery and cascading waterfalls that tumbled over rocky cliffs.

The plane started its descent through the clear blue skies to touch down gently at the lovely resort bathed in sunshine. They taxied along the runway and stopped. With impatient anticipation, Eddie and Micki awaited their turn at the back of the line to exit the plane. The cat and bear tried to chat with the two little rabbits, one real and one plush, that stood behind them, but the bunnies were too shy to talk very much except to say that, although they had recently moved to Scotland, they were actually *Welsh* rabbits.

"Is that Welsh Rabbits or Welsh Rarebits?" said Eddie with a guffaw.

The rabbits were not impressed, and neither was Micki. She clicked her tongue, "That is such a worn-out old joke, Eddie!" she said, embarrassed for him.

Eddie looked downcast as he humbly apologized—he was just trying to be sociable!

The four animals were the last to disembark. They picked up their luggage, which had been set out for them on the tarmac.

"Please make your way to the entrance to the Shady Palms Resort," said the smiling young flight attendant, pointing to the long line up of other passengers. "You will be checked into your accommodation as soon as possible. Those that won the holiday as a prize will be taken care of after all the *paying* passengers are processed."

The four animals stood at the back of the queue with their bags and waited. They waited and waited in the blazing hot sun and were getting wearier, and hungrier, and thirstier.

"I don't think this line has moved an inch in the last hour! Isn't there a concession-stand anywhere?" said Eddie, looking around while he fashioned his large, cotton handkerchief into a makeshift sunhat by tying a knot in each corner.

"Nothing at all," said his friend. "Just that little hut on the wooden pier over there that has a small boat anchored beside it," said Micki, squinting to read the sign on it which said:

FERRY TO SHUTTLE ISLAND

"I'll run over there and take a look—maybe they have bottled water at least," said Micki scampering off.

"I'll wait here with the bags," called Eddie after her wearily.

Micki soon returned empty-handed and looking downcast.

"They don't have anything to eat or drink," said Micki, panting, "They just handle the shuttle boats that ferry vacationers to Shuttle Island when Shady Palms is overbooked.

"I see some of these people in front of us are now being escorted inside the grounds," commented Eddie, hoping that was a good sign.

"I suppose they get priority treatment because they have *paid* status," said Micki, a little miffed.

MYSTERIOUS REALMS

Another half an hour went by and they hadn't moved ahead very far. Just as Eddie was on the point of going to the front of the line to complain, a golf cart with a smallish chimpanzee at the wheel drove up.

"You'll be waiting for ever to get into *that* resort," volunteered the chimp, "Are you prize winners?" he asked.

"Yes," said Micki, "we four animals are."

"I hear they're overbooked again and those at the back of the line likely won't get in," said the wily-looking chimpanzee picking his teeth.

Eddie sighed and sat down on his suitcase, wiping his sweating brow with the tail of his shirt. "Oh, drat it!" he said, "Just our luck!"

"So, what are we to do?" said Micki plaintively, "Our accommodation vouchers are only good for the Shady Palms Resort!"

"If you want, you can go to near-by Shuttle Island where there's another resort, they'll accept your vouchers," said the cart driver confidently. "Nice little place, great food, always has a vacancy, and never a line-up. I can ferry you across for free.

"If it's such a nice place, why is there always a vacancy and never a line up?" asked Micki suspiciously.

"It's just for animals—no *human* vacationers allowed," said the chimp in a hoarse whisper, looking furtively over his shoulder. "And not many animals come this way," he explained, staring hard at Micki and one of the rabbits. "Best option, I would say."

Micki was hesitant, she had always learned she shouldn't take lifts from strangers. The chimp noticed her wary expression and hurried to say, "Hop in the cart! I'll give you a lift over to the boat launch. I have to make a delivery to the Island, so I'll be firing up the ferry pretty soon, and there's plenty of room for all of you on it," he said, deftly lifting their luggage into the cart.

The Highland cat looked at the line ahead of them again—no movement. "Okay," she said jumping into the cart. Eddie complacently climbed in next to her. Then, without a word, the two little rabbits hopped in too. Immediately, they all drove off towards the moored motorboat.

The ape helped the four holidaying animals clamber into the small boat. Eddie sat on an empty crate and looked sulky. Micki sat on the crate beside him, "It may not be so bad, Eddie dear," she said optimistically. "They say we will be well looked after at this other place."

"We'd better be!" said Eddie, or I'll be writing a letter of complaint to the…"

"Yes, I know Eddie, but do try to look on the bright side," encouraged Micki, "at least we won't be stranded on the beach."

☙

The chimpanzee took the helm and introduced himself as 'Sharpie'. Then, without delay, he started the motor and skillfully steered the vessel across the water. Presently, they rounded a spit of land and headed into a quiet bay beneath high, rocky cliffs. The chimp skipper nosed the boat into the small dock and tied it to the wharf.

"We're here, folks," he said matter-of-factly to his passengers as he started to put their luggage, together with the empty crates and boxes of supplies, ashore. When the four vacationers had disembarked, Sharpie yelled to a big, lolloping chimp he called 'Bozo' and told him to start loading the several full and heavy crates sitting on the dock onto the boat. After a quick exchange of a few words and some papers between Sharpie (who was the shipping manager) and Bozo, the latter started up the boat and headed back towards Paradise Island with the load of crates.

The small chimp put his clipboard on a table in the little hut of an office and then turned his attention to the four waiting animals, saying with a toothy smile, "You must be tired after waiting around in this heat. Never mind, I'll have you at the hotel in no time," and he swiftly helped them and their bags into a golf-cart that was parked nearby.

They drove along a wide, dirt road through jungle-clad hills until they came to a humungous set of wooden gates that swung open easily when the chimp pressed a red button on his cart. The huge sign said:

SHUTTLE ISLAND GMO RESEARCH FACILITY

"What does GMO stand for? asked Micki politely of the chimp.

Sharpie seemed caught off guard and struggled to think quickly, "Er… Generously Modified 'Oliday," he said, looking furtively from the cat to the bear, then to the rabbits and back again.

For some reason, Micki was not convinced and squinted her eyes at the driver in suspicion.

MYSTERIOUS REALMS

They drove through the gates and along the dusty road. The passengers looked around them in awe. Lush, jungle-covered hillsides rose steeply above the road on either side. They could hear the chattering of hidden monkeys and see dozens of squawking red and blue parrots perched in the trees. Millions of brightly-coloured butterflies flitted all around.

"This is a real paradise, Micki," ventured Eddie, gazing in wonder at the sight of it all.

"It is, indeed, Eddie," chirped Micki. "Except there seems to be something fishy here," she added in a low whisper.

"What did you say, Micki? Something fishy here?" said Eddie loudly as he cupped his ear.

The chimp shot a funny look towards them at Eddie's words.

Micki noticed the funny look the chimp had hurled at her and nonchalantly said "Oh, I was just saying, I wonder if…they have some fishes here?"

As the cart trundled along the winding road, the inquisitive cat continued to wonder to herself why the twenty-foot high chain link fence with electrified razor-wire at the top was needed—was it to keep something out, or to keep something *in*?

After a while, they drove up to the front of a very impressive-looking, glass and steel three-storey building and stopped.

"Here we are, then," said the chimp amiably as he helped get the bags out of the cart. "You'll be very comfy and well-fed here."

Micki looked up at the huge sign on the front of the building.

SHUTTLE ISLAND RESORT HOTEL

All Animals Welcome!

State-of-the-Art G. E. Happens Here!

"What does G. E. mean?" the cat asked the chimp as they walked up to the large, glass door.

"Er…Great…umm…Excitement," stammered the ape opening the door and quickly ushering the other animals inside. "There's always something exciting going on 'ere. Now, just go up to the reception desk and check in." Sharpie then turned and hurried back to his cart and left.

STEPHANIE JONES

❧

A nice, pleasant, human lady greeted them at the reception desk. She scrutinized their vouchers and verified the microchips embedded in the necks of the two, *real* animals—Micki and Dandelion, the boy-rabbit.

After they were given their room access cards, Eddie asked for the wi-fi code password so that he could access the Net.

"We don't allow guests to have Net and cellphone connections," said the lady, sounding quite harsh. "This is supposed to be a peaceful resort for our guests to get away from all those distracting technologies. I'm sure you understand," she said with a defying glare at the bear.

Eddie was disappointed but nodded conciliatorily.

The bear and cat wished 'happy holiday' to the rabbits, and then went to find their own assigned room on the second floor.

It was a delightful chamber—very clean and modern with big comfortable beds. Each bed had an enticing, expensive-looking, gold-leafed chocolate on the pillow. Eddie immediately ate his with gusto, "Mmm…yummy! Peanut butter and honey!" said Eddie, smacking his lips. "What flavour's yours, Micki?"

"Smells like catnip," she answered, taking a good sniff. But she decided to save her appetite for the promised buffet dinner, and so, put the candy on the nightstand.

The two animals looked out the large window. They admired the enchanting view over the forest and marvelled at the glistening blue sea that could just be seen over the treetops. They hoped the rabbits had a nice room too.

After showering and changing, they went down to the dining room where a splendid all-you-can-eat buffet supper was laid on for the guests. The two friends were shown to their table by a particularly polite waiter. "Please help yourself to the buffet as often as you like," said the waiter. They felt very welcome, and yet were somewhat uneasy seeing two or three burly, chimp security guards lurking in the shadows.

However, they were hungry and wasted no time in attacking the bountiful buffet that sported a variety of delicious-smelling food. They piled their plates high and headed back to their table. As they happily chowed down, Micki noticed that the guests included a large array of many types of animal.

She also noticed that, despite the large numbers of guests dining, it was eerily quiet. She leaned forward and whispered to her companion, "Why isn't anyone talking?"

"Too busy eating, I should think," suggested Eddie, stuffing another forkful of deep-fried, honeyed potatoes dripping with golden ghee into his mouth.

Then Micki spotted a sign on the wall opposite and drew Eddie's attention to it. It read:

RETREAT GUESTS:
As a courtesy to the peaceful, mindfulness practice of all,
please refrain from unnecessary discourse.

"Well, I'm sure that won't bother those two," said Micki, indicating the two rabbits who had been with them on the plane and who were now sat together at the next table. They were quietly absorbed in munching through a huge green salad apiece.

All the other guests were likewise fixated on their food, except for a rat-terrier, dressed as a vampire, who sat alone across the room and kept looking at the newly arrived bear and cat.

"That freaky-looking terrier makes me feel a little uncomfortable," whispered Micki. But Eddie assured her she was just overtired and there was nothing to worry about.

After a wonderful meal, and feeling full and contented, Eddie and Micki left the dining room to take a stroll around the large conservatory that was filled with exotic tropical plants, waterfalls, and fountains. They paused to watch the pretty goldfish swimming under the waterlilies of a little pond when suddenly, the rat-terrier, now dressed as a biker with Heaven's Devil written on the back of his leather jacket, brushed rudely passed them at top speed.

"Here, steady on, old chap!" shouted Eddie after the dog, "Watch your manners, my…" then he felt something in his jacket pocket. "Hello, what's this, then?" he exclaimed, pulling out a piece of paper that the terrier had stuffed into his pocket as he rushed past.

"What does it say, Eddie?" inquired Micki.

"It says, 'Don't trust the CHIMPS!'" read Eddie.

"Why ever not?" asked Micki, her curiosity piqued.

"Probably just some silly dog-game," scoffed Eddie, "You know what idiots some canines can be!"

"Well, we're not going to play along!" said Micki scornfully, "Let's go see what that group of white mice is up to over there!" she said with her eyes glinting and her tail twitching.

And with that, Eddie thought no more of the mysterious note. However, Micki had a gnawing sense that something was amiss.

❦

After a restful night's sleep, Eddie and Micki eagerly made their way to the breakfast buffet for another splendid feast. They ate to their hearts' content and pushed back from the table as a busboy came to take away the dirty plates. As they were leaving the dining room, Micki suddenly caught hold of Eddie's arm saying, "Isn't that the plush rabbit sitting over there? I wonder why she is all alone this morning?"

"Hmm…, maybe her *real* friend is having a lie-in," suggested Eddie, "after all, it is holiday time."

"Or he could be unwell," pondered Micki, concerned, "Let's go over and make sure everything is okay."

They walked over to the plush rabbit's table and said 'hello,' but the nervous little thing just looked at them with a terrified stare. Micki, in an attempt at friendship, had just started to say, "Good morning, I'm Micki. How are you and…" when she was interrupted by a chimp security guard glaring at her and pointing to the large sign on the wall, the same one that she had read the night before.

As they started to walk away, Eddie happened to glance over to the far side of the room where the rat-terrier, now dressed in combat fatigues, was sat devouring a plate of sausages. The dog met Eddie's gaze and shook his head at the bear. Eddie frowned and said, "I'm going to go over there and give him a piece of my mind!"

Micki quickly grabbed hold of Eddie's sleeve and stopped him from his mission, "Let's get out of here," she said quietly, hustling him to the door where they were intercepted by another chimp security guard.

MYSTERIOUS REALMS

"Don't pay any attention to the rat-terrier," the chimp said with a smooth smile, "The dog's mad! We let him stay on here out of kindness really."

☙

The two friends were glad to get out of the eerie atmosphere of the breakfast room and decided to go to the beach for the day. They went to the reception desk to ask about it.

The nice reception lady told them, "Our special beach bus leaves here at 10 a.m. this morning and will bring you back in time for supper. A healthy packed lunch is included. You can sign up for it here."

Eddie looked nonchalantly at his manicured claws and asked, "Ahem, would there happen to be any…ahem…extra charge for these side-excursions?" He hoped that the answer would be a decided 'NO'.

"We are happy to offer ALL our excursions free-of-charge to all our honored guests," the woman assured them with a cheery smile. "Did you bring your bathing suits?"

"Yes, we did," said Eddie, adding their names to the bus roster.

Micki liked the receptionist so much, she ventured to clarify something that had been bothering her since their arrival. "May I ask what G.E. stands for—the sign says it happens here."

A dark shadow flitted across the face of the nice lady like a night-moth flying past a lamp, and after a moment of thought she said, "Good English—we have only good English happening here."

"Oh!" said Micki, not entirely convinced. But she decided not to press the issue, and instead, politely thanked the lady, and with no further comment, she and Eddie went up to their room to get ready for a relaxing day at the beach.

As Micki stood in front of the window, spraying sun-protection onto her fur, she noticed one particularly tall tree in the forest swaying vigorously back and forth. "Eddie," she said, "Why is that tree moving like that?"

Eddie took a look and said with a shrug, "Oh, it's probably just blowing in the wind."

"But it isn't windy, and none of the other trees are moving," insisted his friend.

A few minutes later, they were passing the reception desk on the way to board the bus when Micki thought to question the reception lady about the strange tree, "By the way, we happened to notice a particularly large tree in the forest swaying back and forth just now, and we were curious to know why that would be."

"Probably the wind," said the receptionist.

"But it's not windy, and none of the other trees were moving," persisted Micki.

The nice lady's face darkened, and her eyes narrowed. "It doesn't do to ask too many nosey questions around here," she snapped. "It shows a lack of gratitude."

"Oh, I'm so sorry," apologized Micki meekly. And with that, she slipped her arm through Eddie's and they hustled out to the waiting bus.

꼶

The pristine, sandy beach was full of happy animals bathing and playing frisbee. All was watched over carefully by an abundance of lifeguard chimps that were observing every move.

Eddie and Micki had a delightful time bouncing around in the gentle surf and joining in fun games of tag with other animals. Then, tired out, they flopped down on their blankets and dozed in the sunshine. After a good rest, they ate their packed lunch and then went for a lazy stroll along the beach. They stopped to watch a game of frisbee in which the rat-terrier, resplendent in a Sugar Plum Fairy costume, was avidly chasing the flying discs and outperforming all the other dogs.

"You have to admit, Eddie, he *is* very talented," remarked Micki as the little canine leapt into the air doing a double twist to snatch the frisbee out of the closing jaws of a border collie.

"Humpff," snorted Eddie, "If only he wouldn't dress so weird. He looks ridiculous in that pink tutu."

"He does rather," tittered Micki.

Just then the frisbee came close to them, hotly pursued by the mad terrier. As the diminutive dog leapt up into the air near them, he said out the side of his mouth, "Don't eat the gilded chocolates!" Then he snapped the vinyl disc tightly in his jaws and raced off back to the pack.

MYSTERIOUS REALMS

The cat and the bear looked at one another perplexed by this latest cryptic message.

"Definitely mad as a hatter," said Eddie. "I ate mine yesterday and I'm perfectly fine!"

"Quite so," said Micki, "I feel sorry for the poor fellow."

They continued their walk along the beach and noticed a chimp lifeguard was watching them closely.

❦

When they arrived back at the hotel, they saw a colourful poster surrounded by party lights saying that there was to be a Candlelight Dinner and Fancy-Dress Masquerade Ball that night—free to all guests.

"Wow! That does look exciting!" beamed Eddie.

"But what will we do for costumes?" wondered Micki.

"Perhaps we can borrow some from the rat-terrier!" snickered Eddie.

They both laughed heartily, then they noticed a sign on a nearby door saying:

COSTUMES BORROWED HERE

So, in they went and were amazed at the racks full of fancy costumes of all shapes and sizes. The room was full of excited animals pulling items off the racks and grabbing masks and other accessories from the bins. After much trying on and laughing and giggling with all the other creatures, Eddie felt himself very debonair as the Laughing Cavalier, complete with fake sword. Micki admired herself in a Florence Nightingale outfit that made her feel very important indeed.

At the ball that evening, everyone looked splendid in their fancy dress in the atmospherically-lit room that was decorated with all manner of glistening sparkles and shimmering garlands. A mirrored disco ball spun overhead and shed drops of coloured light over everything. Mesmerized, Eddie and Micki settled at a table they shared with a large, black poodle dressed as the Blue Boy and his partner, a cute, white poodle dressed as the Pink Lady. After a nice dinner and polite conversation, the two canines excused themselves and got up to dance. As the elegant poodles gracefully waltzed past them, Micki, feeling quite starry-eyed, said, "Shall *we* dance too, Eddie?"

Although her friend was not known for his dancing skills, he obliged since this waltz required only slow, simple steps. They were just starting a graceful glide when the music suddenly changed to a polka. The Laughing Cavalier gallantly tried to adjust to the frantic tempo and did his best to steer his Florence Nightingale around the crowded floor without colliding with anything, but try as he might, Zorro and Wonder-Woman-Wallaby who were leaping around, crossed his path a little too close. Zorro's cloak flapped over Eddie's face, blinding him and causing him to trip over his sword, which became entangled with Zorro's. Down they all went in a pile, causing a mass of other dancers to stumble and careen on top of them in a tangled heap.

The Laughing Cavalier wasn't laughing any more. In an attempt to scramble to his feet, he reached up to grab onto something to haul himself up off the floor and his paw closed around a handle of some sort. He yanked himself to his feet by pulling on the handle. Instantly, the fire alarm whooped into action with a wailing that drowned the sound of the screeching melee. Utter bedlam ensued with chimps blowing whistles and waving batons to try and gain control of the madding crowd as the automatic sprinklers kicked into action. Slithering and sliding on the wet floor, Eddie and Micki managed to dodge the guards and flee the dance hall. Flushed with embarrassment, they bolted up the stairs to their room and slammed the door shut behind them.

In the safety of their room, the two chums flung themselves onto their beds in a fit of laughing.

"Well, that was exhilarating!" chuckled Eddie, removing his mask and costume.

"I hope no one recognized us in our costumes," grinned Micki, "We'd never live it down!"

Eddie was hanging up his doublet when a folded piece of paper fell out of the sleeve. He stooped to pick it up and unfolded it, full of curiosity.

"What is that?" inquired Micki, noticing.

"Oh no!" exclaimed Eddie, handing the note to his friend, "It's another crazy note from the mad ratter!"

"That must have been him in the Zorro costume," said Micki, reading the note. I bet he deliberately tripped you just to pass on the message!"

"Well, throw it away, I want nothing to do with his silly nonsense," said Eddie, going to brush his teeth.

"Well, wait a minute, Eddie. What he says is very interesting."

"Rubbish!" said Eddie, frothy toothpaste dribbling down his chin.

Micki sat on the bed and pondered the note very carefully.

"He says, 'Watch the swaying tree, it's a signal!'"

"Poppycock!" said Eddie, spitting toothpaste into the washbasin and taking a swig of mouthwash to gargle.

But Micki took the warning more seriously, "A signal of what, I wonder?" she said with furrowed brow.

"Enough already! I'm tired and going to bed," said Eddie, emerging from the bathroom in his new pyjamas.

"Well, I think he must know something important. How would he know about the swaying tree I saw? Perhaps we should take him seriously and ask him for an explanation of all these cryptic messages?" Micki continued to voice her thoughts, but she was talking to the wall, her buddy was already fast asleep between the satin sheets.

※

The next morning, Micki checked the big tree again. But it was perfectly still. Deep in thought, she picked up the gilded chocolate off the nightstand and turned to Eddie saying, "I wonder why the terrier told us not to eat the chocolates."

"Because he's a daft pooch," said Eddie, "I told you, I ate mine and nothing happened to me. Here, watch!" and with that he took the chocolate and popped it into his mouth. He savored its nippy flavour, smacking his lips noisily. "There! delicious!"

Micki sighed and followed her friend down to breakfast. As they were standing in line for the buffet, Eddie started to talk quite loudly about the food. Micki looked again at the sign that told them to be quiet and mentioned it to Eddie.

She was suddenly startled by a voice behind her, "Yeah, they put that up about a year ago."

She spun around and came face to face with the terrier who had joined the buffet line. Her mouth opened in surprise, trying to find something to say. Her companion beat her to the punch.

"A year ago!" said Eddie loudly.

"Sshhh...!" said Micki.

Eddie lowered his voice and said, "A year ago? Then, you've been here that long? You must really like it here to stay *that* long."

The terrier looked at them in a funny way but didn't answer because at that moment, a guard came sauntering up to them saying, "Move along quietly now, folks! You don't want to hold up the line!"

While the two good friends sat enjoying their eggs Benedict with smoked salmon, a smartly uniformed lady chimp came up to them and identified herself as the Guest Activity Supervisor and said they could call her Ms GAS. "How are you two enjoying your stay? Have you been making new friends?" said Ms GAS.

"We are having a very jolly time, thank you, Miss," said Eddie enthusiastically.

"But we haven't made many friends yet," said Micki a little ruefully, "Other guests seem reluctant to talk very much."

"Except for the looney rat-terrier," volunteered Eddie with a snicker. Micki immediately kicked his ankle under the table and scowled at him.

"Oh, and what has 'Mad Microchip' been saying?" asked the chimp lady with great interest.

"Something about the chocolates not being good to eat," said Eddie, pouting at his friend and moving his ankles out of her reach.

Micki felt like hissing but kept quiet.

"What a silly little nuisance he is," said Ms GAS with a chuckle, "We'll have to take him aside again and tell him to stop upsetting our guests. Tell you what, as a way of apology for his speaking out of turn, I'll make sure a whole box of gold-leafed chocolates is sent up to your room right away for you to enjoy at your leisure."

"Oooh! goody, goody, gum-drops!" said the little bear, clapping his hands as his friend frowned at him.

The cheery chimp laughed again. "Now, let me invite you both to join in our fun day of field games—Egg and Spoon Races, Sack Races, Coconut Shies, and Hoopla-Ring Throwing, and many other thrilling games."

"We'll be there!" Eddie assured her joyfully.

Micki smiled weakly and nodded.

MYSTERIOUS REALMS

After breakfast, the two 'not-so-good-friends' went back up to their room to change for the day of field sports. Micki chastised Eddie for spilling the beans about the terrier.

"We may have got him into trouble," she growled. "I'm sure he meant us no harm."

"Well, it jolly-well serves him right if he does get a stiff telling-off," said Eddie, opening the door to their room.

But their arguing was cut short as both animals stopped and stared in surprise at the lovely box of shiny, golden chocolates on the dresser.

"There!" said Eddie pompously, "See how that kind chimp lady told us the truth and kept her word!" He picked up the box saying, "Here, have one, and don't be such a sulky little cat, then I'll forgive you for bruising my ankle."

Micki did feel guilty for kicking her friend and obediently opened her mouth as her friend popped a chocolate in it. She slowly chewed it and admitted it *was* delicious. They ate two or three more each and then put on their sports gear and made their way to the field behind the hotel where the events were taking place.

They started with the Egg and Spoon Race and Micki almost won. But the effort seemed to tire her and so she told Eddie she would go back to the room and lie down for a while. Her friend escorted her back to their room and, once he saw her safely on the bed, he tucked a blanket around her, fetched her a glass of water, and then left her to snooze.

The bear wandered around the grounds for a while feeling quite bored and sorry for himself; being all alone at the games was no fun. All the other animals seemed to be having such a good time together, laughing and frolicking. He was feeling quite grumpy when he spotted the 'rattie' sat alone near the wading pool. Feeling angry at the mere sight of him, Eddie approached him and said sternly, "Now look here, feller-me-lad, just what do you mean by all these cryptic messages?" The terrier looked beyond Eddie's shoulder and a wave of fear flitted across his face.

"I don't know what you're talking about!" said the dog nervously, "Go away, bear! Leave me in peace!"

"Hello, hello, what's going on here, then?" said a chimp guard, stepping up behind Eddie while slapping a club against the palm of his hand. "This bear causing trouble again, is he, Mr. Chip?"

47

The hound turned on his heel and fled.

Suddenly, rough hands grabbed Eddie and swung him around to stare into the snarling face of the angry chimp dressed in black, "We've been watching you," he growled at the trembling little bear, "and we don't like what we see! You see?"

Eddie indignantly opened his mouth to complain but decided against it—getting into a fight didn't seem like a good idea at this point. So, pulling himself free of the hard grasp, he tottered off quietly.

The poor old bear was feeling very dejected but bucked up when it was time for the Three-legged Race. He was teamed up with Mathilda, the wallaby, which proved to be a most unfortunate match. The less-than-athletic old teddy bear found himself being bumped off his feet and banged down again with a thud at every bouncing stride that Mathilda took until he finally his lost his balance altogether and banged his head hard on the ground as he was dragged to the finish line.

Eddie found little consolation in the fact that they had won—the prize was an orange which they were supposed to share! Rubbing his throbbing head, he sought out a more passive activity and caught sight of the rat-terrier playing hoopla-rings with a delicate Chinese-crested dog. Eddie boldly muscled in between them and snatched up some rings and began tossing them—but he missed every throw.

"Bad luck, Old Feller," said the white terrier with black ears sincerely. He made to shake paws with Eddie and introduced himself. "My name's Chip," he said, looking deeply into the bear's glassy eyes. "Are you enjoying your holiday?"

"I don't see that it's any business of yours," said Eddie curtly, snubbing the dog's offered paw and instead, grabbing another handful of rubbery rings to throw.

"Sorry you feel that way, sir," said the terrier humbly, "I've only been looking out for you and your cat friend." And with a quick salute, he trotted away.

Eddie missed the targets again and slumped away from the game feeling even more depressed. He decided to go and see how Micki was feeling. He thought he would slink in the back door of the hotel as he didn't feel like running into holiday-goers and having to exchange pleasantries with them.

MYSTERIOUS REALMS

On his way to the rear of the building, he was startled by a scurrying movement in the bushes by the path. He stopped to investigate. Something was moving. Something was trying to hide. Eddie cautiously moved some leafy twigs aside with his paw and peered into the deep shadows. He was surprised to see a familiar shape quivering in the darkness.

"Hello!" he said gently, "What are you doing here all alone and hiding like the hounds of hell are searching for you?"

But the little plush rabbit, trembling with fear, just stared at him in silence.

"Oh, you poor '…cow'rin tim'rous beastie,'" crooned Eddie, quoting Micki's favourite Scottish poet. He knelt down on the grass and tried to coax the bunny out into the open. "I shan't hurt you. Come here and tell me all about it. I'm Eddie. I and my chum Micki want to be your friends. What's your name?"

The little bunny felt she could trust this warm, cuddly bear and so crept towards him and allowed him to stroke her head with his big paw. "My name's Daisy," she said in her tiny voice. "And I'm so scared."

"I'm sure you're scared over nothing. Tell me what's bothering you. Where is your *real* rabbit friend—Dandelion, isn't it? We haven't seen him since the first night."

The little stuffed rabbit felt comforted and told how yesterday morning, she and Dandelion were getting ready to go down for breakfast but first, they ate the golden chocolates that had been left on their pillows.

"When I came out of the shower," she said, "Dandelion had fallen back to sleep. I thought it odd, but when I tried to wake him up so that we could go for breakfast, I couldn't wake him, even though I shook him and shouted in his ear."

Eddie looked in alarm at the little bunny, "So what did you do?" he asked, quite concerned.

"I was terrified for him, so I tried to call the desk, but no-one answered. I panicked and ran down to the lobby to get help, but no-one was around. So, I raced back up to the room and…and…" at this point, the little animal's voice faltered, and she started to convulse in a fit of tears.

Eddie tried to soothe the poor creature and gave her a big bear hug. "So, then what happened?" he asked quietly.

The rabbit took a big sniff and blew her nose on the clean hankie Eddie gave her. "When I got back to the room—**Dandelion…wasn't there!** He had vanished!" And with this revelation, poor Daisy broke down into heavy sobs again.

"We have to get to the bottom of this," said Eddie with conviction as he started to get to his feet. Just then he suddenly remembered Micki and then, in a rush, he remembered the terrier's warning about eating the chocolates! He quickly scooped the little rabbit up in his arms and, trying to stay calm so as not to alarm her too much, he explained that he needed to get to Micki right away!

ತಾ

Eddie ran inside the back door of the building and raced to the elevator. Too panicked to wait for it, he put Daisy down and dashed up the stairs two at a time. Daisy followed, running hard at his heels. He flew along the hallway and burst into his room and stopped in abject horror—**Micki wasn't there!** Her shoes and tote bag were sitting at the door. But she was gone!

The bear grabbed the phone to call the desk but, before he could dial, Daisy pulled at his pant leg, squealing for him not to call the humans—the terrier had told her not to trust any of the humans or chimps in this place.

"I'm not sure that we can trust the terrier, either," said Eddie, putting the phone down and sitting on the bed feeling worried sick.

After a minute, Eddie stood up and walked to the window and looked out across the forest to think. To his astonishment, he saw that the big tree was swaying. It was the only tree moving. He called to Daisy to show her.

"Oh, yes!" she said, "I have seen that before. Chip told me it was a signal that the boat was bringing new animals, like us, here from Paradise Island and taking 'modified' or dead ones away in crates.

True terror now gripped Eddie's heart as he suddenly realized what this may mean. That animals who were no longer serving any purpose, were being shipped away somewhere—perhaps in a body-bag—he shuddered. A salty tear ran down his soft cheek as he thought he may never see his precious little friend again. Micki—and Dandelion— may be lost forever!

He shook his head vigorously to clear it. He refused to wallow in his worst fears—that would solve nothing! He looked down at the plush rabbit and it suddenly hit him. Both he and Daisy had eaten the drugged chocolate but neither of them suffered any ill-effects—because they were STUFFED! The drug only affected REAL animals!

"So, the *real* animals are microchipped and drugged so they can be taken away and experimented on in some horrible way," said Eddie out loud, making Daisy cry again.

"Come on, Daisy, let's go and find Chip, I think he's the only one that can help us!"

The bear and the rabbit made their way back to the games field to look for the white terrier with the black ears. He was easy to spot in his hideously patterned Bermuda shorts and garish Hawaiian shirt. He was helping the Chinese-crested with miniature golf.

Eddie walked up to him and hung his head in shame, "Guess I really screwed up earlier. I know now you really were trying to help, I'm sorry, I didn't believe you; and, was rude."

The terrier excused himself from his companion and took Eddie and Daisy aside. There was no reproach in his expression, only a look of concern. "What's changed your mind?"

Eddie's voice was starting to quiver, "It's Micki—she ate the chocolates and now she's gone—disappeared from her room without a trace, just like Dandelion."

Chip looked very grave. "This is serious business indeed," he said, "I'm still trying to locate Dandelion—it hasn't been easy. I lost my main contact and informer some time ago—the Bad Guys discovered her clandestine activities in trying to rescue and smuggle out victims, and I haven't seen her since."

"Is she a rat-terrier too?" inquired Eddie kindly as he saw Chip's eyes moisten.

The terrier shook his head, "No," he said after a brief pause in which he touched a paw to his eyes and swallowed hard. "No, Elsie is a chimp, but a good one. She worked in one of the labs and was horrified at the things she saw happening to innocent animals. So, she vowed to help them in whatever way she could."

Eddie humbly apologized again for his mistrust. The terrier was magnanimous about it and patted the bear on the shoulder.

"We're all in this together," he said, "We're all committed to helping our fellow animals in danger."

"Hear, hear!" cried Eddie and Daisy in unison.

"Elsie and I had planned to whistle-blow the secret wide open. We do have allies out there," said Chip. "There is a world-wide group of scammers who keep trying to trick animals into coming here for a holiday, but it's all a ruse to get them for nasty G.E. experiments!"

"And what exactly does G.E. stand for, then?" asked Eddie, trying to remember what had been told to them.

"G.E.?" said Chip, "It stands for Genetic Engineering."

The penny almost dropped in Eddie's brain and he said, "So it doesn't stand for 'Good English' as the receptionist told us? Nor 'Great Excitement' as Sharpie the chimp told us? But what *is* Genetic Engineering?"

"It's where they take your genes and chop them up into pieces and stick them back together again in a different way," explained Chip as best he could.

Eddie tried to visualize them chopping up the new designer jeans he was wearing and stitching them back together again, "So why do they only want to work on jeans belonging to *real* animals?

"Because 'stuffies' don't have genes," said Chip.

Eddie responded with an indignant retort, "I'll have you know that I certainly do have jeans! 'Cow van Kines' nonetheless!"

Chip smiled graciously and said, "No, not the jeans you wear, but genes that are inside you that make you look the way you do when you're *real*."

This was more than poor Eddie's brain could process so he decided just to nod and pretend he understood. Nevertheless, both he and Daisy were dumbfounded at the terrier's story.

"Why didn't Elsie help *you* escape, then?" asked little Daisy very distressed.

Chip explained, "She did make an escape plan for me, but when I understood what was going on here, I was determined to stay and help others to escape."

Eddie, who had been listening intently, muttered humbly to the terrier, "You're a better man than I am, Gunga Din!"

The dog gave a quick, humble smile and continued, "Elsie and I worked together as a team. I would try to warn animals to resist the attempts of the Bad Guys to deceive, drug, and capture. But if an animal *did* get drugged and captured, Elsie would do what she could to help them. She's a good sort, is Elsie. I heard that they put her in a cage and used her for their wicked experiments too." Chip paused and wiped his eyes, then continued his story, "Eventually, Elsie was betrayed by a traitor. So, I'm fearful that she has disappeared for ever!" Chip could talk no more. He sniffed hard and wiped his eyes again.

Eddie remembered Micki and was beside himself with dread of what may be happening to her right now, "So, what can the three of us do now to find our friends?" he said, clenching his teeth and making a fist.

"Well," said Chip, shaking himself and taking a deep breath, "I've been trying to dig a tunnel into the basement around the back of the building." He paused and looked furtively over his shoulder to make sure none of the guards were watching them. Luckily, the chimps had enjoyed rather a lot of tropical punch while supervising the games and were starting to doze off in the warm sunshine.

"Come with me!" said Chip to his new friends, "I'll show what I've been up to."

He led the others around the back of the building to where the bushes were densely overgrown. He pushed his way under them, and Daisy followed easily, but Eddie wished he was a lot slimmer. A few feet inside the shrubbery, they saw a large stone slab which Chip pushed aside to reveal a big hole in the ground.

"I've dug down deep enough, but now I need to start tunnelling horizontally towards the building and come up in the cellars. But unfortunately, it's very hard for me to turn my body and dig sideways. So, I've made very little progress the last couple of days."

"I think I can perhaps help with that," said Daisy, moving forward and jumping down the hole. "Yes, I'm sure I can!" In a flash, she was digging like fury, sending showers of dirt behind her.

Chip jumped down into the hole and called up to Eddie, "I'll start passing the dirt up to you in a bag I can fashion from my shirt. You can spread it on the ground beneath the bushes so no one will see it."

The animals worked fervently and, in no time at all, they had dug a tunnel wide enough even for Eddie to crawl through. The threesome hurried through the tunnel and found themselves in a dark cellar full of empty cages and crates of all kinds. They scrambled their way over the paraphernalia to a door that they opened carefully. It opened into a large room with all kinds of scientific equipment (that they didn't understand) and more cages—which seemed to be empty. They listened for any sound, but all was quiet and dimly-lit.

"What now?" whispered Eddie.

"I think we should try going up those stairs over there," said Chip, pointing across the room.

They tiptoed past the cages and equipment towards the stairs with the red EXIT sign above them. Suddenly, they all froze! There was a shuffling sound and a low grunt behind them. They spun around to come face to face with… a chimp! Eddie felt his blood run cold and Daisy almost fainted. Chip bared his teeth in his most viscous snarl, ready for action!

As they braced for the attack from the suspected chimp guard, they realized the animal was not coming after them—it was behind bars!

Chip stopped his growling and sniffed the air. He scented someone very familiar.

"Elsie!!" he barked, dashing forward.

The bear and rabbit were struck dumb and stood rooted to the spot.

Chip ran up to the cage and licked Elsie's hand through the bars. "Elsie! You're alive!" said Chip, overjoyed. But then the terrier looked at her scars and became very sombre and said, "Elsie, my dearest friend, what have they done to you?"

"Never mind that now," said the old chimp, "it's a long story. First, can you undo the cage lock and get me out of here, please?"

Chip pulled on the padlock, but it was useless, it was securely locked.

"May I have a go?" asked Eddie, "I've had a lot of practice picking the locks Micki puts on the snack cupboard to keep me out." And sure enough, lickety-split, he skillfully used his long middle-claw to pick the padlock. Elsie was free!!!

After a few heartfelt hugs all around, they quickly exchanged stories. Elsie agreed to take charge of the rescue mission for Micki and Dandelion. She was familiar with the layout of the building, the schedule of the workers, and the placement of the guards and alarm systems. She had a very good idea of where the rabbit prisoners would be kept and how to get to them. They would go through the back way to reduce the risk of being detected.

MYSTERIOUS REALMS

But it was still going to be risky and they would have to be very careful not to get caught!

❦

With Elsie in the lead now, the little group made their way along a corridor where dozens of cages containing hideously mutilated animals and bizarre creatures, the sad results of G. E. experiments, lined the walls. The group couldn't stop; there was no time. They hurried down the long passageway and through a door into a stairwell. Then they climbed up the stairs on their quest to find Dandelion.

Presently, they came to the back door of a laboratory where dozens of rabbits being experimented on were kept in cages. Elsie motioned for everyone to be quiet as she peeked in through the little window of the door. She saw a man in a lab coat and shrank back in fear. But as the man turned around to put something in a cage, she saw his face clearly. She gasped, putting her hand over her mouth. She looked at the others who stood waiting behind her and gave them a big smile.

"It's Marcus!" she said quietly. "What a stroke of luck!"

"He's one of our human helpers, isn't he?" said Chip.

"Yes!" said Elsie, "He arranges the paperwork for our escapees—something I always found difficult to do. He came here as a final-year science student and now he's a lab research assistant. He was going to leave when he found out what was going on, but like you Chip, he stays here because he wants to help the animals in whatever way he can.

Eddie was still a little worried, "But perhaps it was he who betrayed you, Elsie?" he said.

The chimpanzee replied, "I don't think so. It was probably the golden retriever who blabbed. He was overly friendly with humans. Intelligent, but too eager to please anyone who would throw him a ball." Elsie peered into the room again. "Marcus seems to be all alone at the moment," she said.

"Shall we trust him, then?" asked Daisy, hoping that Dandelion would be found in this lab alive and well.

"We *have* to trust him—we need his help!" urged Elsie. "He did feel bad when I was captured. He used to sneak into my quarantine quarters and comfort me. I think it was his caring kindness that kept me alive."

The ape took a deep breath and turned the doorknob and pushed. The door was locked! She tapped lightly on the window, but the man didn't hear as he was talking on the phone. Elsie raised her arm and banged on the glass, but Marcus was oblivious to the sound as he quickly put down the phone and turned out the lights. He then opened the opposite door and left.

Tears of frustration welled up in the chimp's eyes as she explained to the others what had just happened. What to do now!

Little Daisy began to sob loudly. So near, yet so far!

They were all bitterly disappointed and it took a while before they could think of the next step. They decided they must retrace their steps and think of another strategy. They turned to go back through the stairwell door, but it had automatically locked behind them. They quickly raced up to the next floor, but that door was locked too! They raced down to the bottom floor, but same thing—now they were trapped—perhaps forever!

There was nothing else for it but to go back to the door of the rabbit lab and wait in the hope that Marcus would return. They waited for what seemed an eternity but then, suddenly, they saw the light come on in the lab. Elsie ventured to peek through the little window again.

"What do you see?" said Eddie anxiously.

"It's Marcus all right, but wait, he has someone with him this time."

"Anyone we know?" asked Chip.

"It's the young woman with the blonde ponytail who works up in one of the offices," said Elsie.

"What are they doing?" squeaked Daisy, trying to jump up into the chimp's arms so she could look through the window too.

"Sshhh…" said Elsie, "I'm trying to hear what they are saying."

The woman was saying, "I hope they find that mad chimp who escaped mysteriously from her cage in the quarantine section."

"I'm sure they will," said Marcus with little enthusiasm, "and I hate to think what they will do to her when they catch her!"

The girl sighed and nodded.

"Here are all the rabbit reports for you to take back to your office, Josie," said the young lab-assistant, handing her a stack of large envelopes.

"My name's Judy," said the pretty girl with a shy smile.

"Oh, right! Sorry, Judy," said the young man deep in distracted thought.

As Judy turned to leave, she caught sight of the chimp's face in the little window of the door opposite.

"Marcus!" she screamed, dropping the arm-load of reports, "There's something in the stairwell watching us!"

Marcus spun around and looked. He ran to the door and looked through the glass. He stared in speechless surprise at the sight of Elsie and her entourage.

He turned back to Judy who asked with a fearful look in her eyes, "Is it the mad chimp, Marcus?"

He started to pick up the envelopes she had dropped and stammered, "Er…look, Jodie…"

"Judy!" she corrected with a sweet smile.

"Yes, Judy," he stammered, handing the packages to her. "Can you pretend you didn't see anything just now?"

"What are you up to, Marcus Brown!" said the data analyst, narrowing her eyes.

"Nothing! Well, that is…can you keep a secret?

She nodded.

"You won't tell a soul what you think you saw, just now?"

She shook her head.

"Well, if you play along with my little scheme here," he said, taking her by the shoulders and looking intently into her face, "I'll love you forever!"

This last phrase worked like a magic elixir that poured into her ears and swam around inside her head: 'I'll love you forever! I'll love you forever!'—words she had always dreamed he would say one day. A look of enchanted delight spread over her uplifted face. She nodded.

"Good!" he said, ushering her towards the other door, "Now, Julie, you just go back to your office and act like nothing ever happened, okay?"

"It's Judy," she said, glowing all over as she floated out the door in a dream.

Marcus swiftly closed the door behind her and locked it. He ran to the stairwell door and flung it open. "ELSIE! WHAT THE Fff…unky bells are you doing here?!" he said, embracing the ecstatic chimp in his arms. "And who is this motley bunch?" he added, indicating the bright-eyed group dancing around them.

Elsie and the others quickly told him as much as they could and begged him to help them find Dandelion and Micki.

"Well, I did have a new rabbit come in just a little while ago," said Marcus, going over to a cage in the back of the room. "A really handsome little Dutch fellow in his black and white fur coat, but quite nervous!"

"Well, actually, we are searching for a Welsh rabbit," said Eddie, trying to be helpful.

But Daisy, frantically jumping up and down hurried to explain, "But he *is* a Dutch, he was born in Wales and so thinks of himself as Welsh, but of course he lives in Scotland and so he's sort of Scottish too."

Eddie wished people wouldn't speak such higgledy-piggledy nonsense when there was a crisis at hand. He needed to keep a clear head!

Marcus lifted the beautiful little animal out of his cage and gently set him down on the floor. Daisy wrapped her paws around her special friend and gave him a loving kiss on his quivering nose. Dandelion seemed a little dazed and bewildered, but nonetheless, overjoyed to see Daisy again.

"He may be still a little groggy from the drugged chocolate he ate, but otherwise, he should be fine as his experiment wasn't scheduled until tomorrow," said Marcus reassuringly.

With all the stress and excitement, Daisy was feeling quite faint and so it was decided that it would be best for her and Dandelion to return to their hotel room for quiet recovery. Chip volunteered to escort them safely back to their room while the rest of them concentrated on the quest to find Micki. He would try to catch up to them later.

Eddie felt relieved that Dandelion had been safely recovered before he suffered irreversible damage. But now he was even more anxious to find Micki! He beseechingly looked at Marcus and begged him to help them in the search. The young man very much wanted to be of assistance, but he really had no idea where to begin looking.

Before doing anything else, he gave Elsie one of the spare white lab coats hanging on a rack, "Here, put this on, Elsie. Then people will think you're my assistant and not ask any questions."

"What about me?" said Eddie, feeling a bit left out.

"A lab coat won't fit you; you're too small," said Marcus patting the bear on the head, "Just stay close to us and try to look dumb."

MYSTERIOUS REALMS

Eddie wasn't sure how to take this last remark, so he shelved it in the back of his brain to think about later.

☙

Marcus, Elsie, and Eddie stealthily wandered the labyrinth of corridors and stairwells, stopping to peek in this lab or that room in search of Micki. After an exhaustive search, Marcus said sadly, "Well, I hate to say it, but the only place we haven't looked is the mortuary. I am sorry to think it, but she may have succumbed to ill-treatment."

Eddie's heart almost stopped at the thought. His legs trembled, and he would have fallen down had Elsie not caught him in time. She hugged him and kissed the top of his head saying, "We have to consider the possibility. I'm so sorry, Eddie."

The little bear nodded and rubbed the stinging tears from his eyes. It was time for being the bravest he had ever been.

They made their way to the morgue. When they had ascertained that no workers were on site, the three crept into the autopsy room; fearful of what they may find but hoping it would not be their little friend.

They were relieved to see that all the gurneys were clean and empty.

"Better check the body storage drawers," said Marcus grimly, starting to pull them open one by one. You stay by the door, Eddie, and let us know if any one is coming."

Eddie was glad to do only that.

"The drawers seem to be empty too," said the man after he and Elsie had checked most of them.

Just when they had almost finished looking, Eddie whispered hoarsely, "I think someone is coming! Quick, hide!"

Eddie quickly popped into one of the empty body drawers while Marcus and Elsie tried to look like they were investigating specimens in some jars of formaldehyde.

The door opened. A man and a woman entered and looked in mild surprise at the young man and chimp in lab coats.

"What are you two doing here?" said the authoritative woman to them.

"Just checking on these specimens, Yep, everything tallies," said Marcus to Elsie. "We can go back to our lab now and write the report."

Elsie nodded, keeping her face averted in case she was recognized by the pathologist and her assistant.

The pathologist turned to her assistant and said, "Well, that's the last of the dead stuff crated and shipped off for today. Let's just clean up here and then lock up."

Marcus and Elsie left the morgue at once while poor Eddie, unable to blow his cover, cowered in the mortuary drawer. He hoped the people wouldn't notice that the drawer was open just a crack. The two people started to chat about the latest kerfuffle with one of the new felines that had just been brought in for research. Eddie listened intently and gasped. But the assistant who was tidying up, suddenly noticed something amiss. He walked over to the stack of body drawers to see why one was partially open. Eddie held his breath in absolute terror—would he shut the drawer up and trap him for eternity?!

Instead, the man looked inside of what should have been an empty drawer.

"Yuck, what on earth is this?" he said, pulling a face as he picked Eddie up by an ear and lifted him out of the drawer.

The pathologist looked over her shoulder at him and chuckled, "Looks like some scruffy, old teddy bear. Probably the boss's kids have been playing around in here again. We're going to have to make sure we always lock the door when we leave."

"What shall I do with it?" asked the young man.

"Oh, it looks pretty worn and dirty, best just chuck it down the garbage chute."

The man walked over to the chute and opened it. But he couldn't get the bear to fit—it was too fat.

"Won't fit," he said, "If I force it, it'll get stuck halfway down and block everything," he said, frustrated.

"Then just throw it in the organics mulcher and shred it," said the woman casually.

"**Aaaarrghh**!" shrieked Eddie in a voice that would have awakened the dead.

Receiving the shock of his life, the man lost his grip on the animal letting him drop to the floor. Eddie wasted not a second and bolted madly for the open door and ran down the corridor as fast as his chubby little legs would carry him. He opened the first door he came to and went through it slamming it shut behind him. But oh no! He was disappointed to find it was just the janitor's closet full of stinky mops and buckets. Surely, they would have seen him run in here and come after him. He was trapped! But despite his state of panic, he noticed an open vent shaft just above the furnace. He climbed up into it and scrambled along on all fours as fast as he could.

After a few minutes of frantic scrambling, he paused to catch his breath. He listened intently. No sound of pursuit. When he was certain that no one was following him, he relaxed a little and tried to decide what to do next. Should he wait and try to slip out the door when he thought the coast was clear, or should he keep crawling along the vent shaft in the hope it would lead to freedom? He decided on the latter plan.

He crawled quite a long way as fast and quietly as he could, but it was dark, and he had no idea where the shaft was leading; it had changed direction so many times. He felt the panic arising in him again as he realized he could be wandering around in the dark for eternity—or at least until he died of thirst! "And Micki would never know what happened to me," he sobbed. That last thought hit him like a ton of bricks—Micki! In his flight of terror, he had momentarily forgotten his mission—to find and rescue his dearest friend—if it wasn't too late! The renewed sense of urgency and purpose made him soldier boldly onwards.

Presently, he came to a grill that opened into a small office of some sort. He peeked down through the slats. The room was well-lit but empty. There were two desks in it, and it looked like somebody had been working there recently. A possible way of escape he thought!

Carefully, he removed the grill and squeezed through the opening to land with a thud on the nearest desk. He felt relieved. But what to do now? He had no idea where he was or where to find the others. He looked around the desk for some information and then spotted an item that gave him a brainwave. He picked up a pen and wrote something on a sticky-note. Just then he heard voices approaching the door. Quick as lightening, he slapped the note to his forehead and struck a typical 'teddy bear pose' sitting resolutely on the desk pad, staring into space.

The door opened, and two giggling young ladies entered with mugs of hot coffee in their hands.

"Really, Margaret, you are awful! What will he say when he finds out?" said the blonde.

"Well, I really don't care what…" began the brunette.

"I say, Judy, what's that old teddy bear doing sitting on your desk?"

The girl with the blonde ponytail put down her coffee mug and took the note from Eddie's brow. "It says,

'Pleze tek this VIP bare to Markus imeedyately'

Looks like it's been written by some half-witted chimp!" she said with a laugh.

Eddie almost blew his stack *and* his cover at this insult to his literary skills, but he remembered, just in time, his life or death mission to find Micki, and so he bit his lip and swallowed his pride.

Margaret chuckled, "How strange! But aren't you the lucky one!"

"How so?" asked her co-worker.

"Well, you're always trying to find an excuse to get the attention of that heart-throb Marcus who never seems to know you exist," said the brunette.

"Ooh, yes!" said the pert data analyst, "Marcus is so dreamy, and looks so dashing in his white lab coat. If I take him this very important bear, perhaps he'll notice me at last. It could be the start of something big," said Judy, clutching Eddie to her bosom and dancing starry-eyed around the room.

Eddie, feeling as if the breath was being squashed out of him while locked in this amorous embrace, was thinking to himself, "Never mind all that—you, silly wench! Just get me to him!"

Judy wasted no more time. She beeped Marcus's pager to check his whereabouts and then, holding Eddie tightly in her arms, dashed out the door and along the hallway, up a flight of stairs and into a room labelled:

Research Lab—Private. No Admittance

She burst into the room without even knocking. Her most attractive smile adorned her countenance.

"Marcus!" she said, "I've brought you something very important!"

Marcus looked in shock at a very wide-eyed Eddie who was proudly held out to him by the excited young woman. He instantly grabbed the bear and set him on his feet.

"Thank you!" he said, beaming, "I really appreciate your help.…er…er…"

"I'm Judy," said the blonde, a little disappointed, but still riding high in her excitement.

"Oh, yes, right, Well, thanks again for your help," said Marcus, trying to gently hurry her out of the door, "Very good of you, Julie."

"It's Judy," she said, starting to pout a little.

Marcus was very distracted by the urgency of getting back to the life and death matter at hand. He attempted to close the door quickly after the young woman, but she wasn't going away that easily.

"What are you up to with all these animals?" she said, looking suspiciously at the little group consisting of chimp, terrier, and bear.

"It's all part of our little secret. You remember your promise, right?" said the lab worker, searching her face in earnest for a show of loyalty.

"Hhhmm…" she said, "For now, I'll trust you're up to something good,"

"Yes, I am, indeed!" he said, "Thanks for your trust, Jodie, I may need your help later, goodbye!"

"JUDY!" shouted the exasperated blonde over her shoulder as she went on her way.

The youth closed the door behind her and locked it. He then turned to Eddie saying "Come on, we have to hurry if we're going to find Micki before it's too late. We still have no idea where to look, so we'll start again in the…"

Eddie tried to interrupt him, "I've got so much to tell you. I was stuck in the drawer and I …"

"Not now, Eddie, you can tell us all about it later," said Chip who had rejoined the group, "We have to go and…"

"But I *have* to tell you what…" began the desperate little bear again.

"Later, Eddie, please!" said Elsie, starting to unlock the door, "We have no time to waste!" and without further delay, she led the way out into the maze of basement hallways and stairways and rooms.

"But, but…" said Eddie, puffing after them and trying hard to get their attention.

"Never mind, Eddie. You can tell us when we find Micki—there's not a moment to lose!" said Marcus, grabbing the bear by the arm and almost dragging him along.

"LISTEN TO ME!" yelled Eddie at the top of his choking voice causing the others to stop in their tracks. Wrenching his arm free, he glared at the other three who halted and stared at him.

You could have heard a pin drop. Eddie never asserted himself like this. Marcus, Elsie, and Chip stood in silence waiting for their ursine friend to speak.

"I'm trying to tell you," Eddie began, regaining his composure, "When I was stuck in the drawer in the morgue, I overheard two workers talking about a black and white cat that had just arrived in the labs and was causing a lot of trouble. She was tearing the place apart and scratching and biting and screeching such that all the workers were talking about what to do with her." Here he paused to catch his breath.

"Did they say where they were holding her?" asked Chip, his eyes wide in astonishment.

"Yes!" said Eddie, "in cell block E37, wherever that is."

"I know exactly where that is!" said Marcus excitedly. "It's the quarantine block where they keep the madly insane animals. But it's not easy to get to and we will have to have a strategy for making the rescue."

The little group sat for a moment and strategized carefully. Satisfied with their plan, they leapt into action.

❧

Block E37 was where the researchers kept the dangerous animals under extra-secure lock and key. For most of the inmates, it was death row. Euthanasia was administered in what were considered to be hopeless cases.

Marcus quickly went to a phone and made a call. He talked for quite a while and when he hung up, the animals looked at him expectantly.

"I've enlisted the help of Judy who sees all the data on the research animals. She was able to find out the truth about Micki. The cat is suspected of having rabies and is being sent to E37 to be held until she can be checked for the disease. Government orders require that if the test results are positive, she will be euthanized, and all the people bitten by her, sent to the infirmary for immediate treatment. So, here's the plan Judy and I have worked out. There's no time to lose!"

2

Before long, Marcus, Elsie, Eddie, and Chip, after having all put on surgical face masks, made their way to quarantine block E37, carrying an empty crate. Here, they were stopped at the entrance by a chimp guard who asked them for identification. Marcus showed him some important-looking papers and muttered a few words. The chimp's face turned ashen and he held his breath, hurriedly burying his nose in the crook of his arm. He nodded and opened the door for them to enter.

The foursome made their way along the deserted corridor heading in the direction of blood-curdling yowls and screams.

Micki had regained consciousness from the sedatives they had injected into her. Although still glassy-eyed and groggy, she realized she was trapped. Afraid and confused, she began to fight violently all over again. Her captors handled her roughly as they tried to inject her with more sedative, but she broke free and bolted down the corridor lined with cages full of distorted creatures gaping in amazement.

"Help! HELP!" yelled the hysterical Micki, "I'm Micki MacVitie and I'm being held against my will!"

Her captors brought out the dart gun and shot a sedative into her. Almost immediately, the drug started to take effect.

"Help, somebody help me!" cried the little feline, "I'm Micki MacVitie and I'm being held against…my…" her voice faded weakly away as the drug took over. She slumped to the ground…semiconscious, almost senseless.

They put her in a wheelchair and push her along the corridor past the staring deformed creatures lining the hallway. Micki, her mind now rambling incoherently, raised one paw and, in a gesture of blessing, she muttered to the shouting animals who were reaching their paws through the bars of their cages, "I absolve you of all your weaknesses, I absolve you all of your…"

Waiting for just the right moment, Marcus and the others watched in horror from behind the glass pane in the door.

"Now!" shouted Marcus as he flung open the door into the corridor, putting their rescue plan into action. The workers looked up in surprise as Marcus boldly stepped up to them waving the papers in his hand.

"STOP!" he cried from behind his mask, "It has been determined that this feline has a fatal airborne disease of incurable madness. I and my assistants, here," he gestured to Elsie, Eddie, and Chip, "have been ordered to immediately crate her up and speed her away to a special secure facility on the mainland."

Elsie and Eddie rushed forward and lifted the limp Micki out of the wheelchair and put her gently into the crate they had brought. Chip threw a blanket over the crate and secured it with a rope and big labels which read:

Extreme Danger!

MAD CAT!

DO NOT OPEN CRATE!

༄

Little Micki was still sleeping in her crate on the golf-cart that Marcus drove down to the boat launch a few minutes later. Elsie, holding a clipboard and wearing a lab coat, sat on the seat next to Marcus. As planned, Eddie was hidden in another crate next to Micki's. He was feeling very worried for his friend but encouraged that the rescue mission was going according to plan. There would be a lot of explaining to do later when she woke up. Dandelion and Daisy were in a wicker basket close by. Chip was sitting quietly alert in his own crate, listening and watching.

Marcus pulled up at the moored motorboat. He was worried that Sharpie, the chimp shipping manager, may ask too many questions. He planned to tell the sly animal that he had a special shipment on the cart—a very *secret* special shipment. However, when he jumped off the cart, he saw only Bozo—the not-so-bright chimp stevedore.

"Where's Sharpie?" asked Marcus of Bozo, looking around for him.

Bozo told him that Sharpie had hurt his toe while unloading crates from the boat and had gone off to the infirmary to have it looked at.

Marcus breathed a sigh of relief and thought to himself, "Good news! Bozo has been left in charge of shipments—he's not too bright, his job is to just lift the heavy stuff at Sharpie's command."

MYSTERIOUS REALMS

"Papers please," said Bozo to Marcus, trying to sound officious. Marcus handed him the fake forms that Judy had prepared.

Bozo looks at them carefully and said to the young man stood before him, "These items are not on my shipping manifest."

"Last-minute special orders," explained Marcus. He then whispered to the chimp. "Special assignment, Top Secret," and tapped the side of his nose. "Only VIPs who have a 'need to know' can be trusted with this information, but I think you can be trusted, right?"

"Oh, right! Right, Gaffer," said Bozo, anxious to seem important. "Of course, I'm silent as the grave when it comes to state secrets. I know all about these sorts of things," he said as he began to help Elsie load the crates onto the motor-boat. Then he suddenly stopped and picked up the phone, "Better just let Sharpie know that I'm handling this secret shipment properly," he said, starting to punch buttons.

"Oh, no need to create a fuss!" said Marcus hurriedly. "Besides, likely, he hasn't been told about this because it is *so* Top Secret, you see. Best leave him out of it! A smart chimp like you can handle it by yourself, eh?"

Bozo puffed up his chest and considered the matter. He nodded with a proud grin and put down the phone.

Marcus reached into his lab coat pocket and pulled out some pieces of paper—Banana Vouchers! –A valuable commodity among the chimps of the island. The man slyly stuffed a few into the chimp's paws, "But remember," warned Marcus quietly, "mum's the word!"

The dull-minded chimp took the vouchers eagerly, his eyes glinting. He pocketed the papers quickly and grinned "Right you are, Gov'ner. Won't say a dicky-bird!" and he waved congenially to Elsie who was already in the boat. Marcus leapt into the ferry, started up the engine and sped away from the dock leaving a wild wake behind them.

༄

By the time the little group of adventurers reached Paradise Island, Micki had started to come around. As the secreted animals emerged from their crates, Eddie put the blanket around Micki and vowed never to let her out of his sight again. He explained to her what was going on, but she was still too groggy to fully understand.

Marcus easily purchased seats for them all on the next plane flying from Paradise Island to the Inner Hebrides, which was, conveniently, departing soon. The flight was quiet, and the exhausted friends were glad to have a chance to rest.

After safely landing and disembarking at the Inner Hebrides airport, Marcus and the animals immediately took a taxi to the animal rights group GOFAR (Genuine Organization for Animal Rights). The friends spilled out the entire story of what was happening on Shuttle Island—they left nothing unsaid. The spellbound authorities listened to the whole tale in stunned amazement.

After giving valuable testimony, Daisy and Dandelion bade fond farewells to their friends and took the next train to their relatives' home in the quiet countryside of Wales—they would be very thankful to put their feet on familiar turf and take it easy for a while.

The others enjoyed refreshments provided in the comfortable visitors' lounge of the GOFAR building. They whiled away a pleasant few hours chatting over the whole adventure and, in particular, the miraculous rescue plan. Micki was now fully recovered and couldn't express her gratitude enough to her special friends—especially clever, brave, faithful Eddie.

It was an emotional goodbye that Eddie and Micki shared with Marcus, Elsie, and the now beloved 'mad ratter,'—Chip. But after they had all shared friends-forever hugs with each other, Eddie's face suddenly took on an expression of immense gravity. He cleared his throat and turned to Marcus, "Ahem, Marcus my friend, I have something I need to say to you, in private. Man-to-man, as they say."

Marcus looked most perplexed and couldn't imagine what was the matter. "What is it, my dear friend?" he said with great apprehension.

Eddie cleared his throat again and stood on tippy toe to whisper something into Marcus' ear. As the young man listened, his cheeks reddened like boiled beets. "JUDY!?" he exclaimed, "She does? Me? She *is*? My, what a blind, silly, old fool I've been!"

Eddie nodded with a smile.

"Well, I'll have to remedy that as soon as I get back there! If she still feels the same way about me, that is," declared Marcus emphatically as he straightened up tall and put his shoulders back with a big grin creasing his handsome face. "I've always thought she was an intelligent, attractive girl!"

Eddie winked at the other animals who looked on in puzzled amusement. "Fill you in later!" he murmured to Micki.

༄

The authorities immediately sent the strong arm of the law to Shuttle Island and arrested the Bad Guys, including the computer scammers and the collaborating chimps. At the trial, the Bad Guys were all found guilty as charged and sent to prison for a *very* long time. Most of the chimps, who had claimed they were just doing their job and had been afraid for their own safety if they refused, (like Bozo) were sent to a special facility for rehabilitation. The same went for those who plea-bargained their case and provided evidence and testimony in support of the law (like Sharpie).

Of the unfortunate test animals from the GMO facility, those who had a home and caring family to go back to were repatriated with their loved ones. Others, who were alone in the world or too deformed to go out into it, were offered a loving forever home on Holiday Haven Island (formerly Shuttle Island) to live in the new resort which was renovated as a retreat for long-term care and rehabilitation for unfortunate animals. Marcus, Elsie, and Chip were awarded 'custody in perpetuity' of Holiday Haven Island and the hotel which they renamed: The Grand Prize Resort: Loving Home for Mistreated and Abandoned Animals. The Resort, run by Marcus and his new wife Judy (Yes!), with the indispensable help of Elsie and Chip, gained a reputation for being a paradise for animals in need. Sympathetic visitors were always welcomed.

Chip didn't have to act mad anymore, but he enjoyed it so much he continued his craziness for the entertainment of residents and visitors alike. He became renowned and much loved for his dress-up antics.

Eventually, Micki's persistence in entering essay competitions paid off, and she won a genuine competition and was awarded the grand prize of a ten-day get-away for two in the holiday haven of *their* choice. Of course, she and Eddie chose the Grand Prize Resort and had a wonderful time reuniting with their old friends and making lots of new friends too.

[THE END]

THE GYPSY LIFE

ONE DAY, EDDIE BEAR *was* in the garden, but he wasn't gardening, that was because he was reading. It was such a lovely warm, sunny day that he preferred to just sit and read his favourite comic book. Lounging in his deck chair on the patio in the late afternoon sun, he absent-mindedly reached over for another chocolate-covered digestive biscuit from the plate on the little table beside him. Munching contentedly, he then reached for the tumbler of iced tea but his eyes were still on his comic book and so he misjudged the distance and his paw sent the tumbler careening off the table spilling his tea onto the flagstones.

"Oh, drat and bother!" shouted Eddie.

"What? What's happening?" said his best friend and housemate, Micki MacVitie, the black and white Highland cat.

As he mopped up the mess, the cast-off old teddy bear, looked across the lawn to where his friend was busy digging holes in the soft dirt and planting seedlings.

"Why don't you take a break, Micki?" Eddie said. "You've been slaving away half the day."

The cat looked up from the flower bed where she had been industriously gardening all afternoon. "I just want to get this final bed planted out, then I'm done," said Micki, stretching her legs and swatting at a passing dragonfly. "How d'you think it looks, Eddie?"

"Looks splendid, my little friend! A good job well done!" said Eddie, putting another biscuit in his mouth and savoring its milky, smooth, chocolate and honeyed crunch. He then went back to reading. After a minute or two, he threw the comic book down, picked up the local newspaper from amid the pile of comics and magazines strewn at his feet, and began idly browsing its pages.

Presently, Micki put away the gardening tools and set about washing her paws. Then, she joined her friend on the patio taking the other deck chair and helping herself to a cold drink out of the cooler. "Anything of interest in today's paper?" she asked, putting more chocolate-covered biscuits on the plate.

"Not much," replied Eddie, repositioning his sunhat, "But I was just reading this advertisement for that big new RV outfit on the edge of town: 'VANS-4-U'. The new holiday caravans look quite swanky. They have everything inside them, *including* the kitchen sink!"

"The price is probably 'quite swanky' too, Eddie," said Micki, her mouth full of biscuit, "Well out of our league anyway."

"Well, I dunno," said Eddie, flicking a fly off the page, "It says they're having a huge Grand Opening Sale featuring unprecedented discounts." The wheels of Eddie's imagination were already starting to turn. He quoted out loud, **"Unbelievably Slashed Prices**—*We have travelling wheels to suit **every** piggybank! Come and choose the modern caravan that's right for you! Enjoy Luxury Beyond Your Wildest Dreams'.*" His excitement was palpable.

"It does sound idyllic; purring along peaceful country lanes, watching bees and butterflies play among wildflowers," admitted his friend. "But, like I said, probably nothing *we* could afford."

"The model pictured here says: 'With just a few easy payments, this magnificent streamlined caravan, fitted with all *mod. cons.* including icemaker, wine-cooler, soft beds, Persian carpets, dishes, and linens, could be your very own!'" The bear stared off into the distance then wistfully mused, "You know, I've always fancied the gypsy way of life—roaming the beautiful countryside without a care in the world."

"Doesn't sound much like any gypsy caravan *I've* ever seen," said Micki, taking the last biscuit off the plate and slurping the last dregs of her pop.

"Well, nothing wrong with a bit of modernizing here and there," said her friend. "Imagine racing along the country roads, honking to all the denizens of the pastures as they stare at us in awe!"

Micki chuckled, her eyes wide with excitement, "Imagine waving like royalty to all the gob-smacked villagers as they leap out of our way and gape at us with star-struck envy!"

Eddie sprawled back in his deck-chair sighing, his paw searching idly for another chocolate biscuit on the empty plate. "We would blaze along the trail, happy and carefree with not a worry in the world!"

"Yes! Forget about overpriced B & B's, stuffy hotels, and crowded airports!" added Micki, rifling through the cooler for a new packet of biscuits.

"And smelly buses and trains that are never on time!" continued Eddie. "No! we'd rather be on the open road where we'd be in charge of our own destiny!"

"I'd take my sketch pad and pencils," said the cat, triumphantly retrieving the biscuit pack from the cooler and tearing it open with her sharp claws, "I've always envied those artists I see happily sketching bucolic landscapes at sunrise."

"And I'd take my field guides so that I could identify all the marvels of nature we came across!" said the bear.

"Our very own home away from home!" they shouted almost in unison.

"Wouldn't hurt to go look, Micki!" said Eddie, looking pointedly at his companion, his voice and enthusiasm now tempered by very serious consideration.

"Hmmm…. How late are they open?" inquired Micki, her eyes taking on a shimmering glow.

Eddie looked at his watch, "For another hour!"

And without giving another thought to chocolate biscuits, the two friends were laughing and jostling each other, each trying to be the first to get their bike out of the shed and begin pedalling like the wind down the road that led to VANS-4-U.

☙

One bright morning a few days later, the July sun rose above the horizon bathing the countryside of the lower uplands of the Inner Hebrides in a vermillion glow, promising yet another glorious summer's day. As the peaceful landscape warmed, newly emerging butterflies began to dance among the brilliant flowers—blues and fritillaries and clouded yellows bent the heads of harebells and buttercups as they rested upon them to dry their crinkled wings. Hungry bees hummed their morning chants as they yielded to the lure of the wild roses that spilled their sweet intoxicating fragrance into the air. The clarion calls of vigilant feathered visitors filled the azure skies and reminded all those within earshot of their closely guarded territorial boundaries.

With the passing hours, the celestial orb climbed towards its zenith, exchanging its ruby robe for one of gold. The grazing cows settled down in the grassy meadows that stretched beyond the roadside hedges to chew their cud. Pastured horses sought the shade of spreading chestnut trees to stand with drooping heads and locked knees to drowse as they lazily swished their tails to flick away the flies that alighted on their flanks.

But this idyllic harmony was soon to be shattered!

A frantically honking car-horn in the distance was the first hint of pending trouble. HONK! HONK! Then, without warning, the air vibrated with a foreign sound. The roar intensified and became a backdrop to a violently blaring shriek! Cows stumbled to their feet and hurried away in alarm. Horses whinnied and bolted to the other side of the field in terror. Startled birds fluttered up from the fields and hedgerows. Insects deserted the nectar-laden flowers and hid beneath the leaves.

All nature was a-tremble! Then the cause of the hullaballoo burst through the quietude and caught the eye of all who dared to look—a massive black truck with darkened windows yanking along a sleek, chrome and black caravan behind. The vehicles careened along the narrow lane, crushing the delicate foliage of the roadside.

As the roaring intrusion diminished into the distance, the serene drapes of stillness began to descend over the landscape once more, and natural harmony ventured to return.

Emerging from this wounded world came a more peaceful sound. The gentle rumble of cartwheels, blended with the soft rhythmic clip-clop of unshod hooves, held back the closing curtain of silence. Small voices, broken with fits of coughing, rose above the trundling sound hidden amid the choking cloud of dust and fumes that still drifted in the quivering air. The driver, sitting on the weathered wooden seat of an old pony-trap that had once been used to haul apples to market, clicked his tongue to encourage the moth-eaten mule that was begrudgingly pulling it. The bear stole a sideways glance at his chum sitting beside him. They had been slogging around the countryside since the crack of dawn and were already feeling a bit fed up as the novelty of the adventure was wearing off. And now this!

The bear spoke first. "Not quite what we had in mind is it, Micki?" he said gloomily.

"That's an understatement, pal!" said Micki as she picked a piece of grit, thrown up by the passing truck, out of her eye. "Blast that mad driver!" she snapped.

"Jolly inconsiderate, wasn't he?" Eddie said.

"Hope he gets a puncture!" said Micki testily.

"Would certainly serve him jolly-well right!" added her friend, "Almost had us in the ditch back there!"

"Hope the law catches up with him!" hissed the scowling cat.

"They should lock him up and throw away the key!" said Eddie, his jaw set, "By Jove, I'll telephone the constabulary at the first opportunity and file a complaint, you see if I don't!"

"Perhaps the next farmhouse will let us use their phone?" suggested Micki.

"How far is it to the next one, anyway?" asked Eddie.

With a heavy sigh, Micki unfolded their Ordinance Survey Map of the area and scrutinized it. "We need to pull into the next farm anyway to buy our food supplies for the trip," she said. "Eggs, bread, butter, milk, cheese, and maybe some home-cured ham and strawberry jam, and perhaps some garden produce, if they have any."

"Splendid idea!" said Eddie, thinking it had been an awful long time since their skimpy lunch of dried-out sandwiches of potted-meat spread, wilted lettuce, and soggy tomatoes. "Where *is* the next farmhouse?"

"There should be a turn-off just around the next corner. Then we follow the lane until we go under a railway bridge, and then…take a dirt track on the right," said Micki, tracing the features on the map with her paw.

The little farm eventually came into sight. With considerable fuss and effort, Eddie managed to coax the stubborn old mule through the open five-bar gate, bringing him to a halt in the farmyard. They looked around. Everything was unnaturally quiet and deserted. Not even the cluck of a hen or the warning bark of a wary farm dog.

Micki jumped off the cart and cautiously walked up to the cottage door to make enquiries. She noticed a couple of bloated dead chickens covered with flies off to the side and wrinkled her nose at the sight them. Then she spied a hand-stenciled sign on the well in the yard.

POISON

"The water is bad here," called Micki, peeking over the stone wall of the well.

"Probably why it's all deserted," reasoned Eddie. "Best be on our way. Where is the next farm on the map?"

Micki jumped back on the seat beside Eddie and picked up the map again. "Quite a way off," she announced. "There seems to be some sort of old castle ruins a mile or so along the road, and then a farm a couple of miles beyond that." She refolded the map with a sigh.

Eddie eyed the descending sun and said, "We need to start looking for a good spot to set up camp. Hopefully, we can buy supplies and get settled before dusk."

"If this animal doesn't go a little faster, we'll never make it to anywhere before midnight!" observed Micki, tired and irritable with the way things were going.

Eddie slapped the reins on the old, brown mule's rump in yet one more effort to get a little more speed out of the aged beast, "Get a move on there, Jack!" he said, causing the reluctant draft animal to scuff its feet a little bit faster on the dusty road before slumping back into its customary dawdle. After they reached the main road again, Eddie broke the brooding silence, "How were we to know you needed a big truck to pull one of those swanky new caravans," he lamented, waving away the evening midges that kept clouding around his face.

"This is all we could afford anyway," said Micki grumpily. "Maybe it wouldn't be so bad if we could at least get a trot out of this stubborn creature. "Did the animal tell you why he walks so slowly?"

"He doesn't seem to be able to speak," said Eddie with a shrug, "He couldn't even tell me his name! Hey, Jackass! You up front, can you pick up the pace a bit, please?" he shouted.

But there was no response from the old mule, not even a twitch of his ear.

"Doesn't seem to be able to hear, either," said Micki, her patience wearing thin. "Shout louder, Eddie!"

"TROT!" yelled Eddie at the top of his voice. But still the mule plodded.

"I've had just about enough of this!" said Micki, an ugly scowl distorting the features of her usually pretty face. "Let's see if he hears THIS!"

And like a flash of lightning, the feisty feline was atop the mule's neck screeching like a thousand Banshee's in his left ear. "TRRR--A-A-AHHHT!!!!!!!!!"

In less than a blink of an eye, the mule sprung to life, rearing up on his hind legs with a whinnying sufficient to awaken the dead. Micki instinctively dug her claws deep into his neck to save herself from falling. The mule responded to the skin-penetrating needles by leaping ten-feet into the air and lunging forward with a blood-curdling screech! He bolted for his life along the road and around the next bend where the wheel of the cart caught the edge of the ditch causing the contraption to bounce into the air sending poor Eddie on an airborne trip that almost brought him into collision with a passing eagle. He saw the world turning dizzyingly every which way beneath him, and then all went black.

The mule broke free of his harness and was down the road and out of sight in no time. Micki had bailed successfully and landed on her feet with cat-like deftness. She stood for a moment in shock and then looked around for Eddie. He was nowhere to be seen. Then she spotted his seemingly lifeless body in the grassy ditch. She sprinted over to him and stood over the limp prostrate form of her best friend, licking his face in earnest.

"Eddie! EDDIE! Oh, Eddie, dearest most beloved friend, do wake up!" she mewed frantically, fearful that he would never wake up again!

But after a minute or two, one glassy brown eye opened— 'ping!' And then the other one opened, and then both eyes blinked. "Whe...where am I?" murmured the dazed little bear, "What happened?"

"Oh, thank goodness you're all right," sobbed Micki, hers tears of joy dripping onto her friend's nose, "I was afraid you were gone forever!"

Eddie rubbed his eyes, licked her tears off his nose, and sat up still feeling a little woozy. "Where's the mule?" he said looking at the empty shafts of the upturned applecart.

"Run off!" said Micki in disgust. "Probably seen the last of him, the ungrateful animal!" she scoffed, helping her friend to his feet.

Eddie had a blinding headache but otherwise felt fine. Nothing torn or broken except his right ear seemed a little looser than usual. He pulled at the dangling threads to tighten it up a bit. He dusted off his clothes and then gave his buddy a hug. "Well, what do we do now?" he said, putting his paw on the uppermost cartwheel that was still gently spinning in the breeze. "Even if the cart is still useable, we can't get it back upright without help."

The two animals sat dejectedly in the fading sunlight amongst the roadside weeds trying to think of a solution.

"It must be supper time by now," said Micki, pulling herself to her feet and going to where their supplies were scattered in the ditch. "I'll see what I can salvage."

"Yes, I'm feeling quite peckish," said Eddie, getting up to help his friend ferret around in the weedy ditch for their few scattered provisions. But as he climbed the embankment to retrieve a jar of honey, he noticed a speck of something off in the distance coming along the roadway from the direction in which they had been headed.

He squinted into the shimmering light of the setting sun and furrowed his brow, "Who's this I wonder?" he said to Micki, "Maybe we can ask for help?"

As the image got closer, they could see it was a string of a half-dozen gypsy caravans heading towards them. The colourfully painted reading vans were being pulled by handsome piebald horses whose profuse white fetlocks flowed like little waterfalls over big, strong hooves.

"Looks like a group of Romani gypsies," said Micki, anxiously watching the caravans approaching. "I wonder if they're friendly?"

"Let's hope so," said Eddie, "Perhaps they would be willing to help us… for a price that is."

"Look!" said the Highland cat, "Isn't that *our* mule the gypsy boy is leading?"

"By Jove! I do believe it is, Micki," said the bear, shielding his eyes against the sun which was now quite low on the horizon.

A few minutes later, the caravans had reached the stranded animals and their overturned old wagon. A gypsy man stood without speaking and looked at the spectacle.

MYSTERIOUS REALMS

Eddie cleared his throat uncomfortably in embarrassment, "Had a spot of bother," he said to the man. "Blessed mule took a fright and bolted," he explained a little sheepishly.

The man nodded silently and beckoned to some of his fellow travellers. Three or four strong lads set to work pulling the trap up onto its wheels. Then, they began repairing the broken harness while a young boy coaxed the mule between the shafts. Two or three children with grinning faces stood and stared quietly at the scene. They seemed amused with the funny-looking bear and black and white cat dressed in holiday clothes.

The work done and order restored, the gypsies made to resume their trek. Eddie and Micki showered the men with words of gratitude. Micki nudged her friend indicating that he should reach generously into his pocket. Eddie pulled out a thin wad of bank notes and offered a few to the boss man. But the fellow shook his head, and waved the money aside, "Better luck be with you, my friends," was all he said as he clucked his horse forward.

Micki and Eddie nodded to the man in understanding and appreciation. But before the caravans had moved very far, Micki rummaged through their belongings and ran after the travellers with a handful of treats. She looked questioningly into the face of the gypsy woman walking with the children and held out the treats. The woman nodded approval and the cat handed a yummy goodie to each of the mesmerized children.

Back at the cart, the two relieved friends patted the rehitched mule and told him they were glad to have him back safe and sound. The mule smiled and nodded his big head.

"Thanks," he said, speaking to them for the first time.

"So! You *do* speak after all!" said Micki in surprise.

"Yeah, I'm sorry I was so stubborn and unfriendly. You see, I don't like folks very much," he said, drooping his clumsy head humbly.

"Why is that?" queried Eddie, frankly glad that they were finally having some dialogue.

"Well, I get treated pretty badly by some drivers," said the flea-bitten equine, directing a disgruntled look at the cat and the bear.

"I'm sorry for yelling rudely in your ear and for scratching your neck with my nasty claws," said Micki apologetically, hanging her head in shame.

"I was very unkind," said Eddie, taking the point, "I'm sorry I was impatient with you."

The mule shrugged "That's okay, no hard feelings," he mumbled. "But there are those who act like I deserve no tenderness just because I'm an old mule," he continued, staring fixedly at the ground.

"Yes, some people can be very cruel. Even those you've loved and trusted may chuck you out when you start to look patchy because your hair begins to thin, and you get paunchy as your stuffing starts to sag," commiserated Eddie.

"But we're happy to have you with us on our adventure, Jack," said the little cat brightly to their new friend. "My name's Micki, and this is my good friend, Eddie."

"Thank you. But, by the way, my name's not *Jack*," said the draft-animal, his spirits lifting a little.

"So, what is it then?" asked the cat and bear together.

"It's Freddie!" said the mule proudly.

"Well, what d'you know!" said Eddie, offering to shake hands. "That rhymes with my name! We're almost *twins* you and me! Put it there, pal!"

The mule raised a hoof and hee-hawed a laugh, he liked these new drivers after all.

"Well, I suppose, we'd best be off," said Eddie. "Not much daylight left, and we still need to find a place to camp for the night."

"I know just the spot!" said Freddie, setting out at a smart pace.

Eddie and Micki glanced at each other in surprise. "How would you know such a thing?" asked Eddie.

"It's where those gypsies were camped when I met 'em," explained the mule, happy to have something useful to say. "It's a beautiful level meadow near a stream in the grounds of an old abandoned castle!" And with this, he broke into a merry trot with Eddie and Micki sitting on the cart grinning happily.

☙

They soon came to the old castle ruins and pulled into a lovely meadow of sweet grass and summer flowers bordered by woodland. The cool evening air was trilling with the evensong of a myriad of songbirds. Eddie parked the applecart near the spring-fed babbling brook. While he unharnessed and brushed the mule's dusty coat before setting him free, Micki set up camp. They built a little fire and cooked a meagre, but adequate meal. After eating, they sat on cozy blankets and shared stories in the flickering light of the campfire.

Freddie was quite free with tales from his chequered past. He spoke of his glory days of travelling the high roads and low roads, and then lamented on his downfall at the hands of man.

Eddie nodded sympathetically, "Yeah, I hear you, friend," he said, "But I refuse to let others define my self-worth. I can do that very nicely for myself when I have time to think on it."

"Same here," continued the mule, "I'm not a dumb ass like everybody sez. In fact, I'm quite a smart ass," said the old equine quite seriously.

Eddie exchanged glances with Micki and they each bit their lip to stifle a chuckle.

"We take your meaning, Freddie," said Micki, reaching over and patting the mule on the shoulder kindly, "And we love you just as you are."

Eddie, poked at the fire and started to push some marshmallows onto a stick, then began, "I think you just have to…"

"Sshh…!" said Micki suddenly. "What was that?" Her sharp ears had detected an unusual sound near the castle ruins behind them.

"What was what?" asked Eddie, cupping his ear as he looked around him.

"An eerie groaning, moaning sound," said Micki, her eyes wide.

"Oh," said Eddie, rubbing his paw across his tummy, "I do beg your pardon, I hoped no one would hear that!"

"Sshh…, there it is again, a low, haunting growl," said Micki, straining her ears and twitching them back and forth.

The mule spoke up, "Probably just the wind in the castle turrets, or maybe it's a tawny owl hooting for its mate," he said, hoping it was nothing worse.

Hearing nothing more, Micki settled back down again, but not for long—a loud screech cut them to the quick making them all jump out of their skins.

"What on earth was that?" said Eddie in terror.

"I'll kick it, whatever it is!" said Freddie, slicing the air with his hooves.

"I'll scratch its eyes out, whatever it is!" said Micki, flexing her razor-sharp claws.

"*I'll*…just…leave it be, whatever it is!" said Eddie, trembling.

But whatever *it* was, it stayed away from them and they heard nothing more. However, they remained on alert for some time until the long day on dusty roads got the better of them.

"Well, I think it's time for me to hit the sack!" said Micki, yawning and setting everybody else off. "We want to be bright and fresh for our journey tomorrow."

"So where are we headed?" asked Freddie, swatting a tickly night-beetle off his back with his tail.

"To the West Country, where sheep may safely graze in peace and quiet. Right, Eddie?" said the cat to the bear who was nodding off by the dying embers of the fire.

"Huh, what? Yes, yes! Anywhere away from this creepy old castle," said the drowsy Eddie as another shiver ran up and down his spine.

Micki and Eddie snuggled down into their sleeping bags while Freddie found a soft piece of turf to lie on.

"Good night, everyone," said Micki.

"Sleep tight, friends," said Eddie.

"Nighty-night, don't let the bed bugs bite!" chuckled Freddie, delighted to be in good company.

It had been an exhausting day for all concerned and spooky sounds were soon forgotten as they fell into a deep restful slumber. Nothing was stirring except for a curious little fieldmouse that scuttled around checking out the visitors. Soon, the only sound was the contented snoring of three little friends.

☙

After a peaceful night, the animals awoke to another beautiful, sunny morning. Anxious to be on their way, Eddie and Micki were content with a simple breakfast of bread and honey followed a bowl of milk each—pretty much the last of their supplies. Their new friend was happy to chomp the sweet, juicy grasses and wildflowers growing abundantly in the little meadow; washing them all down with a refreshing, deep drink from the gurgling stream.

"If we make good time on the road today, we may even make it to the seaside," said Eddie, loading up the cart again.

"Oh, yippee!" whinnied Freddie, kicking up his heels. "I love the seaside. I remember going to Weston-Super-Mare once when I was a dashing young colt. I ran up and down the beach looking for all the Super Fillies but saw nary a one! All I did was get stuck in that black sticky mud! *So* humiliating, having to get pulled out with ropes!"

"You must have been quite the stud in your youth!" said Eddie, backing the mule between the shafts.

"Ah, yes! My glossy coat was like the finest silk and…"

"Oh, NO!" cried Eddie, looking down at the cart axle.

"It most certainly was!" said Freddie, offended by what he perceived as Eddie's disbelief.

"What's up?" asked Micki, looking up from packing the blankets into the cart.

"Seems we won't be going *anywhere* right now," said her friend, getting down on his knees to crawl under the trap.

Freddie looked down between his legs towards the cart, "Uh, oh!" he said, "Bad news, kids!"

Eddie crawled back out saying, "Must have gotten that big crack in the axle when it overturned yesterday."

"Oh, pooh and bother!" said Micki, looking at it too. "It won't even last another mile by the look of it."

"What are we going to do now!" groaned Eddie, very annoyed.

"We'll have to walk to that farmhouse noted on the OS map and try to get help." said Micki.

"Why don't one of you hop on my back," said Freddie congenially, glad of a chance to show just how useful and cooperative he could be if given a chance. "I can run faster than either of you."

"Good idea!" said Eddie, taking heart.

"You go with Freddie," said Micki to her friend, "I'll stay here to guard our stuff."

"Are you sure you'll be all right by yourself?" said Eddie, worried for Micki's safety even though, secretly, he was glad not to be the one staying behind at the creepy castle.

"Don't worry about me, Eddie; I can take care of myself!" she said, exposing her sharp claws.

The others grinned at the brave cat as she gave Eddie a leg-up onto Freddie's back. Without further delay, the mule started towards the road.

"We'll be back as soon as we can, Micki!" shouted Eddie with a wave of his paw.

Micki waved them off calling after them, "Oh, and while you're at the farm, can you please pick up a dozen fresh eggs, two pounds of bacon, a pound of freshly-churned butter, two loaves of freshly-baked bread, lettuce, tomatoes, and a jug of Jersey milk with extra cream…and maybe a ham and a jar of jam,… and…!" But most of this went unheard as the mule had already galloped far along the road.

☙

Micki sat for a while in the pleasant sunshine wondering what to do with herself. Then, she remembered the art materials she had brought along and retrieved her sketch book and pencils from the luggage. She set about drawing beetles, butterflies, and flowers. Presently, she noticed a solitary rook that sat a long time atop the castle ruins, watching her intently. It puzzled her as to why such an extremely gregarious bird was all alone. She made several sketches of the mysterious bird then, tired of drawing, she put her book down and wandered lazily around the castle grounds, pawing at dragonflies until the sun made her sleepy. She sought the comfy pillow on top of the cart and nestled down for a little catnap.

She was purring contentedly when she suddenly became aware of a distinct chill in the air. Opening her eyes to black, angry clouds overhead, she was almost blinded by a flash of lightning. Then a roll of thunder grumbled not too distant. When she blinked her eyes clear, she was shocked to see a hook-nosed, old hag, dressed in black, standing beside the cart.

"Who…who are you?" said Micki, a little afraid.

"Just an old pedlar-woman," cackled the old crone. "I live in Nemesis Castle," she said, indicating the ruins behind her.

"Well, what do you want?" asked Micki.

"Will you buy a pretty little trinket from a poor old lady," she said, dangling what looked like a catnip-stuffed mouse in Micki's face.

MYSTERIOUS REALMS

The cat hesitated for just a moment. It did smell tempting. Then she remembered she mustn't take treats from strangers, so she said curtly, "Not today, thank you, madam. Please be on your way."

"Cross my palm with silver and I'll read your fortune," said the pedlar coaxingly.

"If my friend was here, he'd say 'stuff and nonsense'! Now be off with you!" said Micki, swishing her tail in irritation.

"Double trouble, boil and bubble," said the hag mysteriously while making a stirring motion with the knobbly walking stick in her hand.

"Rubbish!" scoffed Micki.

But the old woman didn't leave. "Whether it be in wind or rain, never will you see your friends again!" said the witch-like crone as a terrific crack of thunder and another bolt of lightning pierced the air. Micki darted under the pillow and lay there trembling to the core, fearing for her life.

As the thunder rumbled away into the distance, there came the sound of beating wings overhead, which also faded away.

After a long period of quietness, Micki cautiously peeped out from under the pillow. The old crone was nowhere to be seen and the sun shone brightly everywhere again.

"Bah, humbug!" exclaimed Micki, "There's nothing here at all. Likely, I was just dreaming. A nightmare caused by something I ate for breakfast that gave me indigestion. But then she remembered the hag's warning about never seeing her friends again, and she shivered despite the warmth of the sun. She wished Eddie and Freddie would hurry back. In spite of trying to be brave, she felt quite alone and small with the foreboding castle ruins bearing down on her.

The cat sat a while and decided to sketch what she had seen as best she could so that she could show her friends when she told them about it. This made her wonder if they were having any luck at the next farm. It seemed they had been gone an awfully long time. "Probably they're chatting merrily to some hospitable farmer while the farm-wife stuffs them with cakes and pies," thought Micki, starting to feel a bit miffed as well as very hungry.

Miles away, Eddie and Freddie were far from enjoying themselves. Indeed, they were having peculiar troubles of their own.

Eddie said, "Well, this is the fourth farmhouse we've visited. Let's hope there's someone home at *this* one."

Freddie was hot and tired with all that galloping from one farmhouse to another and had now slowed to a lumbering walk while his sweaty hide steamed despite the heat of the mid-day sun. "It's very strange that all the farms are deserted—no people and no animals around, not even a pesky farm dog to bar the way," said the weary mule, all the while praying silently for a cool breeze or a cloud to block the sun.

"It is weird. All the wells having 'poison' signs hanging on them and all the water troughs have been turned over, so we can't even slake out thirsts," moaned Eddie.

"Yes, and that dead cow at the last farm gave me the shivers," said Freddie, shuddering.

The pair dragged themselves up the driveway to the fourth farm, but they had no luck at this place either. It, too, was deserted.

"Drat and bother!" said Eddie, mopping his brow with his neckerchief as he flopped down on the dusty road taking advantage of Freddie's shadow.

"Perhaps we should be getting back to Micki?" the mule said.

"Yes! I hope she's all right and not too bored with waiting for us," said Eddie, "We've been gone much longer than expected."

☙

Back at the castle camp, Micki was becoming very bored and so she started to thumb through some of the books Eddie had brought along. She smiled as she remembered how excited he had been the night before their trip as he packed his beloved books:

"I want to explore nature and learn to identify all kinds of things during our holiday of exploring the countryside," Eddie had said, rifling through their bookshelves and pulling out his *Field Guide to Wild Flowers,* and *Bird Watching in the Lower Highlands,* "…I mustn't forget *Know Your Rocks,* and, of course, I'll need…*Constellations of the Summer Sky*… and…."

MYSTERIOUS REALMS

"Steady on, old feller," Micki had said with a laugh as she eyed the teetering pile of tomes Eddie was building. "We are only going for a week you know! It's to be a trip *of* a lifetime not *for* a lifetime!"

Now, remembering this scenario and the hag's words about Eddie and Freddie never being seen again, the lonely cat started to feel very melancholy and not a little apprehensive. Indeed, she was becoming increasingly worried and thought maybe she should go in search of them. Perhaps something horrible had happened?

☙

Her disgruntled friends were trudging along the winding road back to the castle as darkness began to fall. Eddie, riding on the mule's back, ducked as a particularly large, solitary rook flew annoyingly low over them. Eddie grunted peevishly as the bird scuffed the top of his head a second time.

"Look where you're going, ignorant bird!" he called out after it. "Where are your manners!"

The pair plodded on wearily. Then, around the next bend, they saw what seemed to be an old woman who had fainted at the roadside.

"Probably the effects of a hot day and walking without being able to quench her thirst at the farms," speculated Freddie.

"Poor old dear," said Eddie, tapping her face gently before hoisting her up onto Freddie's back. "We'll take her back to our camp where she can rest and drink some water from the stream."

The old lady seemed to recover as she rode on the mule's back. She sat up and looked at Eddie walking at the animal's head and said, "Oh my, what a to-do! What's happening?"

"Are you feeling a little better, lady?" asked Eddie, turning to look up at the woman. "You had fainted along the road, so we picked you up. We can take you home if you like. Where do you live?"

"Well, if you would be so kind as to take me to Nemesis Castle where I have a lowly little room, I would be most grateful, my dears."

"Where is Nemesis Castle?" inquired Eddie, hoping it was very close.

"It's the old ruins along this road another couple of miles or so, but we can take a short cut across the fields," said the woman.

"Oh, I know the place. In fact, that's where we're camping," Eddie said. "It must be unpleasant living in the old ruins," he added, remembering how scared they had all been the night before. "And don't you get wet when it rains?"

"I live in the one room that still has a roof on it," said the woman. "It's very humble, but enough for a poor old pedlar like me."

After what seemed forever, despite taking a short cut they finally arrived, exhausted and hungry, at the castle that, once again, looked spooky in the darkness. Eddie looked around anxiously for Micki. But there was no sign of her. "Where can she be?" he thought to himself.

The old pedlar was very grateful for the ride and she offered Freddie a pail of fresh water and a manger of sweet apples and molasses. The mule was not only hungry and tired, but extremely thirsty as well so he readily followed the old woman into the barn built into the castle wall. But as soon as the animal started to slake his raging thirst, she locked the barn door behind him.

"Why are you barring the barn door?" asked Eddie in alarm.

"To protect the mule from marauding wolves that are known to roam these parts at night," she answered with a toothless grin. "Don't look so worried, son. He'll be all right!"

"Well, actually, I'm more worried about my friend who stayed behind to guard our belongings. She is nowhere to be seen. We left her here while we went in search of victuals and help in repairing our cart," explained Eddie, peering through the darkness and calling his friend's name.

The old woman tried to console Eddie with regard to his missing friend, "Cats like to roam around at night and she'll likely come home to nap when she's good and tired. Come on into my parlor, my boy, and rest a while."

But Eddie felt uneasy as he knew his friend well, and it was not like her to wander alone in strange places after dark—especially if she could hear marauding wolves nearby. Eddie also felt a little uncomfortable about leaving Freddie locked alone in the barn. Then a new fear tightened his throat, "How did you know my friend was a cat?" he asked the old woman, suspicion stiffening his voice.

"Oh, you must have mentioned it along the way," said the pedlar, looking nervously at the balking bear.

MYSTERIOUS REALMS

Fatigue and gnawing hunger had made Eddie feel faint so he accepted the woman's invitation into her castle room for refreshments. He was easily tempted with the promise of a plate of chocolate-covered biscuits and a glass of warm milk with honey. He yielded as the woman took hold of his arm and led him inside, "I bet choccy-biccies are your favourites, if I know little bears!" she chuckled.

He thought she was smart to guess that! He wasted no time in delving into the plateful of biscuits and chugalugging the glass of sweet milk which she set on the table before him in the dingy little room.

But, no sooner had he smacked his lips and burped in satisfaction than he heard the click of the key turning in the lock of the stout, wooden door behind him.

He spun around to challenge her and demanded to be let out. But the woman was nowhere to be seen, Instead, a big, frightful rook spread its wings with a scream and came at him with its huge, grey beak gaping open.

Eddie suddenly realized with terror what had happened. "You, nasty, deceiving old witch!" he cried, raising his arms trying to protect himself from the sharp, prodding beak.

She chased him around the room, pecking mercilessly at his eyes until he charged into a big iron-barred cage for safety and pulled the door shut against the savage bird. But then, immediately, the rook turned into the hag again and turned the big key in the lock of the cage and cackled.

"Ha, ha, ha, ha! I'm the Wicked Witch of the Woods (WWW for short). I prey on animals for body parts used in my deadly potions," she laughed.

Eddie was mortified, petrified, stupefied, and terrified of what would happen next!

The witch went over to a big vat of something she was boiling over a large fireplace. As she stirred the brewing mixture, she chanted over it:

"Double trouble, boil and bubble...," she cackled. "Now, let me see. I've already added Wart of Toad, Tongue of Frog, and Ear of Bat so now I just need—Wool of Bear, Eyes of Mule, and Heart of Cat!"

Eddie listened in horror and thought of poor Freddie the Mule locked in the barn who was about to lose his eyes. He thought about Micki the Cat who at this very moment may be imprisoned somewhere inside this castle and destined to lose her heart—if she hadn't lost it already!

He jumped to the back of the cage in panic as the WWW came at him with a huge, sharp straight razor to shave off his woolly fur for her brew. Unable to reach him through the bars, she started to open the cage, but he put up a good fight and almost escaped, so she cursed him angrily and turned herself into a poisonous viper and slithered through the bars towards him. Eddie dodged and kicked at her as she tried to bite him hoping to paralyze him with the venom dripping from her hollow fangs. She almost got him, but he dodged just in time!

Just as she was about to strike again, there came a terrible banging crash from the barn! Freddie had kicked down the door and escaped!

The viper slithered out of the cage and turned back into a hag again. She was in a fury as she flung open the door and charged out of the castle to investigate.

While she was gone, Eddie saw his chance of escape too. The witch had left the door of the room open. He desperately tried to pick the lock on his cage with his claws, but he couldn't budge it. Glancing through the open door he caught a glimpse of Freddie passing by at top speed. Eddie yelled to the mule to go fetch the constable. Freddie turned his head to look for Eddie and saw him trapped in a cage. He reared and whinnied and then galloped off. Eddie hoped he was smart enough and brave enough to fetch help.

※

After the Wicked Witch of the Woods ran off in pursuit of Freddie, Eddie slumped back in his cell trying hard to think what he could do to help himself escape. He thought of Micki again and hoped she had not been captured. If only he could be sure.

As the bear sat and pondered in the mouldy old cage, he became aware a dark, irregular shape in the dimly-lit far corner of the room. He peered through the bars and tried to discern the odd shape. As his eyes adjusted, he identified a large, black rat sat in a rocking chair calmly reading a huge tome by candlelight. Eddie squinted to read the title printed clearly on the cover: *The Beginner's Book of Magic Spells*.

"Hey, rat!" yelled Eddie. "Can you do me a favour?"

MYSTERIOUS REALMS

The young rodent stopped reading and looked over his spectacles at the imprisoned animal. "Who are you calling 'rat'!" he said haughtily, "I do have a name you know!"

"Oh, I beg your pardon, no offence!" apologized the bear. "And what would that be?"

"What would what be?" said the rat.

"Your name, sir!" said Eddie, trying to stay calm, "What is your name?"

"Royston!" exclaimed the rat, turning back to his book.

"Good lord!" scoffed Eddie in disbelief.

"What's that you said?" snarled the rat, narrowing his beady eyes at the bear.

"Er…Good, m'lord!" stammered Eddie, quickly realizing that this was *not* the time for an argument, "Good, noble name that…Royston. If I had a boy, I'd call him…er…Royston." Eddie paused to think of his next move. "I say, *Royston,* old chap, you wouldn't care to do me a favour would you?"

The rat peered over his wire-rimmed spectacles at the bear behind bars and ventured in a raspy voice, "What's in it for me?"

"Well, I'll 'Like' you on Physog-book, and…and 'Friend' you," suggested Eddie.

Royston sneered and set the chair to rocking vigorously as he flipped over another page of the illuminated book of spells.

"Or, I'll give you my life savings," said Eddie in desperation, fully aware of just how little his net worth really was.

"I've got everything I need right here," said Royston, waving his hand to indicate the room in a show of nonchalance, "The old lady takes pretty good care of me—plenty of good food, a wizard's outfit, warm bed.

"So, you must be very contented, then?" said Eddie, trying to think of a way to use the rat to his advantage.

"No, actually I'm not," said the rat bluntly.

"Why?" asked Eddie, "Do you have to slave hard for your keep?"

"No, not really," said Royston matter-of-factly. "I just help her with magic concoctions. She's teaching me to become a great magician!"

"How exciting! So, you're a sorcerer's apprentice, then?" said Eddie, trying to sound impressed while an idea was secretly forming in his brain.

"You might say that," said the young rat, looking proud of himself. "I *should* be happy, all my needs are met and I'm on a promising career track, but something important seems to be missing in my life."

"Hhmm…that's too bad," Eddie said. After a minute, while the rat muttered a few partial spells as he read, the bear queried archly, "I suppose you already know how to cast *some* spells?"

"Yeah, but I don't get to practice the really cool ones, the old witch won't let me," said Royston, sounding quite vexed.

"Well, she's not here now, and I'd like to see you do something *really* clever," said Eddie.

"Oh, would you!" said the rat, chucking the book on the floor and jumping to his feet with a toothy grin curling the lips of his scrawny, long snout. "Like what f'r instance?"

"Well," said Eddie, pretending to think, "like say, making the big, brass key turn in this lock on my cage."

"Oh, piece of cake, kiddo! I could do *that*! Stand back! I'll show you just how clever I am!" And so, the budding magician pushed up the floppy sleeves of his sparkly blue robe, adjusted his wizard's hat and grabbed his wand off the nearby table.

Eddie held his breath and stood poised behind the door of his cage ready for action should his plan work. Royston wasted no time in getting the spell underway. He waved his wand and chanted:

"Abracadabra, A-B-C, one-two-three, in that lock, turn that key!"

They waited with bated breath, but nothing happened. The apprentice tried again.

Abracadabra, one-two-three, A-B-C, in this lock, turn this KEY!"

Nothing!

Royston repeated his efforts a few more times with the same result—or lack thereof. Eddie was afraid the rat, now red in the face with humiliation, would lose his temper and give up, or maybe do something worse! So, the clever little bear frantically racked his brains until a light bulb went on.

"I say, Royston, I bet it's because I'm watching. What if I closed my eyes so that I couldn't *see* what was happening?"

The rat saw a face-saving way to salvage his dignity and make the spell 'work'. "Good idea!" he said, "Yes, that's the problem! That key don't like being watched by a 'septic'! Close your eyes real tight and no peeking, mind!"

"I think you mean 'skeptic' muttered Eddie, hurriedly complying by putting his paws over his eyes. However, he was careful to leave a little gap where he could peep out to watch what he hoped would happen. He wasn't disappointed.

"Right!" said Royston, coming very close to the cage door, "Habracadabra, you can't see, how in this lock, I turn this key!" chanted the sly rat as he stealthily stretched out both paws and turned the heavy key in the lock until it clicked. "Voila!" shouted Royston triumphantly, flinging the door wide open to prove his success.

"Bravo!" said Eddie, clapping his paws together as he stepped out of the cage, "Let me shake your hand, my good man!" And before the rat knew what was happening, Eddie grasped the rodent's paw and flung him head over heels into the cage, slammed the door shut, and turned the key—which he then tossed across the room. "Smart trick, Ratty! Have a nice day!"

The rat jumped up and down screaming in rage as he flung himself at the bars, "Let me out!" "I'll get you for this!" he yelled as Eddie ran out the castle. "The old hag will kill me when she finds out! Come back here!"

But Eddie was on a roll and not stopping for anything. He had to find his friends. But where to look? And where, and in what form, was the dangerous old witch?

༺༻

Meanwhile, the Wicked Witch of the West was fully occupied chasing after Freddie who was running for his life. First, she turned herself into a lion as she chased after him. But his adrenaline was pumping, and he raced so fast that she couldn't keep up, so she morphed herself into a dragon and flew after him. As she hovered over his galloping form, she tried to grab hold of him with her talons, but he was too heavy to lift into the air, so she let him go. She came at him a second time trying to remember a spell that would turn him into a fieldmouse. She was poised ready to pounce on his rump when the desperate mule lashed out with his hind hooves and smacked the dragon on its chin breaking her jaw and sending her somersaulting to the ground.

Freddie, panting so hard he was afraid his heart would burst, could run no more. He stood gasping for breath while watching in trembling dread as the dragon, beside herself with anger, slowly morphed into the old hag again. His sides heaving, he backed away as she crawled to her feet and gave him a hellish glare, mumbling a spell that sent a strange quiver through his whole being. But with her injury, she couldn't chant properly anymore. Reeling from the shock of the savage kick, she turned slowly on her heel and tottered off back down the road towards the castle to nurse her wounds; her jaw hanging loosely and jiggling as she walked.

Poor Freddie felt bad in a way, he had never hurt a fly in his life—well, maybe he'd swatted at a few blue-bottles with his tail but….

The kind-hearted equine thought maybe he should follow the witch back to the castle and try to patch things up and maybe negotiate Eddie's release—Micki's too if she was imprisoned there. But he didn't know if the witch had the power to heal herself and come after him again. He didn't dare trust her too much. As he walked along the ditch keeping a healthy distance behind the WWW, he started to feel very strange—a little dizzy. Everything around him seemed to be growing bigger. The grass became so tall it towered above his head. The pebbles on the road looked like big boulders.

It was getting quite dark now as the sun had long since sunk below the horizon and the moon was not quite ready to walk the night in her 'silver shoon'. He pushed his way through the weeds and grasses wishing he had a machete to clear the way.

૭૭

As Freddie pondered deep and weary, an owl swooped low over his head. He ducked and then reared up ready to fight what he thought was the witch in the form of an owl. The large owl swooped noiselessly over the mule again. Freddie leapt away sure it was the witch. "Remember how well I can use my hooves, old woman!" warned the mule, every nerve of his body taut as a bow string.

The witch's spell to turn the Freddie into a fieldmouse was taking its effect on the old equine. But because she had been unable to utter the spell properly, the effect was only partial. So, although he became the *size* of a fieldmouse, he was still in the form of a mule. The barn owl saw him jumping around in the grassy ditch and thought he was a mouse, albeit a strange looking one. After making a few low passes to check him out, the owl caught the funny creature in his talons and took him back to his house in the woods to take a closer look.

Freddie hung helplessly trapped in the sharp talons of the large owl, sure that he was in the clutches of the witch and hence, doomed beyond hope.

Arriving at his treehouse deep in the forest, the barn owl set Freddie down on the flat part of a tree branch and stared at him in wonder. The owl's mate came out of the house to see what had been brought home for dinner. "What is that, Tyto?" she asked quizzically, "It doesn't look like a vole or a mouse."

The couple took Freddie inside their house for a closer look in better lighting.

"Weird isn't it?" said Tyto, "Perhaps we shouldn't eat it?"

"No, it might make us sick," said Alba, his mate. "Throw it away before our children see it, then go out and catch something *else* for supper!"

Freddie's eyes were popping out of his head, "Hey! I'm a mule! I'm not for eating!" he frantically squeaked in a tiny voice, "And if you throw me to the ground, I'll be killed!"

"You can't be a mule, you're too small!" said the barn owl, startled by this sudden outburst. "But you can't be a mouse either because you're too… well…weird looking. Tell me truthfully, are you a mule or a mouse?"

"What difference does it make? I'm toast either way!" wailed Freddie. "I was bewitched by a wicked witch and shrunk," explained Freddie, hoping they would take pity on him.

"Well, I'm not convinced. I'll have to look into this business further," murmured Tyto, donning his reading glasses and reaching for one of his encyclopaedias. "Now, let me see what is says here about bewitched mules and strange mice."

Freddie was glad that at least he'd had a temporary reprieve. He tried to make himself comfortable as he could in the little wicker basket that they had popped him into. He could only hope that some miracle would save him.

☙

It had been some time since Micki had awakened from her strange dream-like experience. She had become very worried about the prolonged absence of her two friends and so had set out from the camp to look for them. Not seeing them on the road despite covering a few miles, she had strayed into the woods thinking they may have gone there. But even though she wandered around for hours calling their names, they were nowhere to be found.

Presently, darkness fell. The little cat realized it was futile to search any longer. Not wanting to be in a strange forest at night, she decided to go back to the camp but as she turned to retrace her steps, a morbid fear seized her; she didn't know the way out of the unfamiliar woods in the dark!

Micki wandered aimlessly around the forest trying first this path and then that. Her ears twitched at every little sound, her eyes bulged to see her way through the spectre-like trees where little pairs of eyes seemed to be twinkling in and out of existence. Dejected, tired, cold, and hungry, she finally gave up and sat and mewed pitifully.

Mrs. Barn Owl had become impatient with her husband who preferred to study his books rather than to go and hunt for supper. She scolded him mercilessly, "Our children are starving while you sit there reading!" she screeched, flapping her wings in his face until he snapped his book shut and flew off again into the familiar night.

He hadn't gone far when he heard a strange mewling sound. He perched on a large branch. He spun his head this way and that, his huge eyes scanning the dark undergrowth of the forest trying to identify the source of the strange sound. He spotted what he believed to be four white mice. Feeling lucky, he swooped down to grab one but was surprised when it sprouted claws that ripped at his feathers. He flew back up to the tree branch and contemplated the issue. "Well, this is a night of strange events," said Tyto to himself. "First a mule-mouse and now a lion-mouse!" It was all very puzzling, but the owl liked to exercise his five wits by having puzzles to solve. He decided to investigate and upon closer scrutiny, he realized that these white mice were attached to a bigger creature.

After pondering deeply and asking the stranger some well-conceived questions, Tyto discovered that this new creature was called a cat, and this particular one, who had white paws, had become lost in the wood while searching for her friends: a teddy bear and a mule. Micki told the inquisitive owl how they had gone missing while looking for help, and now, not only was she afraid for their well-being, she was lost too!

MYSTERIOUS REALMS

"Well," said Tyto after listening intently to Micki's story. "This is a sorry state of affairs but, as luck will have it, I may have some information for you." And so, he told her about the funny-looking non-mouse he had found. He extended an invitation to Micki to follow him back to his tree to see the peculiar creature. Micki wasn't interested in peculiar creatures at that moment and politely declined the invitation.

But the duty-minded owl assured her that she could rest in safety with his family while he flew around the countryside in search of her friends. He explained that he knew the neighbourhood very well, could cover much more ground than she, *and* could see further in the dark. Micki saw the sense in this and so, agreed. Tyto led the cat to his tree home and introduced her to his wife and children. But before Mr. Barn Owl took to the night sky on his mission, he wanted to show his visitor the funny thing they had stashed in the wicker basket.

"We put him in a basket for safe-keeping," said Alba to Micki, "The children are most curious about it and keep lifting the lid to peek at him."

"Go and take a look," said Tyto. So, Micki allowed the baby owlets to lead her by the paw to see the mysterious creature.

Micki peered down into the container and couldn't believe her eyes. "Freddie?!" she yelped in disbelief. She stared in shock. "Freddie, is that really you? It's me, Micki!"

"How do I know you're not the wicked witch in disguise?" said Freddie, his tiny voice tense with suspicion.

The Highland cat said, "Honestly, Freddie, it's me, your friend."

"Prove it!" said the stubborn mule, not taking any chances.

"Well, how do you want me to do that?" said the little cat.

Freddie thought for a moment then said, "What was I at Weston-Super-Mare?"

The reply was a little while in coming. Then came the hesitant answer, "A Stick-in-the-Mud?"

"Hmmmm.... That's not quite the answer I was hoping for, but it does a ring of truth to it. Hee-haw! Micki!" he brayed, now convinced. "How wonderful to see you again! You're not a prisoner of the old crone after all! But what are you doing out here in the dark woods all alone?"

So, Micki told him how Tyto had found her wandering lost in the woods and that he'd offered to help find her friends. "Speaking of which," she said, "where on earth is Eddie and why are you so *small*?"

Freddie was reluctant to give all the scary details of their capture, but Micki insisted on being told everything. So, the mule patiently explained all that had happened since he and Eddie had gone off in search of help at the farms. Micki and the owls listened in wonder and concern. Micki's heart stopped when she heard of Eddie's being held captive.

Everyone agreed that there was no time to be wasted. Eddie was in big trouble and they had to rescue him from the clutches of the WWW at the castle without further delay.

It was decided that Tyto would guide Micki back to the castle while he gently carried Freddie in his talons. However, just as they were getting ready to leave the treehouse, the spell on Freddie began to wear off! He felt himself starting to grow!

"Get me on the ground quickly!" he yelled. "I'm starting to get big again and I don't want to become full-size up a tree!

Tyto wasted no time in picking up the little, quivering mule and flying him safely to the ground—and just in time, for once on the ground, Freddie immediately became full-size again.

He shook himself, and then said to Micki, "Quick, hop on my back and hold on tight—but watch the claws!" They galloped away while Tyto flew a little ahead to guide them out of the woods and to the castle.

༄

Meanwhile, back at the castle, Eddie couldn't find Micki around the meadow, but he did find her sketches that showed her encounter with the witch as a rook and as a pedlar-woman. So now, fearing that she had been captured and imprisoned in the castle, he screwed his 'courage to the sticking place' and crept back to the ruins in hope of finding a secret entrance to the dungeons where he assumed Micki would have been taken. He stopped and stood on tiptoe to look through the little window of the witch's room whence came quite a commotion. He was astonished and dismayed to see the old crone, now with a bandage around her chin, chasing little Royston madly around the room with a fly swat. The poor rat was screaming in terror as he ducked and dodged the flailing weapon begging for mercy and forgiveness. Eddie was sympathetic, he didn't like to see a fellow animal treated so cruelly, but he felt powerless to help.

More anxious than ever, the distraught bear snuck back into the castle through a little side door that stood ajar further along the stone wall. Some stone steps led down into a tunnel. He crept along the dark passage in which he found himself and called out his friend's name as loudly as he dared. No response was heard. He wished his hearing was better; perhaps Micki was too weak to meow or perhaps she was gagged. "Micki! Micki, my dear friend, where are you?" he whispered loudly.

After spending what seemed forever, going down passages and up and down stone spiral staircases, and in and out of creepy cells, he was no closer to learning of his friend's whereabouts than before. Not only that, but a new fear gripped him as he realized that he was so turned around he had no sense of direction anymore. He couldn't find his way back out of the castle!

He was just on the point of panic when he heard a sobbing whimper coming from somewhere nearby. He could see a glimmer of something like metal in the dim, intermittent moonlight that crept through cracks in the masonry. Certain that it was Micki, he tried to hurry towards the sound calling softly, "Micki? Micki, is that you? It's me Eddie." The bear stumbled around in the damp darkness his paws outstretched trying to feel his way, but the whimpering had ceased again. "Micki?" he said tentatively. But there was no reply.

Eddie's heart started to thump hard and fast. Perhaps it wasn't Micki after all! But then, who or what was it? Fear gripped him so hard he felt faint. Something shuffled near his feet. Sweat started to trickle down his fur and the hair on the back of his neck stood up. The sniffling sob came again. He wished he could see, and then the moon obliged by sending a beam of bright silvery light to pull back the mantle of darkness. The delicate light glinted off the steel bars of a small cage. Then, two tiny eyes caught the moonshine and sparkled for a second.

"Royston!?" said Eddie in total shock. "Royston—is that you?"

"Uh-huh," came the feeble affirmation. "Are you the bear I set free?"

"Yes! Did she put you in here as punishment for helping me escape?" asked Eddie while somewhat fearful that this might be simply another trick of the witch and not really the rat at all.

"She was so mad at what I'd done," continued the frail voice. "She beat me with the fly swat and told me I was stupid and useless and would *never* be a magician," sniffled the rat, wiping his paw across his snotty nose. "She burned my cap and robe and broke my wand. Then she locked me in this cage and told me she'd leave me here to die of hunger and thirst."

"Wicked old witch!" said Eddie, genuinely moved at the rat's plight. He then remembered Micki again and asked in a very deep, stern voice, "Tell me the truth, hand on heart, Royston, is she holding a cat here as a prisoner?"

Royston shook his head. "I don't think so," he said, sounding quite honest, "At least I've not seen one. It's just you and me here now that the mule has escaped."

Eddie took a deep sigh of relief at this news. He was glad Micki wasn't a captive, but he was still greatly concerned for her safety. He needed to think carefully at this new turn of events. He not only didn't know where his friends were, he didn't even know where *he* was. An idea came into his head.

"Listen, Royston!" he said, bending his face close to the rat, "are you willing to make a deal?"

The rat nodded, a ray of hope brightening his doleful eyes.

Eddie continued, "I'll set you free if you promise to show me the way out of here—deal?"

The rat nodded again, a look of eager compliance animating his pathetic countenance. Eddie wasted no time in deftly picking the little lock with his claw. Royston stepped to freedom and shook himself like a dog.

"Let's get out of here!" growled Eddie. "Which way do we go?"

"Hold on to my tail," said the rat, "I know this place like the back of my hand."

"Make sure we don't run into the witch!" said the bear, suddenly remembering the danger that could be lurking around every corner.

☙

Right about this time, Micki, Freddie, and Tyto finally arrived at the castle. They waited in the shadows of the great stone walls avoiding the light of the now unclouded moon. All was quiet and still. After a while, when they were sure there was no-one about, they crept up to the lighted window and looked inside. All they could see was the old woman sitting in the rocking chair. She had a big bandage tying up her broken jaw and she moaned miserably as she rocked 'to and fro'. There was no sign of Eddie. The big cage was empty!

"Maybe he escaped too?" said Freddie optimistically.

"Perhaps I should try and sneak in there and have a look around," said Micki, secretly wishing she didn't have to, but would do anything to save her best friend.

"I think it's too dangerous, Micki," said Tyto wisely. "It might be better to go for help?"

Micki was in a desperate dilemma, "Perhaps we can lure the witch out of the castle somehow and then I can slip in unnoticed?" she suggested.

But Tyto shook his head gravely, "I think Eddie likely got away since he's nowhere to be seen in there," he considered. "Maybe he escaped and ran off into the woods to hide?"

"Then he'll be lost for sure!" said Freddie.

"Why don't I fly out to the woods and over the fields to see if I can spot him?" said Tyto, already stretching his wings. All agreed. So, off he went noiselessly into the night.

☙

At this moment, unbeknownst to the others, Eddie was with Royston trying to find the way out of the dank, smelly dungeons. Eddie caught the faint glint of something hanging on the damp wall. It was an ancient halberd. He grabbed it to use in case they encountered the witch along the way. Thus armed, the bear and rat stumbled their way through the maze of crooked passages and crumbling staircases.

"Are you sure you know your way out as well as you bragged you did?" asked Eddie, losing confidence with every dead-end they reached.

Royston didn't want to admit to not having a clue where the door to the outside was, but luckily, he eventually did stumble upon a small hole in the crumbling brick work of the outside wall.

"We can squeeze through here," said the rat, thankful for the miracle. And he immediately wriggled his slender frame through the opening and landed with a light plop on the grass a foot or so below.

For Eddie, it was not so easy a task. He had misgivings as he sized up the hole and then his waistline. First, he passed the halberd out through the hole and Royston grabbed it.

"Come on!" said Royston in a loud whisper, "We haven't got any time to lose!"

Eddie valiantly put his head and arms through the restricted space. His shoulders and chest got through with some effort, but then he was stuck! "Drat! I knew it!" he spat. He looked at the rat indignantly, "Okay, idiot! Don't just stand there staring, give me a pull!" he growled.

Royston grabbed the pudgy arms and pulled for all he was worth, but he couldn't budge the bear more than an inch or two forward. "You're going to have to slide back," said the rodent.

"I'm not going to be sliding anywhere!" wailed poor Eddie. "I can't move backwards or forwards."

But suddenly, from his somewhat inglorious vantage point, Eddie spotted an owl coming towards them. He yelled to his buddy, "Quick, hide! It's the wicked witch turned into an owl and she's coming after us!"

Royston swivelled to face the attacker. He snatched the halberd from the ground and waved it wildly at the oncoming raptor. "Get away! You, ugly beast!" shrieked the rat savagely.

Tyto barely managed to swerve to avoid being hit. He had just embarked on his mission when he had heard the little voices near the base of the castle wall. Swooping in for a closer inspection, he was astonished to see a half-bear protruding from the stones and a rat brandishing a dangerous weapon.

"Whoa! Steady on feller!" called out Tyto in alarm, "You might hurt somebody with that!"

But Royston was not letting up, and Eddie screamed as loud as he could while flailing his arms uselessly.

Micki and Freddie heard the commotion and came running around to that side of the castle to see what was going on. They were horrified to see what they thought was a rat attacking Eddie stuck in a wall and Tyto flapping around in the air beating his wings and screeching, desperate to defend himself against the rat. Micki bravely went for the rat's legs. Royston was terrified and confused with so many strangers coming at him. Freddie didn't know whom to kick first, and Eddie was mortified at being stuck in a hole with everyone around him going mad!

"FREEZE!!!" screamed Eddie. Everyone froze their action. Silence! "Just…everyone calm-down! And for pity's sake get me out of here so we can all talk sense!"

All the creatures took a deep breath and mumbled apologies to one another. Micki took the halberd and used it to pry some of the rotting masonry apart until her friend could crawl out. Eddie stood there dusting himself off. "Now," said Eddie calmly, "Why don't we go and sit down so that everyone can introduce themselves politely."

They all walked over to the pony-trap and sat on the blankets Micki spread on the ground for them. After they had all introduced themselves, they discussed everything that had happened to date and what they should do next.

Royston, who was now disillusioned with the witch and her wickedness, sat brooding quietly until he surprised everyone with an announcement: "I'm ready to spill the beans on what I know about the old witch and her scam!" Now that he had everyone's close attention he began to explain. He told how the old woman had devised a 'get rich quick' scheme for herself. "She cleverly mixed a magic poisonous brew that she put into bottles," continued the rat. "Then, at night, she secretly poured the poison into the farmers' wells."

The listeners held their breath.

The young rat went on, "When the water turned deadly, the farms became virtually worthless. With their water now poisonous, the famers had to walk away from their property and the land was useless. Then, when the farmers were desperate for a buyer, she offered them rock-bottom prices and bought the abandoned land for a song."

"But if the farms were useless, what would she gain from buying them?" said Eddie.

"Ah!" said Royston, "Once she had the deeds to all the farms, she planned on mixing the antidote brew and making the water pure again."

"Then she would be able to resell the land at inflated prices to make huge profits!" said Micki.

"A well-construed scam!" said Freddie in disgust.

They were all astounded at Royston's revelation. They gasped as the full impact of the story hit them. 'My, how wicked she was!' They all exclaimed.

"And did you know all this and keep quiet about it?" said Tyto accusingly to the rat.

Royston nodded, hanging his head in shame. "Yes!" he admitted, "I even helped her stir the brew sometimes."

"Oh, how could you!" said the others.

"She said there was a big reward in it for me. For *me!* Some way to make my mark in life!" said the rat defensively. "You see, I'd never had anything of my own. I was from a big family and orphaned at an early age; a farmer poisoned my mother and his dog killed my father. I was bitterly resentful towards farmers."

The others began to feel sorry for the poor little chap.

Royston continued, "I had no future until the witch took me in. She fed and clothed me and promised to train me to be a great magician! Now I had a chance to be somebody!"

Eddie pursed his lips, "I sympathize with your plight, Royston, yet it's no excuse for cheating folk."

"Too true! Causing harm to others is no way to make your mark in life, young feller-me-lad," grunted Tyto authoritatively.

"I know that now," sniffed the youngster. "She never cared about me really. She just used me for her own ends." Royston choked back a sob and wiped his eyes with a dirty paw.

"Well, perhaps you can make amends by helping us now to turn the witch over to the authorities," said Tyto sternly.

"Yes! But wait a minute!" said Micki handing Royston a clean hankie. "You said she was going to prepare an antidote to the poison and restore the wells once she owned them?"

"That's right!" said Royston, blowing his nose.

"Well, that means there is a recipe for the antidote *somewhere*, so if we could find it, maybe we could prepare the remedy and purify the water ourselves?" said Micki, feeling quite excited.

Royston nodded. "I know where she keeps the *Big Book of Antidotes*," he said. "But first, we need to get her out of that room!"

MYSTERIOUS REALMS

☙

They went to the window to see what the old crone was doing. She was rocking back and forth in the creaky chair mumbling to herself while reading from a book.

"I recognize that book she's reading," said Royston. "It's chants for healing injuries."

"What is the charm telling her to do?" asked Micki.

"I can't see the page clearly enough to read," said Royston, standing on Eddie's shoulders and pushing his long rodent nose against the windowpane.

"I could fly up onto the roof and peep through that little chink in the rotting rafters," suggested Tyto. "I have keen eyesight and should be able to read the print."

Everyone agreed that was a great idea.

So, up he flew silently and perched on the roof. After a minute or so he flew back down looking very solemn. For a while, he stood with his face averted from the group and refrained from answering their eager questions. Then at last he spoke. "It says that to cure a broken jaw, she needs to boil the beak and bones of a freshly killed owl, then grind them up and mix them with its blood, then smear the mixture on the jaw. With this, mending of the jawbone is guaranteed."

Everyone stood in stunned silence. Tyto was the first to speak. "I will act as a lure to get her out. Hopefully, she will morph into the rook again, or at least a creature I can handle."

The others were reluctant to let him do it as it was too risky. But there seemed to be no other way.

Taking a deep breath, Tyto went up to the window screeched and danced around tapping his beak on the glass. His antics immediately caught the old crone's attention and her eyes widened like saucers, in joyful surprise. "What luck!" she thought aloud.

She tossed aside the book and wrapped her shawl over her head and shoulders and ran towards the door. Tyto got ready for fight or flight. Then the hag did something totally unexpected. She reached her hand up for something above the door. Suddenly, she flung the door open and stood a moment silhouetted against the light, in her hands was a long gun with a night-scope attached.

Tyto shrieked off into the darkness of the forest. The animals watched in horror as she ran after him with the gun at her shoulder.

BANG! BANG! Then a morbid silence, heavy with the acrid stink of gunpowder, crept around them. The animals stood paralyzed in dread and shock!

It was the young rat that came to his senses first. He insisted that they had to carry out their plan no matter what had happened. Indeed, Tyto's life would have been lost in vain if they failed. Royston wasted no time in dashing into the castle room to look for the book of antidotes. Eddie ran and grabbed the halberd off the ground and joined Micki and Freddie already standing guard at the open door—the friends were ready to fight to the death if the witch returned before Royston came out with the book.

After a few anxious minutes which dragged liked hours, Royston emerged from the room with a large tome in his arms. They all ran and hid under blankets in the applecart. They had no sooner buried themselves under the cover to keep watch, when the old witch came out of the woods dragging along something bulky wrapped her shawl. A chill ran down each of their spines, a lump stuck in each of their throats, and tears stung their eyes as they watched the hag go into the castle and close the door behind her.

"We can't stand here and let her mutilate the body of our brave and trusted friend," said Micki. She thought of his mate, Alba, and all his babies that were waiting patiently for him to return with supper to feed the hungry mouths that depended on him—their loving husband and caring father.

"There're four of us and only one of her," said Freddie, ready for action.

"But she has magic powers to use against us!" said Eddie, all a-dither.

"Perhaps she's losing power because she can't utter chants with her broken jaw," reasoned Royston.

"We have to go and see what she is doing," said Micki, throwing off her blanket.

"I can't bear to look!" said Eddie, but he followed Micki anyway.

They sidled up to the window again and carefully looked through the dirty glass.

"She seems quite weak and faint," said Micki. "Running after Tyto must have taken the last of her strength."

MYSTERIOUS REALMS

"We have to rush the room," said Royston, "and catch her by surprise."

"Hopefully she didn't lock the door behind her," said Eddie.

"I don't think she did," said Freddie.

The gang put their heads together to devise a plan.

It was decided unanimously that they would all pounce on her at once and wrestle her to the ground. Micki would use her claws, Freddie his hooves, and Royston his sharp teeth while Eddie would grab the shawl containing Tyto's body and run out the door with it and hide. As soon as they believed Eddie was safely hidden, they would release the hag, and all run off. They agreed they would take Tyto back to his house and family with Micki and Freddie leading the way they now knew through the forest. However, the gang dreaded having to present the body of Tyto to his wife and children and explain what had happened.

Summoning every ounce of courage, they stood in a tight group outside the door. In unison, they whispered, "Ready, steady, GO! and burst into the room! At first, everything went according to plan. They quickly and easily knocked the old witch to the floor. Micki leapt on her shoulders and dug her claws into the flesh, Royston sunk his fangs into her ankles, and Freddie planted his hooves on her chest pinning her to the ground. She struggled a while and groaned eerily. Then something very strange started to happen. Instead of fighting, she began to relax and go quite limp. She started to shrink and then slowly fade away—quite literally!

The four stared in astonishment as they watched her melting away beneath them. They jumped back and covered their faces as an evil, greyish mist arose from her disintegrating body. The entire body of the hag evaporated into a thick cloud that drifted through the open door and dispersed into nothingness—hopefully, never to be seen again!

The animals stared after it in wonder and then they looked at each other and gave a little shiver.

Suddenly, Royston's voice startled everyone, "Bing, bong! The witch is dead!" he shouted, jumping up and down waving his arms. The others cheered and clapped.

But the rejoicing was cut short when they remembered the lumpy shawl lying on the table. Eddie and Micki went over to it and opened it up and gently revealed Tyto's limp body. Their feathered friend lay there so still and lifeless. They looked at his placid, white, heart-shaped face. They stroked his splendid feathers carefully avoiding the single drop of blood that had beaded on his breast.

Royston and Freddie came and stared; their heads bowed in respect. Freddie said, "Maybe we should say a few words over him?"

"Yes, I think we owe it to him," said Micki.

But no one knew what to say. Eddie looked around at them all, cleared his throat and began in his most solemn voice, "Dearly beloved, we are gathered here to say goodbye…"

"Wait a minute!" Royston gasped, "Just hold on a bit!"

The others turned and glared at him, frowning at the disrespectful interruption.

Eddie stopped his oratory and growled, "Well, what is it, young fellow?"

"I have an idea!" said the rat, wrinkling his brow deep in thought.

"Well, what is it? Eddie said. "Spit it out man or hold your tongue!"

"It may not work, but it's worth a try," said the rat, looking very contemplative.

"What is?" shouted the others annoyed.

"A magic spell that returns life to good souls who have just departed," said Royston, his eyes bright.

The others exchanged quick glances.

Micki said, "Go on!"

Royston ran to the dishevelled mound of ancient books heaped in a corner of the room. He flung volume after volume aside as he searched frantically for what he needed.

"Here it is!" he said picking up a dusty, leather-bound tome. He spread the old book open on the table and ruffled through the yellowed pages. "This is it!" he said stopping at an ethereal painting with a verse under it. He read it out loud.

> There is a wonderful thing,
>
> That gold cannot buy,
>
> A blessing that's rare and true,
>
> Sincere love of family and friends

MYSTERIOUS REALMS

Shedding tears of sorrow true,

Planting their kisses one by one,

On the corpse just turned blue,

Gives the gift of wonderful life,

Like the life we wish for you.

The four little creatures grinned with joy. They all chanted the poem as they each placed a gentle kiss on Tyto's soft, feathered brow and let a heartfelt tear fall and trickle into the depths of his plumage.

They then stood back and waited, their hearts pregnant with hope.

After some minutes, as they watched in silent pleading to the Great Universe for a magical resurrection, a most peculiar thing started to happen.

The little bead of blood on Tyto's chest began to morph into a tiny, heart-shaped ruby. Then Tyto's chest started to rise and fall with life-breath. His wings began to twitch, then his eyes opened wide like large, gold-rimmed black orbs that shone with the spark of life.

The four watched in awestruck delight as the owl turned his head this way and that to peer deeply into the eyes of his friends. He blinked once or twice and then sat upright.

"Where are we?" he asked in bewilderment. "What on earth's going on?"

"We're in the old castle and we're all safe. You're alive again!" They all chimed as they danced a happy little country jig. Tyto sat in wonder watching the spectacle until he was able to join in too.

༄

The fully recovered owl was soon flying home to his treehouse. He carried some morsels of food Royston had found in the room with which to feed his family. Safely home again, he told his anxious family some of what had happened. They listened quite dumbfounded. Later, while their children were asleep, Tyto told Alba the *whole* story and gave her the ruby heart as a token of his love for her and their owlets. She immediately put it on a silver chain as a pendant that she would always wear around her neck as a constant reminder of his devotion and rebirth.

Back at the castle camp, Eddie, Micki, Freddie, and Royston, all settled down with cozy pillows and blankets to get some much-needed sleep. Tomorrow would be a big day of preparing the antidote and delivering it to all the poisoned farm wells. Royston fell asleep holding on tightly to the *Big Book of Antidotes*.

☙

The next day, the gang of four awakened to warmth and birdsong. They stretched and yawned, then prepared a hearty breakfast from the food Royston retrieved from the kitchen room which had been his home for so long. They rehashed the events of yesterday and wondered how Tyto was doing. The owl had promised to return to their camp the next day to help them with making the remedy. The others were eager to know how his family had reacted when told of the ordeal he had endured.

After eating their fill, Eddie, Micki, Freddie, and Royston, poured over the *Big Book of Antidotes* looking for the remedy they needed to restore the well water. When they eventually found it, it proved to be a very interesting one. They had to create a brew that required many items to be gathered: several kinds of wildflowers, gypsy mushrooms, and cuckoo spit (collected off plants) were needed. These would be stirred into a bowl of pure spring water at midnight under a starry sky. Quartz moonstones had to be collected and arranged on the ground to represent the Big Dipper. The animals were required to sit and concoct the brew under that same constellation.

They were thankful for having Eddie's nature books to help them identify all the items they needed. All agreed that bringing them had been a very good idea.

"I knew my field guides would come in useful," said Eddie proudly. "Never leave home without them!"

The four animals had split into two groups to gather the ingredients. Eddie and Micki wandered around the meadows and woods, searching for the plants and cuckoo spit. Freddie and Royston looked high and low for the rare gypsy mushrooms until they found some in the forest. After a long search, the mule and rat discovered the quartz moonstones in the streambed, and it proved to be quite a scramble to retrieve them from under the rapidly rippling waters.

MYSTERIOUS REALMS

After the sun bid the world goodnight and darkness fell, Tyto arrived on the scene. They were eager to ask him to supply the mournful hoot of an owl which was required to make the new brew vibrate at just the right frequency.

But Tyto had to explain to them that he couldn't hoot.

"But why on earth not?" cried Eddie, "Don't all owls hoot?"

"I'm a barn owl, also known as a screech owl, because instead of hooting, I screech!" explained Tyto.

"So, now what do we do?" said Micki disappointed that, after all their careful preparation, an important ingredient was missing. "Can't you at least try a little hoot or two?"

"Not to worry," said Tyto confidently, "I'll enlist the help of my friend Leo. He's a Long-Eared Owl and has an amazing hoot that will set the water vibrating. I'm sure he'll be glad to help out." And so off he flew to find his feathery friend.

In no time at all, Tyto returned with a big, beautiful owl; speckled and barred with big, golden-rimmed eyes, and feathers that stuck up from the top of his head like big ears.

"He has big ears like Freddie!" laughed everyone.

The animals had a lot of fun identifying the Big Dipper which they found a picture of in Eddie's book. They had never really looked at all the stars before and were quite amazed at just how many there were.

By midnight, they were ready to assemble the glowing moonstones in the pattern of the constellation above them. Then, they stirred the wild plants into the bowl of spring water and added the cuckoo spit. As they mixed the magic potion, they sat and sang the 'Chant for Magic Antidote to Poisoned Water' which went as follows:

> Fill water bowl from bubbling spring,
>
> Then all sit down and form a ring,
>
> Cuckoopint, Coltsfoot, Ladies Slipper,
>
> Stir beneath the sky's Big Dipper,
>
> As above, then so below,
>
> Moonstones, like the stars will glow,

STEPHANIE JONES

> Form a Dipper on the ground,
>
> As owl's mournful hoot doth sound.
>
> Gypsy mushrooms, Shepherd's Purse,
>
> Stir them well, remove the curse,
>
> Add in love and Cuckoo Spit,
>
> Chant the charm now, while you sit.

Then, as they sat around the bowl of spring water and herbs, Leo mesmerized them all with a long, mournful hoot that gave them goosebumps as it set ripples dancing upon the surface of the water. The final ingredient was the healing vibration from chants of love and harmony from the whole group.

༄

The next morning, after a peaceful night's sleep, the gang got up bright and early to begin delivering the antidote to all the farms which had poisoned wells. The day held great promise except for one small thing—they had totally overlooked how they were going to deliver the new brew to where it was needed. They had absolutely no idea.

They thought maybe they could find some clean containers in the old room. These perhaps could be filled and then somehow carried. Someone thought that they could fashion a type of pannier to put on Freddie. Even so, how were they going to be able to walk to all the farms, which were miles apart, carrying a load of water. It was all very distressing, and the strain started to show.

As they rummaged all morning through the rubbishy, jumbled contents of the castle room, cracks in the hitherto friendly alliance began to appear. General irritations with the situation developed into outright bursts of temper.

"That jar won't do, Eddie, use your brain!" said Micki tersely while she considered the potential usefulness of a ladle and saucepan she'd just found.

"Well, it's a good size," retorted the bear, "Better than that silly stuff you've picked out!"

MYSTERIOUS REALMS

"Are you blind or something? Can't you see, it's got sticky goo in the bottom!" she shot back, making a face.

"Yuck! Stupid bear!" scoffed Royston, looking up from the heap of pots and things he was rifling through.

"Quit arguing and concentrate on searching!" ordered Tyto from his perch where he was supervising.

"I'm not carrying anything *that* big!" said Freddie, eyeing a huge cauldron Royston had unearthed from the rubble.

"You'll carry what you're told to!" snapped the rat.

"We need a more systematic plan for searching," began Tyto, "why don't you...."

"Oh, shut up, Owl! You've done nothing but sit there criticizing everybody else!" interrupted Eddie sick and tired of the whole business.

The foray was rapidly escalating to an ugly conflict when the door of the room suddenly blew shut.

"Drat!" said Micki, annoyed at the sudden loss of light. "I can't see a thing now!" Very little sunlight penetrated through the tiny, dirty window and, without the illumination coming through the open door, the dark corners of the dingy room had a sinister look.

"Open the door, somebody!" shouted Tyto.

Royston obliged, but not before he deliberately smashed an earthenware jug on the flagstone floor in a fit of temper generated by the dictatorship of the owl. He went and pushed and pulled on the old wooden door. "It's stuck!" he groaned, yanking at the doorknob with all his might.

"Give him a hand, Eddie!" ordered Tyto.

Eddie gave it his best, but the door wouldn't budge. Micki was sure they weren't doing it right, so she went and gave a good tug and then a push. But still it wouldn't move.

"Freddie, give it a good kick!" commanded Tyto.

"Okay, stand back everyone!" said the good-natured mule, and he turned his rear to the offending obstacle and let fly with the most vicious kick he could manage. But the wooden door stood fast.

Then they all threw themselves pushing and pulling, kicking and beating when the owl, from his vantage point, saw something that turned his blood cold.

"**STOP!**" he screamed at them.

They all froze at the tone of his voice. They looked at him wide-eyed and then followed his gaze upwards to the old roof where a narrow beam of sunlight dug into their eyes and made it hard to see what he saw.

"What's the matter?" said Micki, squinting her eyes against the prick of light. Then she saw what owl saw and choked on the fear that made her legs weak.

"NO!" she cried, trembling to the core, "It…it…can't be!" she stammered, breathless.

All the others turned their heads this way and that, until they too saw the reason for the look of terror distorting the cat's face.

Peering through the chink in the old roof, the very hole that Tyto had looked through that fatal night, was an eye! A familiar black, sharp, glinting eye! The piercing, coal-black eye of a rook!"

The big, black bird cackled that dreaded caw. Its eye moved away from the hole and a big, grey, broken beak poked through in its stead.

"Thought you'd spoil my plans, did you my little darlings?" she croaked, "Heh, heh, heh, not so fast my sweeties!"

As the little gang of animals cowered in the dim shadows of the little room, the rook withdrew its beak from the hole and seemingly went away, at least they couldn't see or hear it anymore.

They didn't know what to do. They had been so busy arguing they hadn't noticed what might be happening outside. They had let their guard down. Panic set in. Had the revived witch destroyed the remedy brew? Had they left the antidote book out in plain view giving her a clue as to what was in the bowl?

Eddie, Micki, Freddie, Royston, and Tyto, sat and pondered their plight. They regretted their peevish quarrelling—where had it got them? What could they do to save themselves and their noble plan? The gang realized they couldn't think their way out of this one. They sat in a group hug of remorse for their earlier outburst of temper and made a commitment to form an enduring, loving friendship. Thus, they sat in respectful quietude and hoped for rescue—but who would rescue them? Nobody knew they were in trouble!

☙

True to form, Eddie eventually felt hungry and began looking around in cupboards for any signs of food. He remembered seeing something that resembled a biscuit tin earlier when he was searching for pots. He remembered those chocolate-covered biscuits the witch had given him, perhaps there were a few left. He found a similar tin and wrenched the lid off. But there were no biscuits inside, just some old folded papers.

"Any luck, Eddie," said Micki.

"No, sorry. Only some old documents," he said, his voice heavy with disappointment as he pulled them out to show everyone."

"Oh, I recognize those," said Royston, taking them in his paws. "These are the deeds to the farms!"

Tyto came over to take a closer look, "Indeed, they are!" he said, reading them over one by one. "And it looks to me as if they could be very important in the case against the witch by showing that she gained title through false pretenses," said the learned raptor, "We must take them with us. Good find, Eddie!"

The thought of taking the deeds with them suddenly reminded them that they weren't going anywhere—they were well and truly trapped—forever, or at least until the witch returned to do nasty things to them.

☙

There was no possibility of escaping through the tiny window. Not only did it not open, but it had an iron grill across it so the space would be too small even for Royston to crawl through.

Without the sunlight coming through the door, an icy chill was wrapping its tentacles around their little bodies, causing them to shiver violently. Micki looked at the cold, bare fireplace and suggested they build a fire to warm themselves. Then she had an idea, "What if I could climb up the chimney and escape and get help?"

"Yeah! Perhaps we can find ropes and rig up something so we all could climb out," suggested Royston jubilantly.

"And I can maybe fly up and out," said Tyto going and looking up the sooty, old chimney. The room was part of the old kitchen and had a huge fireplace where the witch's cauldron sat.

"What about me?" cried Freddie, trembling with fear as well as cold, "I can't climb ropes, and I don't want to be left here all alone!"

"We could climb out and maybe haul Freddie up by a rope," said Eddie, holding up a length of hemp twist and estimating the mule's girth.

"But what if the witch is waiting at the top to pick us off one by one?" considered Tyto, a worried look returning to his face.

"Good point," said Micki, "because we could only go up slowly, one at a time."

Royston suddenly snapped his fingers. "I've got it!" he declared, beaming his toothy grin and grabbing everyone's attention. "There's an old defunct well in the little scullery just off this kitchen that hasn't been used for eons. I explored it once, a long time ago, and remember that a little way down, there was a small hole in the brick sidewall which opened into a tunnel that led to the dungeons. Perhaps we could escape that way?"

Eddie frowned. "I don't fancy wandering around in that dark labyrinth again—and you didn't seem too sure of the way out last time we were there, Royston."

However, they all went to have a look at it, but it was so dark down the well that only the owl's eyes could discern anything at all.

"Hhmm...yes, but the hole looks to be very small, and I don't think anyone except Royston could get out that way anyway," said Tyto thoughtfully.

It was most discouraging.

The pervasive chill engulfing their prison was both literal as well as figurative. They proceeded to build a fire in the hearth to keep warm.

"Do you know any magic spells to help us out?" asked Micki of Royston while they were arranging sticks and paper in the old grate to set alight.

He shook his head. Then suddenly, he had another bright idea, "We could use this fire we're building to make smoke signals! We just need some damp wood—lots of that around, and something to fan the smoke."

Everyone thought that was an excellent idea and quickly set about collecting the damp wood. Eddie found an old Ouija board they could use to fan the smoke. They soon got a good blaze going and then added the wet logs.

As soon as the smoke started to billow, they realized the downside of the plan. As much heavy, grey smoke came back into the room as went up the chimney. They had made smoke signals all right, but almost choked to death as a result.

"This will never do!" said Eddie, coughing violently while his eyes smarted.

"We might as well put the fire out," said Freddie, pouring the dregs of dirty rainwater from a flagon onto it, which only made things worse.

Amid the cacophony of coughing and wheezing, Micki's sharp ears detected an unwelcome sound upon the roof. "Quiet!" she said, pointing up to the ceiling. The others stopped and looked up. "I bet the smoke attracted the rook-witch to come back to see what's going on!"

A few seconds later, they all heard a loud scuffle upon the roof top. There was scraping and flapping, hissing and cawing. There was a loud clacking of beaks and then a brief silence before an eye peered down through the hole again. The animals screamed and shrank back in alarm. "Go away you, nasty old hag!" they yelled as they threw whatever they could lay their hands on at the roof.

But Tyto noticed something different about *this* eye, it wasn't the sharp, little piece of coal of the rook, it was a large, shiny, black pearl. He recognized that eye, "Alba!" he cried in glee at his mate. "Alba! It's you!"

When Tyto was so late coming home, Alba had become very concerned. She knew he was meeting with his friends near the old castle, so she left her brood in the care of neighbour-friend Mrs. Long-Eared Owl and flew off to investigate. As she flew near the old ruins, she had seen the smoke and swooped in to investigate. Upon approaching the smoking chimney, she saw the rook and guessed it was the wicked witch that she had been told about.

The injured witch had been too weak to morph into anything other than a rook. Furthermore, the unexpected sight of the ruby heart, a powerful token of love hanging upon Alba's breast, had drained the last of the old hag's strength. In the body of a corvid, she had been no match for the big, fierce barn owl and, therefore, had been killed outright. The witch-bird's carcass plummeted down the chimney into the grate where it burnt to a cinder in the smouldering embers of the fire the gang had failed to douse.

There was much jubilation in the old kitchen room, but it now was time again for action. "Alba," said Tyto, "we are trapped in here by the old witch's spell—she jammed the door with magic, and we can't get out. Go and get someone to help us, please?"

His clever mate flew off immediately. Earlier, she had spied the gypsy caravans returning along the road to camp in the castle meadow. Now, she quickly soared over to them and enlisted their help in rescuing the poor prisoners. The men made short shrift of opening the jammed door and releasing the relieved gang who all dashed out into the sunlight with whoops of joy at being set free.

☙

The Romanies set up their caravan camp in the little meadow and built their campfires to cook dinner. Eddie and Micki and their friends were invited to sit around and partake of the meal and share accounts of recent happenings. But the travellers also had a story to tell. All the animals were surprised to hear that the witch, years before, used to be a fortune-teller that tagged along with the gypsies. But she proved to be a charlatan who used her powers for bad things—which gave the travellers a bad name. When they banished her from touring with them, she became even more bitter and twisted and took revenge on them by destroying the water they depended on, as well as planning to make herself rich by the scheme.

The animals all told their story of discovering and concocting the antidote to the poisoned water. Then they explained their dismay at realizing that they had no way to deliver it to the needy farms. To everyone's delight, the Romanies were very happy to help the animals deliver the remedy to restore the water in the wells.

It was a very merry party that travelled the countryside with their precious cargo. Furthermore, Eddie and Micki were thrilled to ride in a real caravan.

"A pretty good holiday this has turned out to be after all, eh, Micki!" said the bear with a big smile livening his face.

"And a very exciting adventure too!" laughed the cat, giving her friend a big hug.

☙

One by one, the farmers were all informed of the recent happenings, and the property deeds were handed back to the rightful owners.

Scientists tested the well-water at the farms after drops of the antidote had been added to each one. It was discovered that not only was the water safe, but that it was now the purest water for miles around. The farms in that area became more valuable than ever on account of the enchanted water in their wells. Happily, the farmers recouped their previous losses because their crops grew better and their livestock grew healthier than those of anywhere else.

Additionally, detailed analysis of the antidote potion found that it was a powerful anti-pollutant, so much so that just a few drops of it could be used to purify contaminated well-water around the world. Mrs. Barn Owl took it upon herself to teach others how to produce batches of the antidote for distribution to needy places.

Being the sweetest water that anyone had ever tasted, it was claimed by many to have healing properties and it became customary to make a wish as you drank it. By and by, a free public drinking fountain for all creatures was set up at Nemesis Castle, which Tyto developed into a tourist attraction and renamed Redemption Castle. The old ruins became such a going concern that it was even identified on new editions of the Ordinance Survey Map.

The Owl family was relieved to be able to fly safely around the woods and meadows without fear of the wicked witch and her heinous spells. Tyto wrote a book about the historic events and sold copies of it to the tourists that visited the castle ruins.

The old kitchen room was left pretty much as it was with the huge, black cauldron, in which the deadly brew had been mixed (the incomplete batch of poisonous brew had long since harmlessly evaporated), still sitting in the cavernous fireplace where the body of the witch had burnt to ashes. Visitors could see the iron-barred cage where the famous bear had been imprisoned. The young owlets revelled in giving tours of the creepy dungeons where the de-frocked wizard-rat had been locked up and left for dead. Outside, tourists could view the barn where the brave mule had been shut-up. They could run their hands around the hole in the wall where the courageous cat had used a medieval halberd to free her friend.

At first, Royston felt he had no direction in life now that he would never be a magician. However, the farmers' wives took pity on the demoralized rat and gave him cooking lessons so that he could find employment as a chef. Endowed with new skills, the emancipated rodent joined the merchant navy as a chief cook and bottle washer and traveled the world relishing the magic of faraway places with strange sounding names.

Once again, the gypsies could buy produce from the farmers, camp on their land, and water their ponies at the troughs as they had done for generations. The travellers had suffered as much as the farmers for lack of good water. Moreover, in grateful appreciation for the efforts of Eddie, Micki, and Freddie, the gypsies lent the little gang a beautifully painted and well-appointed reading van to finish their holiday in. The little friends were thrilled to travel with a real Romani caravan.

Freddie developed a yearning for the roaming lifestyle and chatted about his dreams to the gypsy horses he had befriended. Subsequently, the old mule was invited to become a permanent member of this troupe of travellers in whose company he flourished and became known for telling of his travels to anyone who would listen—usually just the children, who would brush and comb him for hours while he blissfully orated his vainglorious narratives.

The broken-down applecart-cum-pony-trap was not worth the expense of repair. Nevertheless, Eddie and Micki felt a sentimental attachment to it so, at their request, one of the grateful farmers hauled it in his truck back to the cottage for them. It was put it in the bottom of their garden and Micki planted an array of beautiful flowers in it making it into a much-admired conversation piece. On summer evenings, the two friends enjoyed looking at the display while they reminisced about their wonderful adventure and all the new friends they had made—something their guests never tired of hearing about.

[THE END]

A WINTER TALE

ONE DAY, EDDIE BEAR, the cast-off teddy bear, was once again not in the garden. This time, it was because it was the middle of winter and he was busy indoors putting up the Mid-Winter Festival decorations. Joining him in this fun task was his best friend and housemate Micki MacVitie, the black and white Highland cat.

Winter weather had come early to the Inner Hebrides where the twosome had their snug little home. The chill winds swirled the snow around the cottage, forming big drifts everywhere. Shovelling a path from the front door to the garden gate had been a daily chore for the little animals. Their garden, so full of life and bountiful lusciousness in summer, was now just a lumpy mass under a white blanket. But indoors, all was warm and merry as it was only a few days now until the festive holiday parties would be held all over the neighbourhood.

The excited anticipation of the two friends was growing daily as they made plans and looked forward to the pleasures the holiday promised. They had worked together to make their own decorations according to popular traditions long held dear. Handmade, brightly-coloured, crepe-paper garlands had been strung from corner to corner across the living room, sprigs of holly and ivy decorated the picture rails, and greeting cards adorned the mantlepiece. The most prominent card was a sparkly one from Micki's Cousin Tabby who lived in Darkest Outer Pongolia.

Now, the finishing touches were being added to the hand-me-down artificial festival tree that had served them well in previous years. Happy, but tired with their decorating efforts, the best mates took a well-earned break for light refreshments. They were in a very merry mood. Eddie sang gaily in his sonorous voice, as he took a treat from the plate Micki was holding out to him.

"Deck the halls with Ed and Micki,

Fa-la-la-la-la, la-la-la, la,

Eat another choccy-biccy,

Fa-la-la, la-la-la, la-la-la,"

Micki giggled and created her own verse:

"Eat too much and you'll be 'sicky',

Fa-la-la-la-la, la-la-la, la."

Eddie continued:

"Dress the tree with Mick and Eddie,

Fa-la-la-la-la, la-la-la, la,

Soon the room will be all ready,

Fa-la-la, la-la-la, la-la-la."

Micki added:

"Almost time to go to 'beddy',

Fa-la-la-la-la, la-la-la, la."

They broke out in a fit of laughter as they danced merrily around the room, admiring their decorating achievements.

"Well, all just about done except for a few more things to go on the tree," said Micki, stopping to catch her breath.

Eddie, feeling a little dizzy from all the spinning around, nodded approval with a big smile. "I'll put the Winter Fairy your old Granny Mittens gave us, up on the very top," he announced, moving the stepladder into position by the ceiling-high, tinsel-bedecked tree. He climbed steadily up the ladder, carefully holding onto the fragile little ornament. As he reached the top and was stretching precariously to place the delicate Winter Fairy on the very tip of the tree, he glanced out of the cottage window. He spied a familiar figure coming up the garden path and started to sing his own version of the lilting

Welsh ditty about an ash grove: "Here comes neighbour spaniel with a face like Mrs. Daniel," he chuckled.

"Don't be rude, Eddie!" said Micki, concentrating on rearranging the string of lights. "Cocky's a decent neighbour and good friend."

"But it's always such a disaster when he comes over to our house, especially when he brings his crowd of boisterous doggy friends, maybe we should lock the door," said Eddie, trying to get the delicate ornament to stay in place. "How does the fairy look here, Micki?"

"It looks very nice, Eddie. Do you think we…?" But Micki didn't have a chance to finish her sentence before the door to their cottage burst open letting in a cold winter blast filled with snowflakes together with a horde of yelping, barking, frenzied canines. She reacted with instinctive terror and charged up the tree in a flash just as the bear was startled into losing his balance and crashed from the top of the ladder to the ground with a body-slamming thud. The fairy ornament was flung across the room to smash against the fireplace fender.

Micki was incensed! "Look what you've gone and done, you stupid animals!" she screeched at the dogs as she clung to the topmost branch of the tree. "You've made the Winter Fairy crash to the floor—it'll be all broken!"

The five dogs stopped in their tracks to stare in amazement at Eddie, groaning on the carpet underneath the fallen ladder. Cocky Spaniel whined and licked the bear's face in apology.

"He's pretty tubby for a fairy, isn't he?" snickered Ruby, the pert King Charles spaniel.

"No wonder he fell from the spindly point," laughed Brittany sarcastically, scratching vigorously at her ear.

"I am NOT the Winter Fairy!" said Eddie indignantly as he pushed away the slobbering cocker spaniel and scowled at the other dogs who stood staring at him in wonder.

Micki had recovered her composure and climbed down the tree. She went over to help Eddie to his feet and put the ladder to rights. She then picked up the fairy ornament and examined its broken wings with a little sniffle.

"We're sorry," said all the dogs variously and sincerely.

"I'll buy you a new fairy," asserted Cocky, lowering his head and putting his tail between his legs.

"Oh, that's all right," said Micki with a sigh. "It was only an old one. It's just that it has special sentiment attached to it. Perhaps it'll mend."

"So, what brings you all here?" asked Eddie, looking quite sternly at the tail-wagging, panting pack of pooches.

"Well, we came to invite you to my Mid-Winter Festival party again this year," said the cocker spaniel neighbour, perking up after his fleeting moment of remorse.

"Oh no!" groaned Eddie under his breath as he turned away to prod unnecessarily at the blazing fire with the poker.

Micki tried to sound enthusiastic. "Oh…well…er…we'd be delighted, wouldn't we, Eddie dear? But…er…." She couldn't think of what excuse to give. The truth was, both cat and bear vividly remembered what a disaster Cocky's party was *last* winter. They had vowed back then *never* to accept another invitation from him.

Eddie quickly came to the rescue, "Well…um…don't we have to go visit… um…your Aunt Mathilda in the Outer Hebrides on that day?" he said, desperately wishing it was so.

The cocker spaniel put his head on one side and looked at Eddie in puzzlement, "But I haven't told you what day it is yet," he said. "Tell you what, you just say what day works for you and that's when it'll be!" he assured them.

Eddie and Micki exchanged crestfallen glances. "Oh, thank you," said Micki, the false enthusiasm draining from her voice. "Well, let's see now…" she said walking over to the Pretty Kitty calendar hanging on the wall by the fireplace. Unfortunately, the day-squares were glaringly devoid of other engagements, their pristine whiteness shone plainly for all to see.

Lost for an excuse to turn down the generous invitation, a day was selected—the day before Mid-Winter's Eve.

"Is there anything you would like us to bring?" asked the cat politely.

"Well, yes there is, please," said Cocky with a grin. "You see, I'm putting on a play this year and you will be given parts in it too, so please bring your costumes."

Eddie's eyes sprung wide in horror. Micki looked aghast, mouth sagging open. None of the dogs seemed to notice—especially Cocky who was bouncing up and down in delight.

MYSTERIOUS REALMS

The happy spaniel gushed, "You will be given your roles shortly. As soon as I've had a chance to cast the characters, I'll let you know when you can start making your outfits!" And with that, all the other dogs started barking and yipping with excitement as they raced madly around the room jumping over furniture as they tried to grab hold of the paper garlands that had been so laboriously hung from corner to corner across the room.

Micki quickly encouraged them to run out the door and into the snow. She gave Cocky her assurance that they would be there to play their part on the appointed evening. The spaniel jumped up and gave her a big, wet lick on the nose before dashing after his friends who were merrily rollicking in the snow drifts lining the pathway. The cat wiped her paw across her nose. She slammed the door closed and locked it. Then she turned and gazed at her best friend slumped in his armchair by the fire. His eyes were fixed vacantly on the ceiling where torn and twisted paper garlands swayed gently in the draught caused by the recent disturbance.

"Chin up, old feller!" said the Highland cat in a valiant effort to cheer up her disgruntled housemate. "Who knows, it might actually be fun. After all, it'll only be for a couple of hours at most. What could be so bad about that?"

It wasn't long before they'd find out!

☙

Within a couple of days after the chaotic visit from the hounds, a neatly folded note was put through the letterbox of Eddie's and Micki's little cottage door announcing the play, the characters the cat and bear would be portraying, and what costumes they would have to make. Mustering as much fervor as they could, the two friends got busy assembling scraps of material, cardboard, coloured paper, and bits of this and that. They became engrossed in cutting and gluing, stitching and taping, painting and crayoning, until appropriate costumes had been rendered wearable.

On the evening of the event, they donned their carefully made costumes and took turns to look at themselves in the full-length mirror and make last minute adjustments here and there.

Eddie looked dolefully at Micki. "I hope no one takes any photos," he said, pulling at the portly snowman outfit that hung uncomfortably around his rotund body. A top hat of sorts balanced precariously on his head, and an orange cone covered his pointed nose.

"I can't seem to get the ruff of my costume to stop twisting around my neck," said Micki, moving her head back and forth above the paper frills. "Do I *look* like a snow-princess, Eddie? It's going to be a challenge to keep up a smile in this get-up."

"Hhmpf!" snorted Eddie contemptuously. "Just keep looking at me and you'll have no problem grinning, in fact, you'll hardly be able to keep from laughing!" And with that they went out of the cottage door, Eddie shuffling and waddling behind his friend along the icy paths that led to Cocky's house.

꼿

As the two friends entered Cocky's house, they were surprised to find it quite chilly and noticed there was no fire in the large fireplace. However, before they had time to wonder why, the cocker spaniel welcomed them with unbounded joy! The candle-lit, over-decorated room was full of guests, mostly canine, dressed in a wild array of costumes. Cocky called his play: *Cocky: Ice King of Wonderland*. He was very proud of his original story and of course, had assigned himself the lead role. He was dressed in a very handsome, professionally-tailored Ice King costume that he showed off with great fanfare.

The bear and the cat already felt it was going to be a *very* long evening.

Eddie leaned his head towards Micki's and growled softly out the side of his mouth, "I wish I could be the Mad Queen character then I could at least have the pleasure of threatening to cut off his head!"

"Let's make the best of it, Eddie. Perhaps the food will be good?" whispered Micki hopefully. "Let's check out the buffet table—looks like an elaborate spread."

They eased their way through the costumed crowd towards the food. "Quite a strange selection," observed Micki, trying to sniff out some salmon but seeing only bowls of brownish gelatin, piles of roasted pig's ears, heaps of rawhide chews, and other such fare. "Mostly dog food, unfortunately," she said.

At the far end of the long buffet table, Eddie spied a big pastry oozing with cream. He pushed his way through the crowd in hopes of grabbing it before anyone else did. He elbowed his way along until it was just within his reach. As he hungrily stretched out his paw to snatch it, Cocky barked sharply to get everyone's attention to the start of the play. He said he was happy to see everyone had stepped up to the mark in making their costumes and he hoped they had done as good a job of learning their lines. The room became hushed.

Eddie couldn't care less about his lines. He held up the selected delicacy to his lips, anticipating that lovely sweet creaminess that was soon to flood his tongue and jowls. With a snap action he stuffed the creamy mass of pastry into his watering mouth, so smooth and— "BLECH...Ugh!... he coughed and spluttered the mess from his mouth and spat on the expensive carpet. Then, gasping for breath he grabbed the edge of the white damask tablecloth and began wiping the foul residue off his extended tongue.

Everyone watched in disgust at the spectacle, especially Micki. Then they all broke out laughing except Micki, who wanted to crawl under the table in embarrassment. She urged her choking friend to take a sip of punch from the glass she held to his lips. "What on earth's got into you, Eddie?" she whispered hoarsely between her teeth. "Can't you behave for five minutes!?"

"How was I to know it was *liver-flavoured* cream—drat those dogs!" said the bear with a shudder.

༄

Order was eventually restored among the company and the play commenced. Everyone took their assigned places, cleared their throats, and nervously fingered crib sheets of scribbled lines. Cocky announced the order of things and explained that he would dominate the opening scene. "I will descend the chimney to the 'mad dream-world of mystery' below—that is, the room you are all presently in," he said with a flourishing gesture of his arm.

Eddie wasn't listening. He was still grimacing from the taste of liver lingering in his mouth. He pushed his way to the punch bowl and took a big slurp to swish around his mouth and after a big gargle, he frantically looked around for a place to spit it out. The nearby potted Aspidistra seemed to be the only viable option and so it got a good soaking of punchy drool. Micki watched out the corner of her eye in mortified horror.

"How are you going to get into the chimney, Cocky?" asked a Weimaraner who was dressed as a knight.

"I'll go outside and climb up the ladder that I've already put in place. Then I'll strut onto the rooftop…." The spaniel halted, suddenly realizing that nobody would witness this wonderful feat. He frowned as he regretted his poor planning of the opening scene. But he needed everyone to be in the room to give applause when he alighted into the large, empty grate; so, he let things be.

"Won't it be awfully snowy and slippery up there?" whined a fluffy little Maltese, trying to look the part of a court jester.

"I'll be all right. I've practiced this carefully," Cocky assured her. Then, taking a deep bow and graciously accepting applause, he marched out of the room sweeping his star-studded cloak around him.

༄

And so, the rest of the 'players' waited for the grand entry of the Ice King into the fireplace. And they waited, and waited, and waited; first in silence, then in fidgety muttering and mumbling impatience. To this was added the restless shuffling of feet with lots of scratching and coughing. And still they waited. Impatience turned to boredom, and boredom morphed into concern as the chimney failed to triumphantly deliver the expected spectacle.

As they all waited, a bright little French bulldog pup was intently watching the drama escalating between the cat and the bear. It upset her to see people not getting along and she wondered how she could perhaps help smooth the troubled waters. Eddie noticed that Micki had moved as far away from him as she could get. A handsome border collie, dressed as a shepherd, was quick to latch onto any damsel in distress and Micki was obviously pleasantly amused by his attentions. Each time the handsome herder nuzzled his black shiny nose to her ear and murmured something, she laughed and looked impressed. Eddie could not hear what was being said, but he winced in jealousy. He considered going up to them and pulling the dog's tail but thought better of it as he sized up the sharp, white teeth glinting in the strong, sleek muzzle.

Then he had a brainwave! Furtively looking around the room to make sure no one was watching, he quickly ducked under the buffet table. Hidden from sight under the draping damask, he took a deep breath and let out a loud bleating, "BA-A-A-H, ba-a-h, be-eh-eh, ba-ah! he cried. In less than a split second, the fooled collie dashed, madly yapping, under the table, ready to round-up the envisioned sheep.

Eddie wasted no time in bolting out from his hiding hoping to mingle innocently among the other guests. It was a good plan except for one unfortunate miscalculation—the bear had forgotten he was in a snowman suit. A suit which weighed him down and pulled him off balance. The sheepdog, blind with excitement, was too fast for him and sunk his gleaming fangs into the little foot protruding from the rotund mass. Poor Eddie, yelping with pain, grabbed the edge of the dangling tablecloth in an effort to pull himself free. Unfortunately, the inevitable happened and the contents of the well-laid buffet table clattered and scattered on the floor all around.

The bear struggled to his feet as the collie, realizing the mistake, released his foot. The red-faced teddy caught sight of Micki's face across the room. He watched in morbid dread as her eyes widened and then narrowed as she took a deep breath and pressed her lips tightly together. She looked ominous as she flexed her claws and began a slow deliberated march towards him. The observant little bulldog held her breath and trembled. Who knows what Eddie's fate may have been had not someone suddenly burst into the cottage yelling that Cocky had disappeared!

☙

Everyone's attention turned to the frantic red setter who had just been outside looking for his host after the spaniel failed to appear down the chimney, "Cocky is nowhere to be found!" he barked in alarm.

A tubby old beagle came wheezing into the room, his costume dishevelled and dirty with snow, "Seems like…he climbed up the ladder…onto the roof," he panted. "His footprints go from the top of the ladder across the roof to the chimney stack, but there is no sign of him there!" the dog declared, his voice tense with anxiety.

Several of the guests ran to look up the chimney. But it was entirely empty. Some called up the flue, but no-one answered.

"He must have gone somewhere else," said the sedate, old otterhound calmly. "Probably had another trick up his sleeve that he forgot to tell us about."

"It should be easy to follow his tracks in the snow," said Micki confidently, her annoyance with Eddie now evaporated. "Why don't we go and look for footprints leading *away* from the bottom of the ladder? Someone, bring a lantern!"

Carrying lanterns and torches, a large group of the guests braved the chilly night air and made their way around to the back of the house where the ladder was propped against the wall. The snow around the base of the ladder was soon heavily trampled making it difficult to discern if Cocky's tracks were among them. After some moments of close inspection and lots of sniffing, it was ascertained that indeed the cocker spaniel had disappeared most mysteriously and without a trace—from the rooftop!

༄

Micki was quick to suggest that two search parties be formed—one comprised of sighthounds and the other, of scent-hounds. She volunteered herself and Eddie to act as 'questioners' who would interview the animals at surrounding farms to see if they had witnessed any strange happenings. She also proposed that a group stay at the house in case Cocky should return there. All agreed that this was a sensible plan and organized themselves according to their talents.

Eddie, his earlier peevishness swallowed by the urgency of new developments, was eager to play his part and strode after Micki only to stumble in his cumbersome costume. "I think I'm going to go home and change first," he said, struggling to remain upright. "I'll be back in a jiffy."

"Good idea!" said his mate. "I'll start at the cow barns over there and you can catch up to me when you're ready," then, turning on her heel, she hurried off towards the dark shapes of the byres across the field.

Halfway across the snowy pasture, Micki had a sense of being followed. She looked behind her but saw nothing. Then a small voice called out, "Can I be part of *your* group please, Mademoiselle MacVitie?"

The cat looked down to see a pudgy little dog valiantly jumping into the hollows the cat's boots were making in the snow. "Perhaps you would be better staying with the house group?" suggested Micki.

"But I want to help ask questions, if you please, Miss," said the cream-coloured, stubby-legged canine wistfully.

MYSTERIOUS REALMS

"All right then," said Micki, not wanting to offend the enthusiastic little helper. "But you'll have to keep up."

The young pup nodded with a grin.

"What's your name, 'Pupsy'?"

"Trixie!" said the little dog, "I'm a French bulldog!"

Micki smiled at the flat-faced pooch and said, "Welcome aboard, Trixie!"

And with that, the cat and the chubby little dog trudged laboriously through the white drifts blanketing the fields.

༺༻

Meanwhile, Eddie was at home ripping off the hated snowman suit and donning warm woollies in its stead. He thought about Micki out in the cold with just her princess costume on and decided to take a warm hat and muffler along for her too. He just was about to leave, when he thought that maybe a flask of warm honeyed milk and a package of chocolate biscuits would be a welcome addition as well—not to mention a bottle of apple brandy. And perhaps the torch needed new batteries, so he hunted high and low for them. "Ah, and my Ordinance Survey Map might come in handy," he said looking for his knapsack to put everything in. Then he thought the little folding shovel might be useful, so he attached it to the outside of his pack. Believing he had everything he needed, he paused a moment with his hand on the doorknob just to make sure he hadn't forgotten anything important. "Oh, my mitts!" he said as he rummaged around in the box of such things until he found the pair Granny Mittens had given him last winter, and he pulled them on enjoying their comforting fluffiness. "Now I'm ready for action!" he declared to himself, opening the door of the cottage. He strode snug and warm along the path to the garden gate that opened onto the lane that led towards the farm where the cows lived.

However, he hadn't gone but a few steps when he stopped dead in his tracks. Something very big and very strange suddenly appeared far above his head and hovered there silently. He stood with his neck craned upwards, staring at an enormous glowing oval of light set against the night sky of twinkly stars. He knew it wasn't the moon.

"What on earth…?" he began. But, before he had time to finish his thought, a bright beam of golden light shot out of the oval and sucked him upwards. He wanted to struggle but seemed unable to. He closed his eyes against the blinding light and trembled as a tingling sensation permeated every cell of his being, paralyzing him.

☙

Unaware of her friend's predicament, Micki had started to interview the cows who were nestled in their straw beds chewing the cud. She had no problem conversing with the black and white Holstein 'milkers'—who spoke excellent English but claimed they knew nothing. However, the Charolais bullock out in the field was another matter. Newly imported from the Continent, he spoke little English. Trixie, using the French she had learned from her mother was, with some effort, able to exchange snippets of conversation in that language with him. He told her what he saw.

Trixie replied, "*Répète nous, monsieur,* slowly please, … er…*qu'as-tu vu…* er…earlier tonight as you were standing out in the pasture?" asked the little bulldog.

"Well, *j'ai vu un gros objet dans le ciel,*" explained the bullock.

Trixie translated for Micki.

"Ask him what happened next, after he saw the big object in the sky?" said Micki skeptically.

Trixie obliged.

The Charolais replied with a shrug, "*Je ne sais pas!* Farmwife bring hay. *J'avais très faim !*"

The cat and the dog thanked the bullock and went on their way; both were puzzled by the Charolais's eerie claims.

"What do you make of all that, Trixie?" asked the cat.

"Perhaps I got the translation all wrong, Miss," said the little dog, wishing she had paid more attention to her mother's lessons.

"We'll see what Eddie thinks of it. We'd best go and question the goats at the next farm," said Micki. Just then they realized that Eddie was taking an awfully long time changing his clothes.

"I wonder what's taking Monsieur Bear so long?" wondered Trixie.

"I hope he's not sat at home sulking because of our little tiff earlier this evening," said Micki, opening the gate to the goat enclosure. "But if he is, he can jolly well stew in his own juice!" she said determinedly as she waved 'hello' to the two Toggenburgs who looked up in surprise at having such late-night visitors.

The Swiss goats spoke French better than they spoke English, so once again Trixie was indispensable. However, little information was gleaned from them other than that the youngest one thought she saw strange lights in the sky.

Having no further luck with their interrogations of the other farm animals, Micki decided it was best to go back and report her findings to the 'house crew' hoping that Cocky had been found safe and sound.

Finding that, unfortunately, the spaniel was still missing, Micki thought it best just to go home and sort things out with Eddie. She bid goodnight to the little bulldog and thanked her for her help.

The tired cat trudged back to her cottage. She turned her key in the lock of the front door and stepped inside expecting the welcoming warmth of a brightly-lit fire to envelop her. But the air was chill and silent. "Eddie?" she called tentatively. There came no answer. She turned on the lights and walked through the little rooms calling her friend's name. But he obviously wasn't there. "Where in the world can he be?" she wondered aloud. She was concerned now but tried to think rationally. She checked for his boots and coat and saw that they were gone. "Surely, he hasn't gone wandering off to look for Cocky all by himself in the dark?" she thought. "More than likely he had been very upset with the evening and therefore had gone to drown his self pity at the 'Mug and Spoon'!"

She made herself some hot milk and built a fire in the hearth, then she sat and waited patiently for the return of her housemate. The tree in the corner with its sparkly ornaments caught her attention, with a sigh she remembered how happily the holiday season had begun just a few days ago.

Suddenly, there was a gentle tap at the cottage door. Believing it to be Eddie who had probably forgotten to take his key, Micki got up and went to open it feeling a mix of curiosity, apprehension, and annoyance. But it wasn't Eddie after all, it was Trixie on the doorstep.

"Has Cocky been found?" asked the cat hopefully.

"No, Mademoiselle," said the little dog mournfully, "No sign of him anywhere!"

"And now Eddie's gone missing too!" said Micki, full of trepidation. "What on earth is going on?"

"I'm scared, now," said Trixie, shivering as much from fear as from the chill night air.

"I think we all are," said Micki, "Come on in and let's stay together by the fire."

※

Eddie found himself inside a very peculiar space. The light beam had effortlessly carried him all the way up into the airborne phenomenon and set him down gently on a solid floor. He tested his legs and arms—all seemed to be moving normally again. He looked around carefully. He was in some sort of room. The walls and floor and ceiling were molded in one smooth shiny black curve. A soft, greenish light shone from somewhere, but he couldn't see its source. The room was empty but for himself and a comfy looking chair in the centre. It was all quiet and nice and warm. He walked slowly around the room when suddenly a portion of the wall in front of him slid open revealing a passageway made of the same material as the room and illuminated with the same greenish light. He hesitated for a moment wondering if he should stay put or venture forth. He decided exploring would be more interesting.

He seemed to have been walking quite a long time and he was curious as to where the passage was leading. The anticipation of a possible great wonder awaiting his arrival encouraged him onwards. So, it was with some disappointment that he found himself back in what looked to be the same room that he had started in. He was tired from such a long walk and thought a good rest in the cozy chair was just the ticket. But to his surprise, as he seated himself in it, he was showered with gently-falling metallic snowflakes—brilliant colours of magenta, gold, emerald green, peacock-blue, and purple. The leaves made a faint tinkling sound as they drifted down around him. He reached out to grasp one, but his paw grasped nothing. Neither did the flakes accumulate on the floor; they simply vanished.

He sat a while bemused before he noticed a large green button on the arm of the chair which said, 'Press for Present'.

"I wonder if I should," he said, wishing there was someone to ask. But he was totally alone. "Well, I like getting presents—especially this time of the year. I wonder what I will get?" he asked himself. "Perhaps this is a massage chair? Well, I could do with a good kneading." And so, he pressed the button and waited. There was no soothing vibration from the chair, and no pretty-papered gift box appeared. Instead, the floor beneath him slowly became transparent.

As he dared to look down between his feet, he felt woozy seeing nothing holding up his chair. He blinked, trying to orientate himself in the landscape revealed below. He was hovering above his house, and as he watched, the cottage roof became transparent also, allowing him to see inside. "There's Micki!" he said out loud. "Micki! Micki! It's me! Look up!" But she was unable to see or hear him and continued to sit in her fire-side armchair sipping her mug of hot milk and staring into the flickering flames. Lying on the hearthrug beside her was a tawny little French bulldog.

Eddie shouted and whistled, and clapped his paws, but it made no difference. Micki and the dog were oblivious to him and anything hovering above the cottage. The bear was frustrated with his futile efforts and became anxious to find a way out. But he was afraid to step out onto nothingness. He looked around the room and noticed the walls were seamless with no door visible anywhere. Then he watched in amazement as the floor slowly returned to its normal solid appearance.

"Drat and bother!" said the teddy as he flopped back in the chair feeling quite tired and sulky. He didn't want to be here anymore. He wanted to go home. He impatiently tapped his paw on the arm of the chair. Then he became aware that there was another button—a blue one. This one said, 'Press for Past.' "Hhmm…," thought Eddie, "what on earth could that mean, 'past' what?" He was carefully pondering whether to take a chance and press the button when suddenly an opening reappeared on his right. He jumped up and ran to make his exit when someone dashed through it into the room knocking him over. Before he could get to his feet, the 'doorway' vanished again.

The newcomer didn't seem to notice the bear at all and ran frantically around the room panting, "I've got to get out, I've got to get out!"

Eddie stared at the familiar creature and was lost for words. He tried to grab the blur of fur. "Cocky!" he said in surprise, "So, you're here too!"

But the spaniel was too frantic to do little more than vaguely acknowledge his neighbour as he dodged Eddie's grasp and continued his mad dashing until another doorway opened and he bolted through it. Eddie made a dash for it too, but he was too slow, and the hole vanished just as he reached it.

"Fiddlesticks!" said Eddie, banging his fist on the wall. "What madness is this?"

He threw himself into the chair again and determinedly smacked his paw on the blue button. If he was stuck here, he reasoned, he may as well see what this button had to offer. He didn't have to wait long. Almost immediately, moving images began to appear all around him, vaguely at first as if forming out of a wavering mist. It made him feel a bit queasy. He peered around trying to make out the shapes. Then the pictures became sharper and the colours brighter. Finally, everything looked so real he reached out to touch things, but nothing had any substance. Holograms!

Eddie gazed at the scene surrounding him and wondered at the strange sense of familiarity that evoked distant memories. Then he gasped in disbelief. "Why, that's *me*!" he said, leaning forward to fix his eyes on the image of a beautiful, golden-haired, young teddy bear sitting on a shelf in a toy shop. "I remember being there. It was my first Christmas! I remember being excited as a steady stream of customers came and bought toys all day long despite the falling snow. I waited so patiently for my turn to be lovingly snapped up and taken to my forever home."

He felt himself becoming one with his youthful self as he drifted back in time.

༄

Young Eddie Bear sat there on the toy shop shelf beaming jauntily, puffing himself up every time a customer's eye passed over him. His glass eyes sparkled, and his mouth turned up in a little smile as he softly sang a swingy tune he'd often heard on Mr. Hodgkins' wireless,

> I'm just sitting here on the shelf,
>
> Happily behaving myself,
>
> Singing to the radio,

MYSTERIOUS REALMS

Doo-di-dum-di, doo-di-dum-doo,

Saving myself for you,

Doo-di-doo-di…"

But alas, other toys were always chosen. By the end of the day, he was the only bear left on the shelf and almost the only toy left in 'Ye Olde Toy Shoppe'. When old Mr. Hodgkins, the shopkeeper, started to close-up the shutters for the night, Eddie felt tears of disappointment, rejection, and loneliness welling up behind his eyes and his chin started to tremble. He sighed and started to bravely sing in a very small, shaky voice,

"So unhappy all alone,

With no one to talk to,

Doo-di-doo, doo…(sniffle)

It's just not fair,

I'm a good little bear,

I want to go…(sniffle) home,

With you…doo-di-doo…"

Just as his song was slipping into a sorry sob, the door clattered open one more time and in came an elderly lady in a dignified dither. "Oh, Hodgkins, I'm so glad you are not all closed up for the night. My chauffeur had a terrible time getting the Bentley through the drifts," she lamented, brushing flakes of snow off her fur stole and her stylish, ankle-length dress-coat. "Such a to-do, all this seasonal shopping for the family. But I do like to do it *personally*. I have been most indisposed of late, and this is the only chance I have to shop."

"How can I help, Your Ladyship?" asked the old man trying not to let his fatigue show.

"I need something for each of my three great grandchildren," she said, looking quickly around the few remaining items in the small premises. "That green tricycle will do very well for Master Alistair, and I think the dappled rocking horse is just the thing for Miss Priscilla." The lady paused as she glanced along the near-empty doll shelf. "Oh dear, so little left to choose from," she said quite distressed, "I was hoping for a big, pretty doll for little Miss Abigail; my youngest great granddaughter."

"Well, perhaps this one would be suitable, m'lady?" said Hodgkins, taking down a rather plainly-dressed, small doll.

"Oh, I don't think so," said the dowager with a frown. Then, she looked up to where Eddie sat watching and hoping.

"Give me that teddy bear!" said the primly-dressed lady, pointing her silver-handled walking stick at the golden-furred Eddie. "It'll do nicely for Miss Abigail."

The elderly shopkeeper slowly climbed the rickety stepladder and took the bear off the shelf. He tried to pack it into a cardboard box, but it wouldn't fit on account of the firm plumpness of its tummy. He sat the toy on the countertop and adjusted the bright red ribbon adorning its neck and brushed dust of its clothes. "Would Your Ladyship wish to see anything else?" asked the old man.

"No thank you, Hodgkins, that will be all. The green tricycle for Master Alistair, the rocking-horse for Miss Priscilla, and the bear for Miss Abigail. I do hope they don't squabble over their gifts this Christmas," said the grey-haired lady, testing the secureness of her large hat before facing the frigid winds that were still swirling snow over the country lanes, "I'll take the bear with me," she said, tucking it under her arm, "but please make sure the other things are delivered directly to the Manor House for Christmas Eve."

"Certainly, my lady," said the shopkeeper following her to the door. As he held open the door for his last customer, he looked at the snow drifts piled high along the road and was thankful that he and his old mare and cart would, on the morrow, have an easier time making their way to the Manor House than the Bentley would.

"I bid you goodnight," said Her Ladyship to the shopkeeper as she picked her way through the whiteness in the darkness with the help of the chauffeur's proffered arm, "and I send compliments of the season to Mrs. Hodgkins."

Mr. Hodgkins, in turn, bid Her Ladyship goodnight and wished her and her family the joy of the season. He then wearily locked the door of his toy shop and turned out the lamps, content that he had made some very good sales that day.

MYSTERIOUS REALMS

☙❧

Despite the well-sprung chassis of the Bentley, the long ride to the Dowager House that night along the bumpy, snowy country roads was so jolty all the way that Eddie Bear feared that his stuffing would be shaken out of him. But he was happy! He had been chosen and was going to his very own home! "I wonder what it will be like?" he pondered to himself. "I wonder what my life is going to be?" He was glad that he had not been able to fit into that box because now he was able to sit, warmly swaddled in the plaid car-rug beside the driver, and watch with excited anticipation, the shapes of trees, big houses, churches, and farm buildings looming out of the darkness along the way.

☙❧

Late next evening, he was bundled up in the woollen car rug once again and driven in the Bentley over to the Manor House where Lord Smedley's children lived. Once inside the grand building, he was placed under an immense, heavily-decorated Christmas tree such as he had never in his short life seen before.

He was left quite alone in the dark, unfamiliar house and was surprised to find himself feeling very lonely. He missed the other toys and the old shop-keeper. But suddenly, he wasn't alone! He heard soft feet approaching him. Then he heard a loud sniffing near his head. He peeked out through a narrow gap in the folds of the blanket and was alarmed to see a black, wet nose on the end of a long snout poking up close. He stiffened and held his breath. With each loud sniff, he watched as a long, plumy tail wagged vigorously at the other end. Eddie kept perfectly quiet and still until the strange creature went away.

The next morning, without warning, pandemonium clamored all around him and his warm blanket was whisked off. He found himself staring into three small smiling faces that were peering at him in wonderment. Soon, yelps of delight from the children and shrill yaps from a leaping brown and white collie filled the room as the rambunctious children grabbed him and threw him up into the air.

"Oww! Ouch!" he winced as the three children tugged hard at him and the collie nipped his foot. They each wanted him. "Don't fight over me!" pleaded Eddie. "You'll pull my arms and legs right off!" And they surely would have had not their great granny intervened just in time.

"You have to learn to share your toys!" gently scolded the elderly lady that had bought him. "Alistair, offer Abigail a ride on your tricycle and maybe she'll let you play with Eddie Bear." The great grandmother shooed away the excited dog as she turned to the older girl, "And Priscilla, if Abigail lets you dance with her teddy, you *must* let her ride your rocking-horse in exchange!"

Amazingly, the children did just that!

Aahhh…, what fun that was for a young bear in his prime! In the ensuing months, as winter lapsed into spring and then summer, he relished the rides in the basket of the green tricycle around the Manor House grounds with the wind rushing in his face. He felt that he could fly like a bird.

Bouncing on the saddle of the rocking-horse in front of the French windows that opened onto beautiful gardens, he could let his imagination run wild—he decided there and then that he wanted to be a gardener.

In the late afternoons, after a tea of yummy scones with raspberry jam and fresh cream, there were strolls in the doll's perambulator around the duck pond. Miss Abigail dressed him in a smart sailor suit as he joined in the fun of sailing paper boats between the waterlilies. The wild geese and ducks entertained him with their swimming and diving. He wished he could try doing that too because, all in all, he was an ambitious little bear. However, all he could do was make-believe. And too soon, even those dreams faded as one by one, the years passed.

The boy, Alistair, went away to boarding school. The nursery became a schoolroom where the young sisters received instruction from a governess. Eddie joined in their lessons as best he could and learned his ABCs and how to do simple sums on his paws. He perused atlases and learned about seas and continents. He looked at pictures in history books and knew about the kings and queens of faraway lands. He even learned to sing a ditty or two and dance a jig. But eventually, even those cherished activities ended. The children came to the nursery no more.

☙

MYSTERIOUS REALMS

Back in the strange floating room, the holographic images faded as smoothly as they had appeared and Eddie, still seated in the comfortable chair, savored the luscious memories that had surrounded him. How petty all the troubles of today seemed now. Just as he was wondering if he would be shown more episodes from his past, the door in the smooth wall appeared again and Cocky burst into the room, as frantic as before.

This time Eddie caught him and forced him to stand still. "For goodness sake, my friend, calm down and take a break from all this hysteria!"

Cocky yapped, his eyes wide with fear, "I've got to get out! I must escape! Let me out!"

"But there *is* no way out!" insisted Eddie.

"There must be! Just around the next corner I'm sure!" panted Cocky frantically.

"But there *are* no corners, Cocky. You're just running around in circles." said his friend. "Stop a while and sit in this chair, you might see some amazing things," suggested Eddie.

"I can't!" yipped the cocker, "I have to escape, I need to get back to the party. What'll they do without me, I'm in charge of everything?"

"Well, the party's over and your friends are searching for you. They were quite worried when you disappeared without a trace, and probably still are. But since you're trapped here you may as well enjoy the experience. Come and sit down a minute and look at…."

"No, no! I can't stay! I must look for a way to escape…I've got to go, so much to do!" and with that, the distraught canine broke free of the bear's grip and dashed off around the room again.

Then a hole on the opposite side of the room opened and before Eddie could stop him, the dog sprinted through it yelping and barking. Immediately, the opening closed, and silence returned to the room.

Eddie shook his head in despair. "Poor kid!" he thought, "I wish he'd just listen to me for a minute." He returned to the chair and cupped his chin in his paw as he leaned his elbow on the arm. He wondered if that was all there was to see. He pushed the blue button again a few times to see if something else would show up—it did. Eddie grunted contentedly, stretched back into the reclining chair and settled down to watch.

The replaying of his life had now jumped forward many years. He was alone in the nursery. The children no longer came to play with him. The governess no longer came to pick him up and smooth out his clothes. Dust was gathering everywhere. His golden fur had lost its gleam, one of his ears was loose, and the gaze of his once glowing glassy eyes started to drift out of focus.

Then one day, he heard footsteps and voices approaching. He perked up but was alarmed as the door of the nursery was flung open and an authoritative man strode in. The housekeeper, looking very efficient, was following him. The two looked in distaste at the neglected room.

"Tell, Jones to come up and clear all this old stuff out!" said the man, tapping this and that with his foot. "Her Ladyship and I will want all new things for *our* young family."

"What should we do with all this then, sir," asked the woman, looking around at the worn-out toys and out-of-date books.

"Burn all the rubbish! But anything worth saving can be given to charity," said the man. Eddie gasped as he recognized the former Master Alistair, now all grown up and lord of the Manor House himself.

"I want the decorating to begin right away," said His Lordship to the housekeeper.

The cast-off teddy bear was filled with fear. Would he be burned or given to charity? But neither was to be his destiny.

"Very well, my lord," said the housekeeper, casting one last look around the old room. Her gaze landed on Eddie and lingered there. She was thinking that the old teddy bear might be a nice Christmas present for Emily, the baby daughter of the newly-hired, widowed cook. And so, a couple of days later, the teddy found himself wrapped in a scrap of worsted blanket and nestled into a wooden box filled with straw in the warm kitchen. His box was placed near the big, black stove where the kitchen cat, Mittens, slept in her wicker basket.

Little Emily was delighted with the golden bear and played nicely with him. She made him a new shirt out of a discarded tea-towel and knitted him a warm jersey from scraps of yarn. And although he no longer was fed fresh scones and cream, he enjoyed the bread and milk almost as much because it was given with such love. Over the ensuing years, his good-natured, curly-haired friend hugged and kissed him very often but then, as with the 'Upstairs' children, the 'Downstairs' girl grew up and didn't bother with him anymore. Eventually, she and her mother went away and never came back. The once-again cast-off teddy bear lay abandoned and forgotten with only the aging mouser for company.

Eddie had always got along well with Mittens, the once sleek, black feline with white paws. They had had many good conversations when they were left alone in the kitchen after all the staff had gone to bed. She had told him many stories about herself and the house. She reminisced about all the kittens she had produced and how she had many, many great, great, great grandchildren who all called her Granny Mittens. She bragged to the bear how she had once been the best mouser the Manor House had ever had. With bared fangs and sharp claws, she had frightened all the mice away. Now, with clouded eyes, dull, broken claws and missing teeth, she had to rely on negotiation to maintain law and order. She managed to keep the mouse population under control by allowing them to help themselves to a certain amount of food and bedding if they promised to send their kids off out into the world far away from the big house. But the most important part of the deal was that they had to keep her informed of the goings-on Upstairs.

"So, I'm quite content to live out my final days in the comfort of this humble kitchen and be fed bowls of fresh milk and soft food that my old jaws can chew," said Mittens with a peaceful smile.

"Well, I'm too young to be cast aside," said Eddie, tightening the loose threads of his right ear. He sucked in his sagging tummy and punched his arms and legs to fluff up the stuffing. "I want adventures! I want to *do* something with my life!" said the middle-aged bear to the cat.

"What would you do?" asked old Mittens, her failing eyes trying to focus on a young mouse poking its nose through a hole in the skirting board near the stove. It was waving frantically to get her attention.

"I fancy myself living in my *own* house and growing prize-winning vegetables in my *own* garden," he said with vigor. Then he sagged and sighed, "But I see no way of escaping from the humdrum existence of life in this dull kitchen."

Mittens was listening to Eddie bemoaning his plight despite her attention on the mouse. "You should go up to the North Country where there are opportunities for an adventurous bear like you," said the mouser. "My great, great, great granddaughter lives in a fine, big, Highland house in the Inner Hebrides, and she has big ideas for herself too—just like you. Not satisfied with catching mice and having kittens, she wants to be a garden designer she says, have her own place in the country. I don't know what the younger generation is coming to, honestly, I don't."

Eddie was instantly envious of this young Highland cat—it sounded like she had opportunities knocking all around her. But how could he get there and get a piece of the action? He had no money, means, or education.

For some reason, it was unusually noisy upstairs in the house that morning with all kinds of 'bangings and bustlings'. Eddie couldn't think straight with all that racket going on, so he decided to go for a walk around the kitchen garden to ponder things. "I'm going for a walk," he called to the old cat as he reached for his hat and jacket. She didn't answer. He looked across the kitchen and saw that she was held spellbound by the young mouse who seemed to have something very important to relate to the ancient matriarch. Not feeling like concerning himself with cat and mouse business, Eddie stepped out into the sunny garden.

Back in the kitchen, Granny Mittens thanked the mouse and, with great trepidation, turned to speak to the bear, but he was already gone. Distressed, she hurried outside to look for him, but her dim eyesight was no match for the bright sun; she couldn't see him anywhere. She quickly thought of a plan, but before she could do anything, ominous footsteps were heard coming down the stairs.

☙

Unaware of the looming crisis in the house, Eddie wandered around the gardens where the thyme and mint yielded up their fragrances as he walked over them. He stopped to sniff at the lavender and sage. He watched the fish in the little pond and read the sundial. It was all very nice, but he knew that he wanted more from life.

The day was bright and sunny, and butterflies were flitting everywhere teasing him to dance after them. He followed the taunting insects down the lane and into the flowery meadow. The exercise and warmth made him feel drowsy, so he lay down in the sweet-smelling grass and fell asleep bathed in the smiling sunshine that filtered through the rose-covered hedgerow and made dappled patterns on his fur. He dreamed leisurely dreams of growing prize-winning vegetables and roaming Highland hills where mounds of honey-roasted parsnips and carrots swirled their aromas around him until he awoke and realized he was very hungry. Stretching luxuriously with a big yawn, he rubbed his eyes and then scrambled to his feet. Whistling jauntily, he returned to the lane and headed towards home confident that somehow, he would secure a passage up to the North Country. But first, he needed a good meal.

He was almost at the gate of the kitchen garden when he met an old cat in the roadway. A tattered, paisley-patterned, woollen shawl was wrapped around her shoulders and a pair of large sunglasses hid her eyes. She waved a cane in front of her, tapping her way along the dusty road. A little tin cup and a musty carpet bag were in her other paw.

She became aware that someone was passing by, "Will you take pity on an old, blind mouser, kind sir?" she muttered, her gummy maw trembling. She put down the heavy carpet bag on the gravelly ground at her feet and rattled the tin cup lightly at him. "If you can spare a penny or two, if not, a farthing will do."

Eddie reached into his pocket for his only coin, a worn-out halfpenny. He was about to pop it into the tin cup when he peered closely into the face of the old cat. "Granny Mittens!" he said in surprise, "What on earth are you doing a-begging in the street?"

The old cat removed her sunglasses and squinted out of her milky-pupiled eyes, "Is that you, Eddie Bear?"

"Why, yes!" said Eddie. He repeated his question, which she answered simply by shaking her head slowly and silently. He noticed a little liquid diamond creep out of her left eye and drop onto the rusty black fur of her chest where it hung trembling, as if it was not sure where to go from there. "Let's go into the kitchen and you can tell me all about it!" said the concerned bear, picking up the carpet bag. He gently took hold of Granny's arm to guide her safely back through the gate of the kitchen garden of the grand Manor House.

"Oh, no! We can't go back in there," said the beggarly cat sharply pulling back in fear.

"Why on earth not?" inquired Eddie quite puzzled, wondering if the old girl had gone senile all of a sudden.

"It's too dangerous for us now," she said.

"How so?"

"The family is selling the house and moving to a villa in the South of France," she explained. "The Upstairs mice heard them talking about it this morning at breakfast."

"Well that sounds pretty exciting," said Eddie feeling quite animated. Things were looking up, he thought! "You'll enjoy your days sleeping in the warmth of a sunny veranda while I go exploring all the beautiful gardens. Maybe I'll even be able to have a little plot of my own to grow veg…"

"No, no!" said Mittens still resisting his efforts to make her go through the gate, "You don't understand! The mice told me they overheard them saying…" she paused finding it hard to continue, "…they…don't think I'm worth taking—too old for the journey they say!"

"Never!" said Eddie quite alarmed. "Surely they wouldn't think of leaving you behind?"

"No, they wouldn't…it's worse!" said granny cat, "They plan to take me on a one-way trip to…to *that* place! They brought the nasty carry-basket down to the kitchen to get me, but because the mice had forewarned me, I was hurriedly packing a bag for myself and a little suitcase for you too. But I had to leave those, quickly grab whatever I could, and make my escape right away."

Eddie was very upset at what he was hearing. "How awful that they would want to…to do away with you like that! I will go and have a word with them at once. I'll speak directly to young Lord Smedley; you see if I don't! I'll get something straightened out! They can't treat you like this after all your years of loyal service."

"There's no point. They won't listen to *you*," said the old cat, wiping her eyes with a corner of the grubby shawl.

"Why do you say that?" asked the bear, puzzled.

"You see that bonfire over there?"

MYSTERIOUS REALMS

Eddie looked towards where she was pointing her cane. A large bonfire was blazing in the bottom of the kitchen garden near the compost heap. He watched as a servant man came out of the back door with a big box of old books and worn-out toys and threw them into the flames. Eddie shuddered as he watched in horror. He glanced back at Mittens. Salty tears were now obscuring her already cloudy eyes. The kind bear swallowed hard and struggled to find his voice, "No, no…they wouldn't, they couldn't…could they?"

The old cat nodded. "They *can* and they *will*," she sniffled. "Neither of us is safe here anymore!"

As Eddie began to digest the sickening truth, he squared his shoulders and declared with a boldness he didn't feel, "We'll go far away from here, right now! Just as we are, with only the clothes on our backs. We'll take a train somewhere. Perhaps we could go and stay with your great, great, great, granddaughter in the Inner Hebrides for a while?"

"But how much money do you have?" inquired the cat.

The bear's shoulders drooped. "Well, just this old ha'penny I was going to give to you," said Eddie, turning his pockets inside out just to make sure. "How much money have you collected in your tin cup?"

With a sigh, the old granny turned the tin cup upside down and a little pebble fell out onto the gravel. Eddie looked at it dolefully. "We'll think of something," he said reassuringly while kindly putting his arm around her shoulders, "Don't worry, Granny. We'll think of *something*."

༄

The two homeless animals hurried along the country lane as fast as they could. The village train station was still a long way off, and they were tired and hungry. But as luck would have it, just as they sat to rest on an old milestone at the crossroads, a horse and cart loaded with trunks and boxes came jogging along the road that led to the village. Eddie hailed the driver. "Excuse me, sir! Would you please be so kind as to give me and my friend here a lift to the train station? I'm afraid we will not be able to pay you but a ha'penny though."

"Would be most happy to oblige, sir! And no charge," was the cheery reply. "It so happens that I am just going there myself to forward all this luggage on the next train to the Inner Hebrides."

Eddie beamed as he helped Mittens up onto a secure spot between himself and the driver. He then settled himself next to her. The man chatted amiably to them but asked no awkward questions. The bear listened to the driver's monologue politely and, despite being desperately hungry and his tummy gurgling, it was a happy ride.

✺

Several dusty miles later, they arrived at the station. The two animals alighted and thanked the driver, then bustled their way up to the ticket window of the busy station. Eddie placed his halfpenny on the counter saying, "How far can we two travel on a ha'penny, sir?"

The ticket seller laughed showing an uneven row of tobacco-stained teeth. "Get along wi' yer!" he sneered, "That won't even get yer onto the platform. Now scram! You, rogues! Yer 'olding up the line of *serious* passengers."

Indeed, the other passengers scowled at the two paupers and shoved them aside.

Feeling both rejected and dejected, the cat and the bear sat down on a nearby bench and wondered what to do next. Their situation seemed hopeless once again, and the big, flashy posters of holiday 'get-aways' pasted on the outside walls of the ticket room seemed to mock them.

Adding to the bustling noise of the busy station was the jarring sound of an organ-grinder's creaky, old machine playing a desultory tune. Eddie listened for a while to the simple music and watched as a few passers-by dropped a copper or two into the cloth cap the musician had set on top of the instrument. The bear thought it unfortunate that the man didn't have the usual monkey or dog dancing act to accompany him. Then he suddenly had a brainwave! He went up to the man and said, "I say, sir, I think you may collect more coins if you had a dancing animal to go with your music."

"Indeed, I'm sure I would, my dear fellow," responded the musician, "But you see, Bessie, my old fox-terrier, passed away last week and I can't afford to buy another dog."

"Well, I'm sorry to hear that, sir. But perhaps we can come to some agreement that would benefit each of us."

The man listened with interest to what the bear had to say. Minutes later, as the organ ground out a merry jig, Eddie danced around flicking his feet into the air and flinging his arms every which way in time to the music. Mittens chuckled and joined in as best she could. She placed her walking stick on the ground and jigged over it, remembering the country dance she had learned many years ago in the land of her birth. Soon, a small crowd of people had gathered around and began clapping and laughing, urging the little band to a frenzy of sound and movement. As hoped, the onlookers were generous in their appreciation of the entertainment. By the time the panting performers needed to take a break, the money cap was full to overflowing with cash.

The organ-grinder gave Eddie and Mittens their share of the earnings—ten whole shillings! They felt rich and ready to conquer the world!

Eddie now boldly approached the ticket-wicket and loudly demanded two tickets to the Inner Hebrides. After paying for the tickets, there was enough money left over to indulge in a little something at the station restaurant. With a good half-an-hour before the train's arrival on Platform 3, Eddie was able to enjoy a full fry-up breakfast dripping with honey, while Granny Mittens delighted in a plate of kippers smothered in best butter on soft bread that she could chew easily with her few remaining teeth.

༄

The train journey was long, but pleasant. At first, there were towns and cities to pass through, then rolling countryside became predominant. Grassy fields of cows and then stony hills of sheep. They passed ocean glimpses with grassy shores, shimmering lochs and glens full of fragrant heather and yellow gorse. Mountains and forests rose up before giving way to windswept rocky pastures, criss-crossed with grey stone walls enclosing the little fields that surrounded whitewashed cottages. Eventually, the train reached its remote destination beyond the Lowlands and into the Highlands of the West Country. Mittens was rejuvenated to be back in familiar territory; it had been a very long time since she had last laid eyes on her homeland.

Eddie was ecstatically absorbing every detail of his adventure and felt overwhelmed with all the new sights, sounds, and smells. The vastness of the landscape made him consider a possible problem. "I hope we have enough money to take the bus to the MacVitie place?" said Eddie to his companion.

"We have only a few coins left," he said, counting them out in his palm. "How much is the bus fare?"

"Perhaps there is no bus to MacVitie Mansion anymore," said Granny, "I'm sure most people have a motor-car these days."

"Then we'll have to see if we can hire a taxi," said Eddie, doubting very much if they could afford such a luxury.

Mittens thought the same. "That is sure to cost us more than we have, like as not," she said sullenly.

Upon their arrival at the station in the Inner Hebrides, they made inquiries about buses and found that there *was* a country bus that went very near the MacVitie place. It should be along in about an hour.

They made their way to the spot where the bus would pull in to pick up passengers. There was no one else queuing up in that desolate place. A chill breeze snaked its way through the gullies of the barren hills and the animals steeled themselves against it as they shivered in their scant clothing. Eddie raised the collar on his jacket and turned his back to the wind. Mittens pulled her threadbare shawl tighter around her shoulders and huddled close to her friend for warmth. Eventually, a lumbering green and yellow vehicle approached and, with screechy brakes, pulled up in front of them. Eddie inquired the price of the fare of the bus driver.

"Fare to MacVitie Mansion? One shilling and ninepence for you, laddie, and one and thruppence for the old lady," announced the gruff driver.

"Oh dear," said Eddie, looking at the few coins in his paw. "That's three shillings, but we have only two and tuppence ha'penny altogether," said Eddie, lifting his wistful gaze to the surly driver.

"That'll only get ye within two miles of the big house," growled the driver, impatient to be moving on.

Mittens spoke up, "If you will drive us right up to MacVitie Mansion, I know my family will pay you the shortage promptly."

The driver squinted intently at the old cat, "Are you one of the MacVitie clan then?" he asked.

"I most certainly am, my good man," said the Old One proudly, "I'm Granny Mittens MacVitie and I'm home again at last!"

"Well, bless me!" said the man, his countenance lifting, "If it isn't Micki MacVitie's old, old, old grandmother come home! And you've brought a special friend, I see," he said, indicating the bear that was hanging back in hope. "Well, climb aboard both of you, I'll pay your fare, don't you worry, and I'll have you both safely home in no time!"

And with that, the bus rumbled off along the rough road with two very happy animals on board.

☙

At the gateway to MacVitie Mansion, the two travellers clambered off the rickety bus and, with sincere hearts, thanked the driver. They walked across the cobbled yard to the big grey-stone country house. It loomed large and austere amid misty, green pastures that stretched away in all directions. Woods, copses, and farmhouses lurked in the murky distance. Eddie stood in awe. A variety of cattle and horses, sheep and goats, ducks and chickens were busy going about their daily routines everywhere. "So many creatures to make friends with!" he mused to himself.

Granny Mittens's great, great, granddaughter, Millie, was the current owner of the mansion and met them in the yard. Overjoyed at the surprise visit, she welcomed both animals into the house and made them very comfortable. She was adamant that they would live with her as long as they wanted. As she sat them by the blazing fire, and rang for tea and oatcakes, she assured them that nice cozy rooms for them would be immediately prepared, new clothing would be soon provided, and hot meals would be enjoyed every day.

Eddie was duly introduced to a swarm of black and white cats: cousins, aunts, uncles, nephews and nieces, all of them of the MacVitie clan. The poor bear was overwhelmed with all the names to remember—Mollie, Muggins, Mary, Maggie, Moocher, Moggy, and countless more. He was hugged and kissed and squeezed until he was quite in need of some fresh air so, after tea, while Mittens and her large family caught up on all the news, Eddie politely excused himself and went outside to explore his new surroundings.

He ambled over to the paddock where he could see a couple of Shetland ponies grazing lazily. Then he suddenly spied a pretty, young, black cat with white bib and paws sat on the paddock fence, sketch book in hand. She was so intent on sketching the ponies that she didn't notice him. Not wanting to disturb her by calling out, he approached quietly from behind until he could see her picture.

"You're really a good artist," he said, admiring her sketches of the ponies.

She turned in surprise and smiled at him. "Do you think so?" she said. "I'm using them to base a painting on. Then I'll sell the picture and use the money to buy a little cottage where I can design and grow my own flower-garden."

"Really? I don't know much about art and selling things, but is it true that selling a painting would give you enough money to buy such a place?"

She laughed, "Well, maybe not quite, but you see I intend to go to college where I can learn to be a garden designer. I will earn good money with *that* occupation."

"You're very lucky," said Eddie wistfully. "I would like to go to school too and learn to—well, I would like to be a gardener and have my own vegetable patch."

"Say! Why don't we team up then?" said the cat, her eyes shining with enthusiasm. "You can practice in *our* garden here. I'm sure John, our old gardener, would be glad to have you as an apprentice. He'd probably appreciate the extra pair of hands." Then she jumped down off the fence and held out her paw to shake Eddie's. "I'm Micki MacVitie!" she announced with a cheery grin.

☙

Eddie sat in the chair deep in thought as the holograms vanished and the room went still and dark again except for the faint green glow. He stared at the blank wall in front of him for a long time deep in thought. He had indeed worked hard and become a knowledgeable grower of vegetables and had even won prizes at the local county fair. He had earned a respectable income helping others with their gardens while his best friend Micki, had earned a goodly amount designing gardens until they could afford to buy a little cottage together and have their own splendid gardens which were a source of great joy for them both. But most of all, he realized just how much he loved his cat friend. She really was a star to him, and they had had so many wonderful adventures together. He wished they hadn't scrapped at the party this evening. It was so horrible when they snapped at one another. Yes, he was clumsy sometimes; he couldn't seem to help it. But he decided that tonight's tiff had been partly her fault because she took offence so easily.

MYSTERIOUS REALMS

As he sat there thinking about his dearest friend, he wondered when he would see her again. He really *did* want to go home. He punched the 'Present' button on the chair again and was rewarded immediately in the same way as before. He could see into the living room of their cottage, but now it was empty!

"Where has she gone?" he wondered. "It's one thing for me to disappear without a trace, but I don't think it's right for her to do so! Wait a minute, perhaps she's gone to bed?" But, like before, no matter how hard he shouted, no one heard him—it was like they were in different dimensions. Frustrated, he sank back into the chair and, as the present scene became obscured again, he remembered the snacks in his pack. He pulled out the apple brandy, milk, and chocolate biscuits and munched and slurped his melancholy mood away.

After finishing his snack, he started to grow nostalgic about all the dubious but exciting adventures he and Micki had had over the years. Perhaps one of the most memorable was that first one. As he lay back in the reclining armchair, he pushed the 'Past' button again and he waited to see what would be revealed this time. The holographic scene kicked in just before the start of that first great adventure.

☙

It was only Eddie's second day at MacVitie Mansion and although he and his new friend had planned to go riding with the ponies, the weather had proved too inclement. A severe storm had blown in quickly that morning and forced them to find amusement indoors. Micki had been drawing and Eddie had been crayoning in his new Mantis Man comic colouring book when the tea bell rang. The family gathered in the front parlour to enjoy homemade oatcakes and sip warm cream. Eddie helped himself to lots of heather honey which he found to be incredibly delicious.

"Do have another oatcake, Eddie, my dear," cooed Micki's mother, "Don't be shy!"

Eddie *was* shy but couldn't resist the offer and helped himself to yet another biscuit although he had already had three. He was just careful not to choose one of the catmint-flavoured ones as he found them a bit tangy.

"These are delicious oatcakes, Mrs. MacVitie," said Eddie politely, even though his mouth was impolitely full.

"Thank you, my dear," said Millie. "I just wish I could offer you the once famous MacVitie smoked fish."

The bear looked at her quizzically.

She explained, "It was the best smoked fish in the Inner Hebrides, but the recipe was lost long ago, and no one remembers it. Not even Granny Mittens."

"Well, it was such a well-guarded secret," chimed in Granny, "And a most peculiar business was its disappearance!"

"Nothing was ever the same after that family of French bulldogs moved in next to us," lamented Mrs. MacVitie with a sigh.

"It was nothing to do with the bulldogs," said her great, great grandmother passionately, "It was that MacTabby clan that caused all the trouble!"

Micki was tired of listening to the inevitable scapegoating arguments about the 'Frenchies' and the MacTabbies that her family indulged in at every opportunity. Everyone fell silent for a while and the big, old clock on the mantlepiece ticked loudly and tiresomely. The disgruntled cat took another oatcake off the plate and nibbled at it dispassionately as she sighed against the weather—the heavy rain splattered on the windowpanes and the wind howled around the tall chimney stacks that arose from the slate roof of the ancient house.

"FIDDLESTICKS!" said the restless young cat going to look out the window for the umpteenth time. "I wish there was something *fun* we could do."

"Why don't you do some painting, Lovey," said her mother pacifyingly, knowing only too well how cranky her daughter could get when she was confined indoors.

"**POOH!** I'm fed up with doing art, I want to do something *exciting*!" pouted her daughter coming back to the warmth of the crackling fire.

"Watch your language, young lady!" said Mrs. MacVitie. "I'll have none of that talk in *this* house!"

Micki made a rude face as she flopped into a nearby chair and kicked her feet irritably against the innocent footstool. "Mothers!" she said to herself as she scowled in the direction of her mater. Then she looked lovingly at her great, great, great grandmother who was now dozing blissfully in the big armchair by the fire. "Would you like some more cream, Granny?" she said going over to her and awakening the beloved matriarch with a kiss.

MYSTERIOUS REALMS

Granny Mittens awoke with a start as her favourite granddaughter slid another bowl of fresh, creamy whiteness into her paws. "Wha…what were you saying, my dear?"

"We want something exciting to do on this rainy day," said Micki.

"Why don't you and Eddie go a-hunting for the lost MacVitie treasure?" said Granny slurping the warm cream. "But of course, you'd have to be careful of the ancient curse that afflicts all those who get close to it."

Mrs. MacVitie huffed scornfully, "Don't fill their young heads with all that nonsense!" she said. "There are better ways to pass the time."

"Ooooh, cursed family treasure!" cried Eddie and Micki together. Indeed, what could be a better way to pass the time than searching for that!

After much coaxing and badgering, Granny Mittens was able to recall enough of the old family legend to make the bear and cat determined to begin the hunt immediately. The two friends hurried away up the flight of wooden stairs that led to the attic where they could plan their search away from prying ears.

୧୨

The old grandmother had remembered something about a secret panel somewhere in the attic being talked of. There was supposed to be a clue hidden behind a panel, but she had never found it despite searching with her brothers and sisters long ago when they were kittens.

Eddie and Micki soon got busy pushing on the panels of wainscoting and feeling the backs of built-in cupboards. While they searched, they speculated as to just what the treasure might be—gold coins?… priceless jewels?… silver ornaments?

After a good hour of searching in vain, they had nothing but sore fingers and aching backs to show for their efforts. They sat dejectedly on one of the bare wooden steps leading up to the attic to reconsider the situation.

"Perhaps your mother was right," said Eddie, tightening the threads of his right ear again and brushing dust off his clothes, "it *is* naught but a fanciful tale."

"I'm sure Granny believes it's true, and that's good enough for me," retorted his friend. "We have to keep looking."

"Well, I don't know where else to look except perhaps along the walls of this staircase," replied her companion, poking at the crack in the step by his feet. "Looks like these old steps need repairing."

Micki looked down at the crack with little interest until suddenly a light-bulb went on in her head.

"Wait a minute," she said pushing Eddie's feet aside. "That crack is very straight and runs all along the top of the riser as well as down the sides."

They both jumped down to the step below and started pushing and pulling at the step until, to their amazement, the whole step and riser swung outwards revealing a small dark room beneath.

"Wow!" said Eddie, sticking his head through the space and looking around.

"What can you see?" said Micki, trying to shove her head through too.

"Nothing!" said Eddie, "It's too dark. Why didn't we think to bring a torch?"

It didn't take long for the twosome to fetch a torch. They were careful to avoid everyone downstairs; they didn't want to share their secret and have someone else finding the treasure first. The friends decided the hidden closet under the stairs would be their 'War Room' where they could come to discuss their treasure hunting strategies together in secret. No one would know they were here, so their plans would be safe.

The newly discovered space turned out to be a small room furnished only with a cot and a little table. "Perhaps this is where MacVitie clan members would hide if the house was being invaded by the MacTabbies in ancient times?" guessed Micki. "I have heard of stories of these old mansions having hidey-holes."

"What was all the fighting about anyway?" asked Eddie with great curiosity.

"Well, it all started a very long time ago back in the olden days and had something to do with territorial claims, water rights, and jealousy. I've been told the MacTabbies were envious of the MacVities making a fortune with their special smoked fish," explained Micki, "But I'm not sure of all the details. Perhaps Granny Mittens could tell us more?"

Eddie listened with interest as he prodded through the dusty bedding and peeked under the mattress. "Well, there doesn't seem to be any treasure hidden in here. So, where is it then?" he asked, turning his attention to tapping the walls and listening for hollow sounds.

MYSTERIOUS REALMS

"Maybe Mother *was* right; there isn't any treasure after all," said Micki, fruitlessly searching under the cot and table and checking for false floorboards.

They discovered nothing!

Having discovered no treasure, they sat on the bed, disappointed and weary, but as they wiggled to get comfortable, they heard a crackly sound in the old eiderdown. They felt around with their paws. Yes, definitely! There was *something* hidden inside. Ripping excitedly at the seams with their sharp claws they stuck their paws in and pulled out a big piece of folded paper. It was some sort of ancient map covered with wobbly lines drawn in black ink. A big 'X' was strategically placed in one square.

"That has to be where the treasure is!" said Micki, her voice squeaky with excitement as she put her paw on the 'X'.

"By Jove!" exclaimed Eddie, "Now we're onto something!"

They turned the map this way and that until they recognized it to be a floorplan of all the little rooms and cubby-holes of the attic. They soon figured out which room was represented by the 'X' and, rushing to it, they quickly spotted a section of mis-aligned floorboard. It was easily lifted to reveal a small hole. With a cry of jubilation, Eddie grabbed the little tin box hidden there. He tried to yank it open, but it was securely locked! Believing it to be full of valuable treasure, they took turns to pick the lock, and then they banged and smashed the little box until the lock gave way and the lid sprang open. But how disappointing! No gold or silver treasure, only a piece of yellowed paper with a mysterious riddle written on it in old-style Gothic writing. They read it aloud together:

> Riches are waiting to be found by you,
>
> Follow your nose is what you do,
>
> Over the wall and through the maze,
>
> Past the graves of olden days,
>
> Past the rose briar prickles and worse,
>
> Treasure is protected by an old curse.
>
> Abandon all cares if you want to succeed,

Enter the cave where you stop and read,

Keep going on, you'll soon be there,

If you do not stop to stand and stare.

They puzzled for a long time over the riddle but could not solve it.

"It's no good, Eddie. We're going to have to ask for help with this, there's no two ways about it," declared Micki.

"But who can we trust to share our secret?" asked Eddie.

"Perhaps Granny Mittens?" suggested his friend.

Just then the dinner gong rang so Micki refolded the bit of paper and stuffed it into her pocket. Then they both put on their best poker faces and obediently went down to supper.

"Well, did you two find a treasure trove?" Micki's mother chuckled sarcastically to Micki as soon as everyone was seated.

Micki's cousins giggled and made faces. Her aunts and uncles shook their heads dismissively. Only the old matriarch looked Micki in the eye with earnest questioning.

"No, we didn't find any treasure," said Micki truthfully. She winked slyly at her old granny.

No one said anymore about it.

And so, to bed, but the cat and the bear resolved to work on the riddle on the morrow. If they couldn't solve it by midday, it would be time to ask Granny Mittens for help.

༄

The following day the friends wanted to get an early start on solving the riddle, but Granny had to go to the doctor about her eyes and Mrs. MacVitie had to take her, therefore, it was required of Micki to run the weekly errands in town. Then Mrs. MacVitie reminded her daughter it was time to sign up for her college courses. Not only that, she would need to take Eddie to register at the government offices as a resident if he was planning on staying in the Inner Hebrides. That was the law and the sooner it was taken care of, the better.

MYSTERIOUS REALMS

So, Micki and Eddie dragged themselves from one place to another across town. Firstly, they took care of all the errands for Micki's mother. Secondly, they went to The College of Landscaping and Design where Micki signed up for her first term. Thirdly, they headed to the Inner Hebrides Office of Residency to sign forms galore—Eddie as the newcomer, Micki as the sponsor. Lastly, they trudged to the Ministry of Health and Animal Welfare where they had to fill out a very special form upon which the granting of residency depended. And so, the whole day was lost as far as treasure hunting or solving riddles went; a disappointing time in that regard, but the two chums were sure tomorrow would be a more interesting day.

However, as luck would have it, the next day brought another problem. At breakfast the next morning the servant brought in the mail and handed it to Mrs. MacVitie who shuffled through the pile to see if there was anything very important. "Here's a letter for you, Micki dear," she said, handing a large business envelope to her daughter.

Micki looked at the return address rather puzzled, "It's from the Ministry of Health and Animal Welfare," she said, ripping it open and taking out an official-looking letter. As she read, her brow wrinkled and her whiskers quivered, "WHAT!?" she shouted in alarm. "What on earth…?"

Everyone looked at her in surprised anticipation. They waited with bated breath for an explanation. Her mother spoke the words on everyone's lips, "What is it, dear? What does it say?"

Micki crumpled the letter in her paw. Instead of answering, she jumped up from the table and went to the window that looked out onto a generous prospect. She stood silently staring into the distance. Blindly, she looked at hawks soaring over the fields. She saw without noticing, small birds flitting about the hawthorn shrubs and heard without listening, their avian squabbles about this and that. Her mother's voice pierced the vacuum.

"Micki! Tell us what's wrong! What does the letter say?"

"Nothing," answered the forlorn cat blandly. Then, claiming a headache, she hurriedly left the room.

Eddie was very concerned for his special friend and as soon as he could politely do so, he excused himself from the table and went in search of her. After checking her room and various other parts of the house without finding her, he took his search outside and eventually spied her sitting alone under the weeping willow tree in the farthest corner of the property. He approached her slowly and quietly until he stood in front of her so he could look directly into her reddened eyes. She looked away but didn't send him off.

"What's happened?" he ventured gently, sitting down beside her and putting his arm around her shoulders.

She slowly unravelled the letter that was still tightly clutched in her clenched paw. "How can this be?" she said, her voice weak with emotion.

Eddie took the letter and tried to read it. But the words were too hard, and he couldn't understand most of them—just enough to make his tummy turn with apprehension as he thought it might be something to do with him— "old bear...does not...we are sorry but..."

"I...I can't read it," he said plaintively, handing the letter back to her. "Please tell me what it says."

She hesitated for a few moments and then sighed as she read aloud,

> Ms Micki MacVitie,
>
> MacVitie Mansion,
>
> Inner Hebrides
>
> Dear Ms MacVitie,
>
> Our recently updated security check has detected that you have an old bear residing in your household. This bear does not meet the requirements specified under the new Animal Health Act of the Ministry of Animal Health and Welfare. Therefore, we are sending a team to your residence for the mandatory removal of said bear immediately for environmentally approved disposal. Upon our receipt of same, the item will be checked off our list and the matter will be considered closed.
>
> We warn you that failure to comply with this process may result in undesirable consequences for you and your family.
>
> Cordially,
>
> *Will Gettit*

MYSTERIOUS REALMS

Officer in Charge,

Ministry of Health and Animal Welfare

Micki scrunched up the letter again and stared ahead of her.

"What…what does all that mean?" asked Eddie, still uncertain as to what all those big words meant. "Does it say I'm going to be sent away from here?" He felt his tummy twitching in a funny way.

Micki nodded. Then, her eyes flashing angrily, she jumped up and yelled with bold assuredness, "How *dare* they treat you with such disrespect! How *dare* they threaten us like that! We won't let them do it! We won't! We can't!" The pupils of her yellow eyes billowed into deep, black *cenotes* and her lips pulled back, baring clenched fangs. "We'll hide you! We'll run away, we'll blow up the Houses of Parliament, we'll, we'll…I don't know what we'll do…" she broke down sobbing despite her burst of fiery determination.

Eddie gave her his warmest bear hug. "Maybe it's all a big mistake?" he wondered out loud. "Perhaps if we go and explain things to the authorities, they'll see things differently."

Micki sniffed and dried her eyes. "I doubt it," she said in a small, halting voice. "Perhaps we can tell…Granny Mittens. She'll know what to do. She's so wise about everything."

Eddie agreed, so they went to look for the Old One to seek her sage advice.

They went into the house and looked for Granny by the fire, but she wasn't there.

"Perhaps she's tired and has gone back to bed, she often does so after breakfast," said Micki.

They went up to her room but were surprised to see only the housemaid there, changing the sheets.

"Oh, your grandmother left right after breakfast," said the maid.

"To go where?" asked Micki in astonishment, "Grandmama never goes anywhere by herself!"

The maid shrugged and continued with her task.

"Let's ask your mother, she'll know," said Eddie.

They went in search of Mrs. MacVitie and found her discussing dinner menus with the cook.

"Granny's gone to stay with your great uncle Mathew MacVitie," said the parent, passing the menu back to the cook.

"Uncle Mathew!" cried her daughter in shock, "But he lives far away in the Big City! Why on earth would she go all that way by herself just for a visit?"

"Er…Well, she wants to see him and have a little holiday," said her mother, trying to sound offhand as she waved away the cook.

"When will she be back?" demanded Micki, quite peeved.

"We'll have to wait and see, won't we," snapped her mother with a frown. "Now don't go all sulky again, Micki. It's nothing to do with us where she goes and what she does."

Micki was not impressed and stomped off with Eddie close on her heel. The tenseness of the discourse made the conciliatory bear wince with embarrassment.

"Maybe she just felt like seeing her other relatives for a while," suggested Eddie, trying to mollify the feisty feline. "All we can do is wait for your grandmother's return," he said, trying to think sensibly while puffing hard in an effort to keep pace with the angry cat.

"Huh!" said his friend, her tail twitching with irritation. "Why do people go off without saying anything? It's so inconsiderate. I bet Mother knows more than she's letting on."

"Perhaps so," said Eddie, looking up at the sky as he felt a drop of rain on his nose. Storm clouds were gathering again.

"Why would Granny go so far away unless there was a good reason?" pouted Micki.

"Maybe she's gone away to give birth to kittens?" said Eddie with a cheeky chuckle.

Micki was not amused, she spun around on the spot to look him in the eye, "May I remind you that is my great, great, great, grandmother you're speaking of!" she hissed as she stomped off.

Eddie took a deep breath and followed, thinking what a roller-coaster ride life with his new buddy was becoming.

MYSTERIOUS REALMS

The rest of that day was a restless one for Eddie and Micki. They had little to say to one another. Micki was annoyed and worried that her granny had gone away without saying goodbye to her. Why was it all so secretive? Why wasn't she being told the whole truth?

Eddie was upset about the sudden departure of Granny Mittens too, but he was also very fearful that he himself was going to be soon whisked away to an unknown fate. Micki was likewise very concerned for Eddie, but she just couldn't think straight anymore and only wanted to be left alone. Eddie went down to the pond by himself and tried to sail a little paper boat he had made, but it became water-logged and sank.

It was the events of the following day that dispersed the melancholy air that had descended over the MacVitie household. Breakfast had been cleared away and the family had all left for a day's outing to the seaside. Micki and Eddie hadn't felt like joining them; instead, the young cat showed her new friend the vegetable garden behind the house and introduced him to John the gardener. Eddie was delighted to have the secrets of growing perfect vegetables explained to him and he was watching intently as John showed him the right way to stake peas and runner beans when suddenly, the interesting conversation was disturbed by the arrival of a strange vehicle at the house.

Leaving Eddie and John, Micki went to investigate. She intercepted the driver and his companion before they reached the front door of MacVitie Mansion. "May I inquire as to your business here?" she asked coolly of them.

"We're from the Ministry of Health and Animal Welfare," explained the driver waving a clipboard with papers attached, "We have orders to pick up a sick, old bear from this address," he said as the other man began lifting a crate out of the back of the van.

Micki's heart skipped a beat, but she thought quickly and announced with authoritative calmness, "There must be some mistake! We have not requested the removal of any bear from here," she said, staring the man in the eye.

"Not your choice Miss! Mandatory government requirement," said the man matter-of-factly.

Micki swallowed hard and tried to maintain a self-assured demeanor despite her rising panic. "You'll have to wait here while I make enquiries within," she said, going through the front door and leaving the men on the doorstep.

She bolted through the house and out the back door where she ran to the garden and grabbed Eddie by the arm. "Quick!" she said, dragging him along and ignoring his cries of bewilderment. "Quick, run up to the hidey-hole under the attic stairs!" she said as she pulled him through the back entrance into the house. "I'll explain later! Quickly now, go and hide!"

Eddie, quite panicked, ran at top speed up to the wooden staircase, jumped into the dark hole, and pulled the movable stair closed again. He sat trembling on the bed in the musty blackness, his heart thumping like the hooves of stampeding horses on frozen turf.

Micki returned to the men on the front step and said truthfully, in a very measured tone, "Only the servants are home, and none of them has seen a sick, old bear this morning."

"Well, we have a warrant to search the premises if necessary, Miss," said the driver, showing her a badge and a card with something written on it. "We have the legal right to enter the house and look for the animal."

"Be my guest," said Micki nonchalantly, stepping back and holding the door open for the men to pass into the lobby. "Search all you want and find what you will."

The men scoured the whole house from top to bottom but discovered no bear anywhere. They even went up the attic stairs. Eddie had sat in terror on the little cot in the dark listening to the heavy footsteps above him. He heard one of the men go into the attic rooms:

"Anything in there, Joe?" called the man who was standing on the very step that covered the hiding hole.

"Nah, nothing but bits of junk and such, Bill," answered the man searching the room. "Waste of ruddy time is this! Let's get out of here."

Frustrated, and thinking that there had, indeed, been a careless mistake on somebody's part back at the office, the men left the house and threw the crate back into the van. "We'll have someone look into this," said Joe, getting back behind the steering wheel, "Someone's obviously screwed up somewhere."

"Well, it *is* hard to get good help these days," said Micki with a grim smile, "Hope you have a better day!" she called after them as they drove off. As relaxation rippled through her body, she closed the door and went to tell Eddie he was safe—for now.

MYSTERIOUS REALMS

☙☙

The chums figured that at least they'd bought some time, but they were still worried about an inevitable return visit from the Ministry 'henchmen'.

"Perhaps it's time to tell your mother everything, Micki?" said Eddie, feeling quite shaken up. "I may not be so lucky next time. We need help to deal with this."

"No way!" said Micki emphatically, "I don't trust her now, she probably sent Granny away against her will to some deadly fate and so she certainly wouldn't hesitate to give *you* up!"

Eddie was starting to feel very depressed. He had, thus far, been lucky with dodging bullets in life—being cast off time and again but always managing somehow to survive another day. Why did people have to make life so difficult for him? After all, he was a good-natured bear and only wanted to live in peace and harmony like anyone else. He sighed heavily.

There was nothing more the two animals could do about the matter at that moment, so they turned their attention once again to solving the riddle they'd found in the tin box. They were more determined than ever to find that treasure! If they were the richest people in the land, they reasoned, no one would dare push them around!

It was too hot and stuffy to sit in the hiding place to swot over the riddle, so they chose a spot under the spreading apple trees where they could lie sprawled on the grass among the daisies. With the warm sunshine on their backs, they were so engrossed pouring over the piece of paper that they failed to notice John coming by with a wheelbarrow full of weeds and refuse.

"Hello, young'uns." he called to them as he walked by. "What have you there that's so taking up your interest?"

Startled, Micki quickly snatched up the paper and hid it behind her back as she sat bolt upright.

"Nothing!" she said unconvincingly while feeling the colour rise in her cheeks.

"It's just an old poem we found," said Eddie in response to the look of surprise lighting up John's old eyes as he put down the wheelbarrow and wiped his face with a dirty kerchief.

The old gardener nodded with a knowing smile. They couldn't fool him; it was obvious they had some big secret they didn't want to share with him. "None of my business," he decided silently as he took up the wooden handles of the barrow again and made to walk off.

"Just a minute, please, John!" shouted Eddie, getting to his feet. He liked John and felt that he could be trusted. "The poem is old fashioned and we're not sure what it means, perhaps you can help us to understand it?"

Micki scowled her worst frown at Eddie and pulled at his arm. But it was too late to retract the disclosure and the gardener was immediately fascinated.

"Well, I don't mind having a look, Master Bear," said the old man.

Eddie ignored Micki's scowl as he handed the riddle to the servant.

John rubbed his chin thoughtfully as he read the words out loud. "*Riches are waiting to be found by you.* Sounds like it could be a treasure chest somewhere with something very valuable in it," he muttered.

"Oh, I'm sure it isn't," said Micki quickly, upset that someone was onto their secret. "Probably means nothing at all!" She reached out her paw to take back the paper, but John held onto it and continued to read:

"*Follow your nose is what you do, Over the wall and through the maze,*" he read. "Ho, ho, I bet that means go to where the disused fish-smokehouse sits in the old walled garden. Wonderful smell that used to be!"

"Where is that?" asked Eddie, quite curious.

"The old abandoned garden over yonder where the MacVities had huge smoke ovens for drying all the salmon and other fish they caught in the big loch that used to be in the valley." The old man looked quite wistful as he remembered. Then his face darkened. "That was before the Great Feud between the clans," he added, looking down at the ground.

Micki seized the opportunity to take the riddle into her paws and said, "Well, thank you, John, I'm sure none of it means anything, and we have to go in for tea now as I'm sure the family is back from their excursion."

"Yes, thank you, sir," said Eddie politely. "Good-bye!"

"And please don't bother telling anyone about this poem, it's really of no importance," shouted Micki over her shoulder.

The gardener touched the peak of his cap, and with a smile, he continued along the path to the compost heap.

MYSTERIOUS REALMS

Micki had to admit that they now had a place to start their treasure hunt thanks to John's information, so she forgave Eddie for his moment of indiscretion.

Although it certainly was tea-time and Eddie hated to pass up a good feast of oatcakes and scones with cream and honey, he was as eager as his friend to hunt for the secret walled garden that held such promise. And so, off the pair went in search of the mysterious place.

They spent a long time wandering about the extensive grounds of the MacVitie estate looking for a promising structure. They passed Lucy, the laundry maid, hanging out the washing on the clothesline and waited while Jock, the shepherd, penned a little flock of the MacVitie's Galway sheep.

Eddie took note of these workers and said to his companion, "Are *all* your servants humans?"

Micki looked astonished at the question, "Of course," she answered. "Why wouldn't they be? They're always so willing to serve us cats—it seems to make them very happy."

Eddie said, "Are *all* humans like that?"

Micki replied, "Many are, but there are those who are not—those ones usually find employment amongst themselves." Then she scoffed and added, "Some of them even find it hard to get along with their *own* kind."

"A bit like cats then?" suggested Eddie, thinking that the Great Feud between the MacVitie and the MacTabby clans was a good example of that!

Micki was quickly humbled and admitted quietly, "Hhmm… I guess that's true."

☙

They had almost given up ever finding more clues to the location of the treasure when dusk began to creep over the countryside and the nightjars started to warble. But as the friends made their way back towards the house, they stopped to smell the honeysuckles climbing among the thick ivy growth beneath some very old trees.

"Just a minute, Eddie," said Micki, "What is all this ivy growing on? Perhaps it's a wall, a wall around the old orchard?"

They pulled and yanked at the ivy and peered into its dim depths.

"It *is* a wall!" yelled Eddie in delight, "I can see the red brickwork."

"Let me see!" said Micki, excitedly pushing past the tubby bear. "Oooh! Wow! So, it is!"

Together they frantically tugged and pulled at the tough stems of the vegetation until they could squeeze through and touch the wall.

"I wonder where the door would be?" said Eddie, "Maybe we can come back tomorrow and look further along the wall for it? We should start heading home for tea now."

"Pooh!" said Micki, too excited to wait until tomorrow, "Who needs tea and who needs a door! We can climb up over the wall right here." And without a moment's hesitation, she clawed her way up to the capstones. "Come on, Eddie! Hurry up!"

Eddie, not wanting to be left behind, scrambled awkwardly up and over the top to plop to the ground amid thorns and nettles on the other side. Micki had sprinted ahead and was already out of sight.

The other side of the wall was full of gnarled espaliered apple and pear trees that had long since failed to yield any significant harvest. Beyond the trees was a maze of very overgrown pathways among what had once been neatly-clipped hedges. With some frustration, they eventually found their way through the maze and followed a path past once-stylish perennial beds until they encountered the old smokehouses—now derelict but with the smell of smoked fish still lingering in their collapsing structures. Micki happily sniffed the air— "Aahh…" she murmured with her eyes closed.

"We'd better keep moving if we want to find the treasure before dark," said Eddie, giving a little shiver in cool evening air and rubbing his growling tummy. He was less keen than the cat to bask in the ancient stink of smoked fish.

"You're right," said Micki, fishing the riddle out of her pocket, "We should look at the poem again and check off what we have discovered so far and see what we should look for next."

They peered in the fading light at the words on the paper. "I think we've found everything up to this line," said Micki before reading aloud, *"Past the graves of olden days, Past the rose briar prickles and worse, Treasure is protected by an old curse."*

MYSTERIOUS REALMS

"Oh, I don't fancy stumbling around a graveyard in the twilight nor pushing through prickly rose bushes in the dark to face an old curse," said Eddie, suddenly feeling very uncomfortable.

"Don't be such fluff-ball!" said Micki, abruptly folding up the paper again and stuffing it into her pocket. "Where's you sense of adventure?"

"Thinking about supper!" thought Eddie silently wishing that he was safely warm and snug in the big house with a heaping plate of tasty food in front of him. He saw that Micki was leaping ahead so, he pulled himself together with a deep groan, and valiantly trudged after his friend through the ugly, grey shapes that formed the overgrown shrubbery.

"**Ouch!**" yelped Eddie suddenly, "Oooh, ... my toe!"

"What did you do?" asked Micki who was some way ahead of her friend.

"I don't know. Stubbed my toe against something hard it seems," cried Eddie, sitting down and holding his foot as he rocked back and forth.

Micki backtracked to where he sat. "It must have been this big rock," she said, touching the tall grey stone poking through the weeds.

"It may be broken, it really hurts. Not sure if I can walk on it," whimpered the bear.

"Hey, look at this!" said his friend more interested in the offending rock than in her friend's toe.

Eddie looked at the granite rock quite unimpressed. "What about it?" he grumbled.

"It's a grave marker with an inscription on it," said Micki, her voice breathless with excitement. "We've found the old graves!"

Eddie jumped up quickly, suddenly fearful that he was sitting on someone's grave. "I want to go home," he whined.

"I can see lots of gravestones now, and mounds of rose briars behind the cemetery," squealed Micki, overjoyed at the discoveries her splendid cat's night vision were revealing.

"Oh, bully for you!" pouted the bear, "I can't see anything! I can't walk, and I won't be able to find my way back in the dark and climb back over that wall. Furthermore, I'm cold, tired, and hungry!"

"Stop whingeing and follow me!" commanded the cat, now pushing her way through the tangle of rose briars. "The treasure chest must be close at hand now."

Eddie reluctantly hobbled after his companion as best he could, feeling that no treasure in the world was worth *this* much effort. The prickles ripped at his fur and scratched his nose. His loose ear was dangling by a thread. His toe was throbbing mercilessly. "Wait for me, Micki! Don't go so fast! Don't you think it's time we made our way back home for supper?"

The cat stopped to wait for her friend to catch up. As she waited, she took the riddle out and, with the newly risen moon enhancing her night vision, she was able to read aloud: *"Abandon all cares if you want to succeed,"* she shouted loudly to Eddie. "So, shut up and get a move on!" she added impatiently. The crashing and grunting of her companion as he struggled through the snaring shrubs seemed to quicken.

"I'm coming…ooh…ugh…as fast as I…**AA**AAaaahh!"

Then all went silent.

Micki strained to peer through the thick growth. There was no sign of her bear friend. She made her way back cautiously through the tangled briars calling nervously, "Eddie? Eddie, where are you? Hello? Eddie! Speak to me!" But there was no reply.

༄

Without warning, the earth had seemingly opened up and swallowed him whole. He had felt the air rushing past his face, then felt the shattering thud of his body hitting the hard ground. His thoughts drifted into oblivion.

Up above ground, Micki cursed the tangled briars herself as she tried to hurry along while scrutinizing every inch of ground. Suddenly, she felt her foot slip into nothingness but, quick as lightning, she grabbed onto a thorny branch, "Ouch!" she yelped but hung on despite the stinging pain. She scrambled to rights and looked down. In the shifting moonlight she saw a large, gaping, round hole that was still partially covered by a rotten, wooden lid. "Eddie!" she called, "Are you down there?" She listened, taut with apprehension as she awaited a reply or some sign that her friend was down there; but nothing came.

As the moonlight brightened between passing clouds, she noticed a glint of metal on the side of the brick-lined shaft. Iron rungs! Hurriedly, but carefully, she climbed down the shaft into the damp, musty darkness. As soon as she stepped onto the rocky bottom of the shaft, she spied a light-coloured heap nearby. "Eddie!" she cried as she went over to him. She knelt by his side and touched his brow. He didn't open his eyes but emitted a faint moan. Her paw felt the wound on his head. "Oh, poor old bear!" she said softly as she straightened his left arm that was bent at a weird angle under his back. She cupped her paw under the water dribbling down the side of the shaft and doused his face with it. The cool gentle touch seemed to revive him a little.

After a minute or so, he struggled to sit up. Dazed and confused he muttered, "Where…where am I?"

"You have a large tear on your head that looks like it may need stitches," she said, pushing some white stuff back in through the ragged hole.

He put his paw up to his aching head and felt around. He suddenly cried out in alarm, "Where's my ear?!"

Micki looked at him and her eyes widened as she saw only one ear sticking up. She scouted around in the dimness and spotted a small lump in a muddy puddle of drip-water. She picked up the soggy piece of cloth and squeezed out the water before holding it out to her friend. "Here it is," she said.

"What?" said Eddie, still a little dazed and his hearing greatly reduced.

"It's your right ear, Eddie, we need to patch it on again," said the cat.

"Uh? We need to catch a train?" said Eddie

"No! I said we need to…oh, never mind. Here, stick this in your shirt pocket until we get home."

He took the misshapen morsel, and with a little sniffle, he placed it carefully in his top pocket, then he looked around him and said, "Where on earth *are* we, Micki?" His eyes were still unadjusted to the lack of light.

"I don't know," she answered, helping him to his feet, "Seems like we're down some kind of shaft—perhaps an old well or something?"

They were in a roughly-hewn, rocky cavern at the bottom of the brick-lined shaft. A single tunnel stretched away into the darkness. Eddie swayed on his feet. He was feeling a bit better but had a raging thirst. They moved along the passage towards the sound of trickling water. Within a few paces they came to where a small spring emerged from the rocky wall and ran in a small shallow stream along the path. They both drank long and gratefully and felt much refreshed.

"Should we try to go back up the shaft or should we carry on and see where this tunnel leads?" asked the teddy as he wiped his mouth on his sleeve.

"Perhaps this passage leads to the treasure trove?" suggested Micki. "It could be an old smuggler's tunnel coming up from the sea."

"That's a thought," said Eddie. "perhaps we could explore a little further? Oh, if only it wasn't so dark."

"Hold onto me," said Micki, "I can see my way, and there seems to be a faint light up ahead."

They soon reached the spot where a little moonlight filtered down through a small air shaft that had been chiselled out of the roof of the tunnel. Eddie's head was now much clearer. "What about our riddle poem?" he asked his companion, "Is there enough light for you to read it? It might give us a clue as to whether we're on the right track."

Micki read from the paper: "*Enter the cave where you stop and read*. Well, that sounds promising, let's keep going."

They crept along the dank tunnel until it opened up into a large cave. Another hole in the roof let in the intermittent moonlight—enough to enable even Eddie to see. There, clearly scrawled on the rock face in white chalk were the words:

Keep going on, you'll soon be there, if you do not stop to stand and stare.

"Wow!" they both cried, "That is the same sentence as in the riddle!"

Now they were *really* excited as there was no doubt in their minds that they were on the brink of discovering the long-lost MacVitie treasure! They took a moment to imagine what they would do with all the sparkling jewels and gold coins. How rich they would be!

"I hope there's a jeweled crown," said Eddie with a grin, "I fancy myself wearing that!"

"I'd like some twinkly diamonds to wear on a collar, and lots of money to spend however I want!" declared Micki excitedly.

The friends tarried on along another tunnel, which led away through the opposite wall of the cave. This was difficult going, the way being very narrow in parts with treacherous footing everywhere. Sometimes, they even had to wade up to their bellies in dark, cold water.

"I hope there're no crocodiles hidden beneath the surface," said Eddie, envisioning scary creatures with big jaws skulking around his legs. He recalled pictures of crocodiles he had seen in books.

"Or something worse!" said Micki seriously.

"That's not helpful, Micki," said Eddie, tensing up.

Micki was about to tease him about his fears when she audibly caught her breath as she squeezed through a very narrow part around a bend.

"What is it, Micki?" said Eddie, not sure if he wanted to know.

"Boy, oh, boy!" was all the cat could manage, "Just look at that!"

Her friend bravely stood on tiptoe and peeked over her shoulder. "Wow!" he exclaimed, equally mesmerized. "What *are* all these things?"

"These are…well, they're called something I can't pronounce but they are formed by dripping mineral water over centuries," explained Micki as best she could. "And look, Eddie! There's a 'frozen waterfall' of the same stuff."

Micki had seen photographs of stalactites and stalagmites in a brochure one of her cousins had brought back from caves he had visited down in the South Country. But these here were even more impressive. Shafts of moonlight pierced their way through numerous natural cracks in the roof of the huge cave and sparkled on the massive calcite formations. The motionless pools of water on the cave floor mirrored the formations so that it seemed like an impenetrable forest of glistening cones lay before the two intruders.

The animals couldn't help marvelling at the beautiful 'cathedral' before them and stood in silent awe for a very long time. After some minutes, Eddie remembered their mission, "The riddle said we would soon be at the treasure if we didn't stand and stare."

"Yes, you're right!" said Micki, breaking her reverie. "Let's move on!"

So, they cautiously picked their way through the maze of formations until they exited the spectacular cave by means of another dark passageway.

୭୨

Presently, they arrived at another, but smaller cave, where a strong smell of saltwater filled their nostrils. The roar of crashing waves forcing their way into narrow spaces among the rocks rumbled in their ears. A pale light came up through a hole in the rocky floor. Cautiously, they inched to the brink of the hole and, crouching, looked down. A scintillating, bluish-green circle of marine bioluminescence swirled at the bottom of a deep, natural chimney in the rock.

Both animals stared into the churning spectacle for some time, quite mesmerized. Then without warning, Eddie became very dizzy, lost his balance, and fell forward. Micki grabbed him in a flash and yanked him back from the edge just as he almost tumbled into the frightening depths.

Regaining their composure, they looked around them at the damp knobbly rock walls until their eyes adjusted to the dim glow which enabled them to see a large wooden door set into the rock face. It had a big iron lever on it.

"This must be the treasure vault!" they whooped together, "It has to be!" Excitement mounting, they both pulled at the lever with all their might expecting the door to open and reveal a mass of treasure or at least a huge chest, but it didn't budge. The door remained impenetrable.

"Drat and bother!" said Eddie, his wave of excitement waning.

"I wonder if we could…" began Micki.

"WHAT ARE YOU DOING HERE?" suddenly boomed a loud, deep voice behind them.

The two little animals jumped in fright and spun on their heels expecting to face a huge sea-monster—but there was no monster. In fact, there was nothing at all to be seen!

"Who's there?" shouted Micki, puzzled and unnerved.

The pinkish-brown, knobbly, rock-face then began to quiver. Something strange and organic slowly started to separate from the stone on which it had been fixed in perfect camouflage. The animals stared at it in stupefied amazement as it slithered down to the floor and then started to morph into a lumpy, mottled, brownish-red mass of jelly-like substance. Then, several tentacles started to emerge, and two large watery eyes opened above what appeared to be a sharp, beak-like mouth.

"Er…we are…uhm…sort of looking for something," Micki managed to stutter in sheer terror while Eddie stood in speechless dread.

"Well, there's nothing here for you to find," said the creature, shuffling forward on tentacle appendages. "Go away, or I'll bite you with my venom-filled beak so that the enzymes digest you from the outside while my suction tongue sucks up your life juices before I feed your bones to the fishes!"

Eddie quickly grabbed Micki's paw. He didn't like the sound of this at all.

Micki bravely stood her ground and tried to sound courageous. "I'm Micki MacVitie and this is MacVitie territory, so I have every right to be here!" said the little cat bravely. "What's more, I have every right to invite my friends here too!"

"Here, here!" added Eddie, taking heart from his companion's lead.

"Oh, so you're a MacVitie?" said the sea-creature. "Why didn't you say so! I've been expecting you."

"Expecting us?" cried Eddie in astonishment. "Why on earth would you be expecting us? We didn't even know ourselves that we were coming here today."

"Well, I thought it must be soon. It seems like a hundred years since I was put in charge of guarding the MacVitie treasure. A family curse bestowed upon me by Laird Morogh MacVitie."

"So, the legend *is* true!" said the bear.

"You're guarding the MacVitie treasure for my many times great, great grandfather?" said Micki.

"I am!!" said the marine monster. "And I'm fed up with doing it."

"But why did Laird MacVitie put the curse on *you* in the first place?"

"Caught me stealing *his* fish out of the loch," admitted the octopus. "He spared my life but said he would cause me shrivel up and die if I didn't guard the MacVitie treasure until he came to retrieve it."

"Well, we would be very glad to relieve you of your guardian duties," said Micki. "If you would please open the treasure vault with no more delay, your vigil will be over!"

"Oh, not so fast, my friends," said the octopus with an unpleasant chuckle, "There's the treasure hunter's curse for you to deal with first!"

Eddie had been hoping *that* part of the legend was *not* true.

"What curse?" asked Micki defiantly. "I think you're bluffing."

"I always tell the truth," said the octopus. "I know all things. You can ask me any question you wish, and I will answer it truthfully." The hideous creature shuffled menacingly closer and continued. "You will have to pass the test to gain access to the treasure vault! You must stand on that trapdoor in front of the wooden door. Your feet will be locked in place by an electromagnetic field generated by the crystal energy within the granite rock, and then you'll be required to ask me the 'Right Question'."

"Sounds like a lot of stuff and nonsense to me," said Eddie, unconvinced.

The octopus shot him a nasty look and went on, "The lever you see here is programmed to open the vault door only if you ask the Right Question. You are allowed only three attempts. After each question, try to pull the lever. If the lever fails to open the door after the third attempt, the trapdoor will open instead, and you will fall down into the raging sea and be lost for eternity!

Eddie turned a funny shade of green. "I think we should quit while we're ahead and go home, Micki," he pleaded, shaking like a leaf. "Your mother may have saved us some supper."

"But the good news is," continued the monster, waving its tentacles jubilantly, "Whatever happens, I will finally be set free!"

"I'll give it a try," said Micki and with bold determination, she moved into position on the trapdoor.

Eddie's heart sank.

There was a short buzzing sound and Micki's feet became fixed to the trapdoor. She took a deep breath and then hesitated. She asked the octopus innocently, "So, do you get to be relieved of your guardian duties regardless of what happens?"

"That is not the Right Question! You'll have to do better than that, my friend," smirked the sea-monster. "You have only two chances left!"

"But that's not fair!" exclaimed the cat, outraged. "That wasn't meant to be a question." She pulled on the lever anyway. But it wouldn't budge.

"Let's go home, Micki!" beseeched Eddie, tugging roughly at Micki's arm with his sweaty paw.

But Micki's feet were stuck fast; she couldn't move even if she had wanted to. She shook her arm free and scowled. After steadying herself, she said to the octopus, "Can I wait until tomorrow to ask the next question?"

"That is not the Right Question!" said the fiend gleefully. "Just one more question and I'll be free of the curse!"

Micki was very angry, feeling she had been cheated out of the chance to ask the Right Question. She yanked on the lever but, once again, it refused to budge even though Micki pulled on it with all her might.

Micki started to feel sick and panicky. She looked at the trapdoor beneath her feet.

"You are so mean and horrible to us!" she said with a sob, "I think you're absolutely, unforgivably, wicked and nasty!"

MYSTERIOUS REALMS

"But, it's not *my* curse, is it?" said the octopus self-righteously, "It was Laird *MacVitie* that created it—he was so afraid that one of the MacTabby clan would get their hands on the treasure. And he was so sure that he *himself* would be the one to come and retrieve it once his rivals had been defeated in the Great Feud. He couldn't foresee how life's twists and turns would make it otherwise."

Micki groaned as she tried to carefully formulate a 'real' question—the Right Question. But her brain had fogged, and no thoughts would come. Her voice faltered as she turned to her loyal friend. "You ask the last question, Eddie. I've failed us twice. It's only right that you should have a turn."

"Me!" shouted Eddie, his eyes popping out of his head.

"Yes, you, Eddie. Please ask the Right Question," said Micki in a very weak, shaky voice.

Eddie gulped. Trembling from head to toe he slowly stepped valiantly forward onto the trapdoor. His feet immediately became fixed. He started to hyperventilate, making his paws tingle before going numb. Then the wheels of rationalization spun around in his bear-brain. He thought carefully and addressed the guardian with a calmness that belied his inner feelings. "You said that you know *everything*, and that you *always* tell the truth," said the bear, making sure this was perceived as a statement, not a question.

"It is so!" assured the octopus.

"Then, you must know the Right Question," stated Eddie carefully and deliberately.

"Indeed, I do!" claimed the guardian.

"And, you said that we can ask you any question," Eddie said, keeping his voice steady and even.

"That's true!" said the octopus.

"Then," said Eddie, looking the octopus straight in the eye while his heart pounded fiercely, "I'm asking you: 'What is the Right Question'?"

The sea-monster broke into a fit of laughter and twirled around madly, "That was your last chance!" he screeched "I'm out of here! Good-bye, kids!" Then the octopus slithered off down the hole and splashed in the depths of the boiling ocean.

Micki turned to her friend and glowered in frustration and terror, "Oh, Eddie! You've wasted our last chance by asking a stupid question!"

"I'm so sorry, Micki, my beloved buddy. I did my best! I know you'll never be able to forgive me for being so silly, therefore, perhaps it's just as well that we are going to be lost forever in the sea!" And with that, he took a deep, tremulous breath and reached forward to pull the lever that he knew would drop them into a watery grave.

"Wait!" exclaimed Micki suddenly flinging her arms around the tubby bear, "There's nothing to forgive you for, my soul-mate. We're in this together, forever!" They hugged tightly in silence for a minute or two, tears wetting their cheeks. Then, Micki clasped the lever with Eddie and together they counted solemnly out loud: "One…two…three!" They pulled the lever and waited, clasped in each others' arms, cheek to cheek, eyes squeezed shut, prepared to enter their doom.

A harsh grating sound of rusty metal hinges screeched in their ears They waited in anguish for the inevitable drop of the trapdoor. They anticipated the feel of the cold, black, turbulent ocean engulfing them, pulling them down to a briny grave. But the trapdoor didn't move! They stood there clasped in each other's arms, unspeaking, unmoving for a full minute, but nothing happened!

They cautiously opened their eyes, anxious to see what sight awaited them. In the near darkness, a gaping black hole yawned before them. The huge vault door had swung inwards revealing a small cavern. So shocked were the pair, that they just stood and stared—unsure if they were still alive or had been transported to never-never land. The friends slowly released their death-grip on each other.

Incredibly, but smartly, Eddie had asked the Right Question! That would give them both something to ponder for a long time to come. Indeed, Eddie promised himself he would think on it carefully as soon as he was safely home and had had a good supper.

When they regained their senses and realized that their feet could now move freely, they stepped into the darkness of the vault. Micki was the first to speak, "Can you see anything, Eddie? she asked trying to catch the glint of sparkling jewels and gold coins in the dim interior.

"No," said Eddie, peering around. "I don't see anything at all! You mean to say that we went through all that for nothing!" In heart-wrenching disbelief, he slumped heavily back against the rock wall. As he did so, a light suddenly came on—he had accidentally leaned against a switch.

"Oooh!" they cried in delight. But their ecstasy immediately became muted. No mound of jewels or gold appeared before them. No treasure chest. They saw nothing but an old leather satchel lying on a stone ledge. It was the only item in the cell.

Micki grabbed it and tried to open the tab—but it was firmly locked with a big brass clasp!

"Grrrr! Drat!" snarled the cat in frustration. She had had just about enough of problems for one day!

Disappointed beyond measure, but thankful to be alive and well, they decided to carry the bag back home and try to open it there. Micki shouldered the satchel and strode through the door, ready to march back along the tunnel. Eddie was right on her heels when, suddenly, "AAAGGGHHH!!!" they both screamed as a myriad of tentacles squirmed around them—the guardian had decided that he was entitled to some of the great treasure too after all these years of guarding it. The cat and bear frantically fought, and bit and scratched, and screamed until they were able to free themselves long enough to make a dash back into the vault and pull the door shut behind them, but the heavy door stuck and wouldn't close all the way. Terror sparked in their brains forcing them to scan around for an escape.

Eddie spotted something whitish high up on the rough-hewn wall of the cell. He pointed to some white chalk marks and could just make the words 'WAY OUT' scrawled in uneven letters. A chalked arrow pointed upwards. Then he saw rough footholds chiselled into the rock face.

"Micki, there's another escape up through the roof of the vault!" yelled Eddie.

"Quick, Eddie! Climb up," yelped Micki.

Eddie wasted no time in hauling himself upwards as best he could while his buddy left the door to push him up from below. There was not yet room on the wall ladder for Micki to start climbing up. She returned to the oak door and threw her weight against it just as a rubbery arm was pushing its way through. "Hurry, Eddie! For Pete's sake hurry! I can't hold it much longer!"

Despite her valiant efforts, the octopus was too strong for her and she felt something squeeze around her ankle. Screaming manically, she smashed at it with the satchel, bit down hard on it and dug in her claws until the tentacle released its grip. In a flash, she let go of the door and sprang for a foothold in the rock on the opposite wall. Her claws struggled for a grasp on the hard, impenetrable stone, and with all her strength, she pulled herself up out of reach of the flailing limbs.

In a matter of seconds, the panting pair found themselves in a passage that switch-backed upwards. They ran around several bends until, with immense relief, they saw the rosy-grey light of early dawn creeping through the dense foliage which hung over an opening a short distance away.

With a whoop of joy, the two friends rushed out into the open air. Nothing followed them. The octopus had discovered that actions had consequences and so had hurried back to the safety of the sea, far away from frenzied feline fury.

The emancipated chums ran with their last ounce of energy over the flower-filled meadows that spread around MacVitie Mansion. Grazing ponies looked up in surprise as the pair rushed past the paddock. "Good morning, friends!" the ponies shouted.

"Good morning, indeed!" yelled Eddie and Micki with a vigorous wave. But they didn't stop to chat. As they ran, the sun peeked over the horizon turning the sky a rosy gold that was reflected in the kitchen windows of the MacVitie house. The cat and the bear burst through the back-kitchen door, startling the cook who was preparing breakfast.

"Good morning, Miss Micki and Master Bear," said cook as the animals rushed through.

"Good morning, Mrs. McCullough!" responded the frantic pair as they dashed into the hallway and up the stairs to their War Room. Once safely in their very own hidey-hole, they collapsed on the cot, exhausted, but incredibly happy to be safely home.

"What should we do with this bag?" asked Eddie.

"Let's leave it here until we have time to force it open," answered Micki.

They hid the leather satchel under the mattress and then went to their respective rooms to make themselves presentable for breakfast. They wasted no time in devouring a hearty breakfast as they made light conversation with the rest of the family who looked at them questioningly but said nothing.

MYSTERIOUS REALMS

◈

It was sometime later in the morning, after they had had a good nap that the two friends went to the War Room to tackle the satchel. But the lock protecting the secrets within, defied them still.

Shortly before lunchtime, they ventured out of their secret place and went downstairs. They had decided to tell Micki's mother about their recent adventure, but when they arrived in the sitting room, where they expected to find her, they learned that she was outside talking to a visitor in the front driveway. Venturing out the front door to see what was going on, they were surprised to see Mrs. MacVitie talking to an important looking man in a pin-stripe suit.

Micki's mother turned around and spotted her daughter and friend just as they were coming out the house. "Oh, there you are! Come here, you two!" she called, "I have something very important to say to you both."

Micki looked at her mother who held some official-looking papers in her hand and then she looked at the businessman who stood by his shiny, black car with a familiar emblem on it. Panic immediately seized the little cat. "Run, Eddie, RUN!" screamed Micki, "Run for your life! It's the man from the Ministry!"

Poor Eddie almost fainted but managed to find his legs and run in blind terror towards the gardens. Micki ran ahead of him and led the way to the walled garden hoping to scale the wall before her mother and the man from the Ministry saw them. She reached the ivy and briar-clad wall and scooted up it in a flash. Eddie was not as agile, and fright had made his legs weak.

"Come on, Eddie! Hurry, or they'll catch you!" screamed Micki.

The terrified bear took a flying leap into the vines and brambles but missed the wall completely. He fell heavily into the tangled mess of prickly vegetation and hung there helpless. He started to simper.

Mrs. MacVitie came panting up to them, "Eddie! Micki! What on earth's got into you two!" she cried in alarm.

"No, please!" begged the poor little bear. "I don't want to die!"

"Leave him alone Go away!" screeched Micki.

"For heaven's sake, Micki, come here and help your friend. Have you gone completely mad?" said Mrs. MacVitie, desperately trying to reach the hapless teddy ensnarled in the brambles.

"Help my friend, you say?" said Micki, scrambling back off the wall and standing guard over the entangled bear who was still stuck fast. "When you are trying to destroy him! Why don't you leave him be!"

"Destroy him?" said her mother bewildered, "What in heaven's name are you babbling about, my girl? I just wanted to tell you that you filled out the wrong Animal Welfare form at the Ministry the other day and it has created a lot of confusion."

"What?" said her daughter, taken aback.

Eddie ceased his struggling and weeping. All became still and silent. The dulcet twittering of a little house wren clanged like a cow bell in the palpable silence that descended upon the scene of suspended animation.

By now the portly man in the dark suit came puffing up to them with a befuddled expression on his face, which had drained to the colour of boiled tripe despite the patches of unhealthy red flush on his cheeks. "Did… did you tell them about the mistake?" he wheezed.

"I'm trying to!" Mrs. MacVitie declared as she carefully tried to free Eddie without causing him more pain. "Micki, you filled out the form for *real* bears, instead of *stuffed* bears. But they corrected your mistake and have granted him permanent residency here, if he wants it," explained Millie as she set Eddie back on his feet, only a little worse for wear despite the tufts of fur left on the thorns. "You should have taken more care, dear. That would have saved a lot of trouble."

Micki felt very foolish, not only for filling out the wrong form, but for mistrusting her mother and not sharing her earlier concerns with her. This could have been sorted out days ago and saved a lot of worry and fear if only she had gone to her with the problem in the beginning.

"I'm very sorry, Mother," said Micki meekly and honestly, "And I sincerely apologize to you, Eddie. Can you forgive me?"

Eddie was only too glad to forgive *everybody* after discovering the truth and knowing that he was safe after all. He gave Micki a special hug and thanked her mother kindly. He even thanked the Ministry man for all his effort in setting the record straight and shook his hand. They all went back to the house where the man quickly took his leave and drove off, scratching his head at all he had just witnessed. "Cats!" he said aloud, his face regaining its usual fresh complexion.

Micki, Eddie and Mrs. MacVitie ascended the steps to the front door to join the rest of the family for luncheon. But they had no sooner reached the top step when another big, shiny, black car purred up the driveway. All three stopped to see who *this* was now.

"Oh, goodness me!" cried Millie MacVitie in delight. "Look who's here!"

Micki immediately broke into a big grin and, with a yelp of pleasurable recognition, she dashed forward to meet the dignified big cat alighting from the vehicle. "Uncle Mathew!!" she squealed, running up and giving him a loving hug and a big kiss. And then her eyes fixed on the figure emerging carefully from the passenger side. "Granny!" she yelled again and almost knocked the poor old girl off her feet as she flung her arms around her and showered her with kisses.

"Ho, ho... steady on, my girl! You'll have me in the dust!" said the old matriarch.

"Hello, Granny Mittens!" said Eddie, also rushing forward to greet his old friend. "How wonderful to see you again!"

"And how wonderful to see you again, Eddie," said Granny, beaming ear to ear, "In fact, how wonderful to see you all again—*really see* you!"

Eddie and Micki stared at Granny in great astonishment. "Why, Granny!" said Micki, looking with a big smile at her grandmother's eyes. "You're not wearing your dark glasses and your eyes are so clear!"

"By Jove, so they are!" said Eddie with a wide grin.

"She's had her cataracts removed in the Big City," announced Mrs. MacVitie obviously very happy that the operation had been successful.

"You knew about it?" said her daughter in surprise. "But why didn't you tell us that's what Granny went away for? It would have saved us a lot of worry about what had happened to her."

"I didn't want to worry you until I knew everything was okay," said her mother.

"But Eddie and I have been worried sick for days about what had happened to dear Granny, we even thought the worst!"

"You're right, it *would* have been better if I had just told you the truth to begin with. I should have trusted you to handle the uncertainty," said Mrs. MacVitie apologetically to her daughter who readily accepted the contrite apology.

Just then someone came out of the house and announced that luncheon was ready to be served. Everyone trouped inside ready to indulge their very good appetites, especially Granny Mittens who had another big surprise for her family. She had received dental implants while she was staying in the Big City so now she could enjoy chomping her food as well as anyone! She got a round of applause from all the family as she flashed them a grand smile of sharp, new teeth.

After a splendid meal with the whole family, Micki took Eddie aside and whispered something in his good ear to which he readily assented by nodding vigorously. Micki politely excused herself to the others who were still eating dessert and ran up to the attic and fetched the satchel, its stubborn lock still unopened. As she brought the bag into the dining room, she took a deep breath and made a startling announcement, "We, Eddie and I that is, have been keeping a very big secret too. But now we would like to share our story with you all."

The others looked around at each other in questioning surprise. Micki and Eddie then took turns in relating the whole adventure they had experienced. The orations culminated in the presentation of the locked satchel for everyone to scrutinize.

"Eddie and I agreed that whatever is inside this bag, should be revealed in front of all the family," declared Micki. And with that, the two buddies forced open the lock with the aid of Uncle Mathew's penknife. They then reached into the bag and pulled out its contents, which amounted to nothing more than a large, leather-bound book of some antiquity. They placed it reverently on the dining table.

The title, in hard-to-read old-fashioned lettering, was embossed in gold leaf on the brown, leather cover:

THE SECRET TO PRODUCING THE BEST SMOKED FISH IN THE WORLD

The MacVitie Treasured Secret, Compiled by Laird Morogh MacVitie

MYSTERIOUS REALMS

They all gasped at the thrilling discovery!

Wow! *This* is the MacVitie treasure! Not gold, or silver, or precious gems, but the secret recipe and procedure for producing the world renowned MacVitie smoked fish. They carefully turned the yellowed pages where all the information was clearly laid out including drawings which illustrated how to prepare and cook the fish with ling heather, rare herbs, and exotic spices, and how to build the perfect smoker to cook the fish to intoxicating perfection.

With great excitement, everyone began fervently yakking about building the smokers again, smoking the fish, and selling it. All except Granny Mittens that is. She was silently shaking her head and looking quite serious. "To think, this knowledge had been handed down through generations of MacVities until it was all lost to sight because of the Great Feud, which also resulted in the draining of the loch and the loss of its fish," declared the old cat. And now we have the recipe but without the loch, there is no fish, and without the fish, there's no point in rebuilding the smokers."

All nodded and muttered in acknowledgment and regret.

"Please tell us all that you know about the Great Feud, Granny," said Micki.

"Yes, do, please!" chimed various other members of the family—young and old alike.

"Well, I only know little bits of the story—just what I've heard from our own family over the years. We really need to hear what the MacTabbies have to say on the matter to get the *whole* story," said Granny.

Uncle Matthew agreed and was eager to do something about that. The wise old cat cleared his throat and stood up to address the family. "I vote that it's high time we called a meeting of the two clans and see if we can't talk about our old issues. Hopefully, we can all come to a sensible agreement about the whole business."

While some of the family thought that was pointless, most agreed that was worthwhile trying. Micki and Eddie really wanted to give it a go and so, at their insistence, the members of the MacVitie clan invited all of the MacTabby clan to meet with them to repair their broken relationship.

The MacTabbies gladly accepted the invitation and agreed that the meeting should be held in neutral territory— the dried-up valley where the fertile loch had once been. This was the first time any members of the two clans had seen each other since the Great Feud for they still lived on opposite sides of the valley. So, it was with great trepidation that the MacVities ventured down into the desolate spot to meet the strangers. They didn't know what to expect and there was much speculation. It was with great anticipation that they sat and watched as the unfamiliar figures of foreign cats appeared on the opposite hillside and made their way down into the valley.

Micki, with tremendous curiosity, cautiously moved towards the MacTabbies as they approached. She was surprised to see that they were not scruffy wild savages with three-inch fangs like she had been led to believe all her life, but instead, beautiful cats with long, silky, striped hair.

Likewise, the MacTabbies cautiously, but full of curiosity, approached the crowd of MacVities and were impressed by the smart appearance of the black and white, short-haired cats that bore no resemblance to the bird-brained bullies with bloated bellies and bad breath that *they* had always believed them to be.

Soon there was much shaking of paws and greetings with smiles and nervous laughter. Before long, everyone was sitting on the parched grass sharing the picnic foods that each family had brought. There was much exchange of information about their histories and the Great Feud, albeit with some differences of opinion, so that a fuller story emerged. Granny Mittens was particularly overjoyed to become acquainted with the grizzled, old patriarch, Grandpa Tam MacTabby. He was the same age as she, so they had a lot in common and it wasn't long before the two old-timers lit a happy twinkle in each other's eyes!

༄

The Great Feud had begun generations ago when the fecund, stream-fed loch had been claimed as territory by the two rivals—the MacVitie and the MacTabby clans. The dwellings of each clan were up among the hills on opposite sides of the valley wherein lay the loch from which *both* groups of Highland cats enjoyed the most abundant fishing in the region. But while the MacTabbies enjoyed eating the fish they caught, it was only the MacVities who learned to smoke the fish to such perfection that it was claimed by all who tasted it to be the finest smoked fish they had ever eaten. It had been in such demand that the MacVities were able to package and sell it far and wide enabling the clan to amass a great fortune.

MYSTERIOUS REALMS

The MacTabbies were extremely envious of their rivals' success and resultant accumulation of abundant riches. The jealousy made them not only very bitter, but also very vengeful. The striped clan wanted to get their paws on all this information so that they could produce this special fish too and become wealthy just like the MacVities. But the black and white cats were having none of that! They wanted a monopoly of the smoked fish trade and they would go to any lengths to protect their secret. However, the MacTabbies wanted this secret so desperately that they planned to attack the MacVitie's and steal the famous award-winning recipe and procedure for smoking fish.

Fearing theft of the valuable book, Laird Morogh, head of the MacVitie clan at that time, hid the only copy of it in a cave to be guarded by a sea monster. The recipe and procedure were stored in the memories of those who did the smoking, so there was no need for the written copy to be available to them.

On learning that the information was out of their reach forever, the MacTabbies retaliated and blocked the flow of water to the loch. They created a diversion of the stream across their *own* land, and although that meant that they, too, could no longer harvest much fish themselves, they felt it was worth the loss as long as the MacVities were brought to their knees.

Over time, the loch drained completely dry and the arable land of the MacVitie clan became dusty and infertile. The big lush gardens and orchard where the smokehouses were located became useless. Eventually, the MacVitie's abandoned that part of their property and, over the succeeding generations, their smokehouses were forgotten. Over time, the skilled workers who had processed the fish passed away and the knowledge was lost to future generations.

But that wasn't all there was to the tragic story. Granny Mittens remembered hearing another very sad tale when she herself was a young kitten and not supposed to talk about such things. But now she was going to tell it all.

At the time of the Great Feud, the beautiful young Moira MacVitie and the noble Tobias MacTabby had fallen in love with each other and eloped. Intermarrying between the clans was forbidden so the new family was shunned by both clans and banished to Darkest Outer Pongolia forever. The interbred family remained taboo and was never mentioned in any household of either clan of the Inner Hebrides until this very day.

As the members of both clans now sat and talked, they recognized the futility of holding a grudge against each other. It served no useful purpose. Much more could be achieved by cooperating and sharing than by selfishness and greed. They all concluded that sometimes, keeping secrets may serve a useful purpose, but most often it doesn't, and only leads to further trouble.

An agreement was made, and the two clans immediately started working together to restore the flow of water to the valley. The resultant loch was restocked with fish and before too long, the new smokehouses, that were built on *both* sides of the loch, were producing an abundance of the famous fish, which was marketed under the new name of 'MacCats Stupendous Smoked Fish' and sold across the land and beyond.

Micki tracked down her cousins in Darkest Outer Pongolia and shared family news and photos with them. She was thrilled to learn that instead of fading away, the new family had actually flourished and mixed with the local population of magical snow cats producing some very beautiful offspring—some golden striped, some silver striped, some with short, black hair, some with long, silky hair, and many with magical abilities.

When the first batch of special smoked fish had been produced, Micki had suggested that a package of it should be sent to their estranged Pongolian family with a formal apology as an olive branch. Both clans agreed on that being a terrific idea.

෴

As the movie of his past life vanished, Eddie sat a while longer in the chair thinking about how things had turned out. Since the Great Reconciliation of the Great Feud, all the families had remained on good terms and their smoked fish business had flourished.

While Micki had studied garden design, he himself, had apprenticed under John the gardener and learned to grow some of the best vegetables in the country. He had been able to sell his produce to acquire sufficient seed money to invest in joint-ownership of a country cottage and garden with Micki. At this recollection, Eddie wondered sadly if he would ever be with his dear buddy again and he tried to imagine what she was doing right now.

At that very minute, unbeknownst to the bear, Micki was in Cocky Spaniel's cottage keeping vigil at the dog's bedside while he slept in medication-induced slumber. Trixie was there too, and while she held his paw, Micki stroked his forehead to comfort him.

"And so, that's how I met my best friend and housemate, Eddie Bear," explained Micki to Trixie in answer to the little dog's earlier inquiry as to how Mlle. Micki had met M. Bear. Then she thought again about where Eddie could possibly be right now, and what he had been doing all this time.

Micki and Trixie had joined one of the search groups and had been thankful when they spotted Cocky wandering in a daze about the grassy common behind their cottages. But initial joy quickly turned to concern as he mumbled incoherently and didn't seem to recognize them or his own house when they took him home.

They had tucked him into bed and tried to find out what had happened, but he had been unable to tell them anything that made any sense. Something about floating upwards in a beam of light and then running frantically around in circles trying to escape until he had truly seen the light.

The doctor had been summoned and a sedative administered. His friends had decided they would take turns to sit at his bedside and watch over him until he fully recovered. Micki and Trixie had taken the first shift.

❦

Meanwhile, Eddie was anxious to go home so he got up from the chair and looked in vain for a way out. He wanted to be with Micki. "Was she worried about him by now?" he wondered. He was also curious to know what had happened to the spaniel as he hadn't seen him in a while. "I just want to go home now, please," he said to no one there. "I want to be with my loved ones again."

Then, before he could say 'Jack Robinson,' he found himself on the path in front of his cottage door whence he had been taken the night before. He landed softly on his feet and looked upwards to see where he had been, but the glowing white oval of light was nowhere to be seen. "Has it all been some kind of dream?" he asked himself. "Was I affected by the cold?"

He tentatively opened the door of his home, unsure of what might be waiting inside—it had been such a peculiar night. He hoped Micki would run to greet him and listen to his amazing story but instead, the cottage was dark and chilly, with no sign of his friend. He took off his coat and boots and began to kindle a fire in the stone-cold grate.

⁜

At that moment, Micki was tramping home through the snow wondering if Eddie had come home yet. She had been glad when replacements had arrived to relieve her and Trixie of their bedside watch as she was anxious to get home and talk to Eddie. As she walked, she pondered Cocky's strange, rambling phrases uttered while she had sat at his bedside and now she wondered if something similar had been experienced by her best friend. But, as she neared the front door of their cottage, she began to rationalize that it was more likely that he had simply skipped along to the 'local' for honeyed mead and biscuits. "The patrons could easily have persuaded him to stay in the warm and play a game of darts rather than search for his missing neighbour out in the cold," she told herself. And the more she thought this thought, the more she believed it to be true; and, by the time she reached the cottage, she was convinced of its veracity.

⁜

Eddie had managed to coax a cheerful, flickering flame from the tinder when he heard the front door open. "Micki's home!" he thought, gleefully jumping up to go and greet her with a warm hug.

Micki opened the cottage door and was at first relieved to see a glimmer of firelight coming from the living room. "Eddie's home!" she thought happily. But almost immediately, with the fear evaporating on seeing him safe and sound, her joy quickly mixed with anger to form her first words.

"Where have you been all this time?" she demanded of the bear in a harsh, dry voice that sounded like autumn leaves scratching across cobblestones.

"I was taken up a golden beam light into this glowing, white thing—like a cloud, that was hovering above our cottage," gushed Eddie, jubilantly holding out his arms in greeting and ready to blurt out his whole adventure to her.

"Don't talk such rubbish!" snapped Micki, brushing past him. "You've most likely been sitting in the 'Mug and Spoon' stuffing yourself with brandied milk and chocolate biscuits while the rest of us were out searching in the cold and snow for our friend!"

"I have not!" retorted Eddie indignantly.

"Yes, you have, I can smell them on your breath," said Micki as she threw her hat and coat on the floor and kicked off her snow boots. She stormed off into her own room and slammed the door shut.

Eddie turned to the fireplace and threw a log onto the burning sticks, creating a shower of orange sparks. Then, with a deep sigh, he plonked himself down in his armchair and gazed unseeingly at the bright specks of soot that glowed momentarily on the flue before vanishing into oblivion. He was inconsolably distraught at his housemate's outburst of temper and disbelief. She really could be so hard to get along with at times.

Alone in her room, Micki contemplated the stories she had hear that evening—the sightings and rumors of the farm animals, Cocky's mutterings, and now Eddie's revelation. There seemed to be a common thread running through them. Mysterious and unbelievable as they were, there surely must be some truth to the stories?

Presently, Eddie's hypnotic state was penetrated by the sound of the door to Micki's room slowly creaking open. He heard the soft shuffle of slipper-shod feet moving across the floor towards him, then a gentle voice spoke.

"You're telling the truth aren't you, Eddie." It was more of a statement than a question.

"I'm telling it the way I understand it," said the miserable bear, "It's the best I can do."

His friend nodded, saying, "How about I make us some hot cocoa and we'll sit here by the fire while you tell me all about it?"

Eddie cheered up immediately and gave her a warm smile and she returned it. And so, over a several steaming mugs of cocoa, the bear related all the peculiar events of that evening as he recalled them. Then Micki related all the puzzling things told her by the farm animals and Cocky. By the time they were done, the grey light of a new day was intruding through the curtains. Exhausted, the animals took to their beds and slept soundly until the sun was nearing its zenith, filling the little cottage with the bright hope of a cheery mid-winter's day.

The pair ate a hurried brunch of poached eggs on toast. They both agreed that after such a tumultuous time, they should celebrate Festival Day in a big way.

"Why don't we put together a wonderful feast this evening and invite our friends and neighbours to join us?" said Micki as she cleared away the dishes.

"What a fun idea!" said Eddie, rolling up his sleeves to begin the washing up. He put the dish soap in the hot water and began scraping dried egg off the plates. "Probably everyone, including Cocky, will be too tired after yesterday's fiasco to fix much for themselves."

"Let's go and invite everyone personally," said Micki. So, they abandoned the dishes and pulled on their coats and boots and scampered off on their mission.

They were thrilled to find Cocky showing signs of good recovery, but it was soon quite clear that he was a very different dog than the one who had disappeared the previous evening. He was not his usual bombastic, cocky self and he was delighted to accept the invitation.

All the other invitees were very grateful for the invitation to the impromptu feast too.

By early evening, as the appetizing aroma of delicious food filled the little cottage, a cheerful Cocky arrived ahead of the other guests. "I wanted to bring you a little gift of festive treats," he said, offering a decorative tin of delicious looking biscuits. "They're not *dog* biscuits!" he added quickly with a chuckle.

His hosts graciously accepted the present and bade him sit and warm himself by the fire. Eddie was secretly glad of an opportunity to converse privately with his neighbour. "I'm relieved to find you so well. I was worried about you dashing around in circles the other night," said Eddie, feeling a little uncomfortable at raising the subject. "How did you finally escape?"

Cocky spoke in a tranquil tone. "I became exhausted with that endless, aimless running around in circles trying to find a way out. I finally broke down and begged for deliverance from the futility of it all. Then, almost immediately, I found myself back down on the ground. I was confused at first, but as time went by under the attentive care of my friends, my mind started to become clearer."

"How so?" asked Eddie quietly.

MYSTERIOUS REALMS

"I realized that I needed to follow a different track in life. I began to see that I had been trapped on a frenetic treadmill and it was doing me no good," explained the dog.

Eddie nodded, feeling empathy with the spaniel's story, having just reviewed his own past in considerable detail and come to appreciate some important values. He glanced at Micki, his soulmate through many a year, and smiled.

Micki had been listening intently and now spoke, "But the experiences of both of you are still shrouded in great mystery."

"I suppose we have to accept that some things are simply unexplainable," suggested Eddie.

Before anything more could be said, the other guests, including Trixie, began to arrive. Soon, everyone was seated at the dining table, ready to enjoy a stupendous banquet. But as the guests started to fill their plates, there was a loud knock at the door. Eddie and Micki exchanged puzzled looks as no one else was expected. With great bewilderment, Eddie got up from the table and went to see who it was.

"Well, lo and behold!" came his exclamation. "What on earth are you two doing here? Come on in, we're just about to start eating."

While the guests looked at each other with excited anticipation, Micki jumped to her feet and ran into the hallway eager to see who had arrived. Suddenly, there was a squeal of delight. "Granny Mittens! *And* Grandpa Tam MacTabby! What a wonderful surprise!"

There were hugs and kisses followed by many cheery introductions as the aged visitors were ushered into the warmth. Eddie quickly found two more chairs, and everyone moved up to make room for the newcomers at the table. It wasn't long before the merry crowd were tucking into the fabulous repast with great gusto.

"So, Grandpa Tam," began Micki after a while, "Was it terribly hard for you to drive the car all this way on icy roads?"

"Not really," said the old MacTabby cat, "I had a lot of good help," he said grinning at the mellow old MacVitie cat at his elbow.

With raised eyebrows, Micki looked at her great, great, great grandmother. Granny laughed, then her face took on a modest air as she said with twinkling eyes, "I took driving lessons this summer and did very well."

Grandpa spoke admiringly, "Yes, and I promised her if she passed her test by mid-winter, she could take turns with me and we would drive all the way to visit her favourite granddaughter!"

"So here we are!" said Granny Mittens proudly.

Everyone raised their glasses and toasted the intrepid matriarch. "To Granny Mittens!"

There was also a toast proposed by Cocky to all those who had helped rescue him, his friends who had stuck by him through thick and thin. It became clear to all that the spaniel was eager to listen with sincere interest to others and be considerate of their feelings.

After enjoying a lovely evening, the invited guests thanked their hosts, claiming it was the best Mid-Winter Festival they had experienced in years. They waved good-bye as they went to their respective homes, stuffed full and very contented.

It was too late for Granny and Grandpa to drive all the way back home in the dark, so they were to be made comfortable in the spare rooms. Eddie and Micki went out to the car to fetch the luggage and got quite a shock for there, on the boot-lid, was a large placard boldly announcing:

JUST MARRIED!

They looked at one another with raised eyebrows, then giggled.

"I suppose we need to prepare only *one* bedroom!" said Eddie with a wink.

"So, it seems!" said Mick with a big grin.

After a long day of fun, flurry, and activity, and with the two newlyweds safely stowed in the spare room, Eddie and Micki took advantage of the quietness of the cottage to sit alone by the glowing embers of the fire to sip a last cup of mulled punch and chat about recent events.

"Well, Micki," began Eddie, "We do have a jolly good winter tale to tell!"

"Full of laughter and tears," said Micki.

Eddie stared into his drink and then looked at his friend ruefully, "I'm sorry my behavior at Cocky's party embarrassed you, Micki. I just don't know what comes over me sometimes."

Micki smiled and shook her head, "You were the life of the party!" she laughed. "I'm sorry I got into such a snit. *My* behavior was not at its best."

Eddie reached over and squeezed her paw, "No hard feelings, eh!"

They both leaned back in their comfy chairs enjoying the glowing warmth of the fire as the logs settled, sending sparks dancing upwards.

"Just think," mused Micki after they had been quiet sometime, "It's almost the beginning of a new year. I wonder what it will have in store for us."

"Hopefully, nothing but peace and quiet," murmured Eddie sleepily.

"What!" said Micki with a chuckle, "don't you want anymore dubious adventures?"

Receiving no answer, she glanced over at her best friend, but he was drifting asleep with the corners of his mouth tweaked upwards in an enigmatic smile.

[THE END]

ACKNOWLEDGMENTS

A special thank you to Afiena and David for reading my manuscript with keenly discerning eyes, for offering their constructive advice, and for giving their tireless support and encouragement.

Thanks also to Suzanne and Cliff for reading my stories and providing supportive feedback.

Also, many thanks to the members of my production team at Friesen Press for their guidance and advice throughout the publishing process.

These valuable contributions helped to make this book possible and for them all, I am truly grateful.

CPSIA information can be obtained
at www.ICGtesting.com
Printed in the USA
LVHW030718130220
646766LV00001B/2